JOURNAL FOR THE STUDY OF THE NEW TESTAMENT
SUPPLEMENT SERIES
159

Executive Editor
Stanley E. Porter

Sheffield Academic Press

Crisis and Continuity

Time in the Gospel of Mark

Brenda Deen Schildgen

Journal for the Study of the New Testament
Supplement Series 159

For Jacob, Dawn and Alexander

Copyright © 1998 Sheffield Academic Press

Published by Sheffield Academic Press Ltd
Mansion House
19 Kingfield Road
Sheffield S11 9AS
England

Printed on acid-free paper in Great Britain
by Bookcraft Ltd
Midsomer Norton, Bath

British Library Cataloguing in Publication Data

A catalogue record for this book is available
from the British Library

ISBN 1-85075-851-4

CONTENTS

ACKNOWLEDGMENTS

Without Professor Elliott, Theology, University of San Francisco, this study could never have been dreamed, begun, or finished. Quite simply, in showing me how to read the Bible, Professor Elliott retaught me how to read. Professor Mazzotta, Italian Language and Literature, Yale University, read the first draft of the manuscript, several years ago. Whereas Professor Elliott taught me what to look for when I was reading the Bible, Professor Mazzotta helped me to realize that what I saw was worth writing about. Both possess that special generosity that develops the work of others and that encourages others by sharing knowledge and precious time. Many have supported my work, but especially Professors Hamilton Hess, Fr. Frank Buckley, S.J. and Fr. Paul Bernadicou, S.J., all from the University of San Francisco. They taught me, encouraged me, and showed me how the study of theology could deepen my literary studies. Professor Emmy Werner, emeritus, University of California, Davis, a fellow commuter from Berkeley, CA to Davis, was a force to be reckoned with on our regular van trips back and forth. Her own great accomplishments, her weekly interrogations about the status of my various projects, and this one in particular, and her constant encouragement are inspirations beyond measure. Professor Werner models how to be a successful teacher, writer, and friend. Finally, my husband's continual intellectual challenge, astute editorial advice and domestic understanding made this work possible.

PREFACE

> Time can become constitutive only when connection with the transcendental
> home has been lost.
>
> Georg Lukács, *Theory of the Novel*

In *The Theory of the Novel*, Lukács argues that 'Only in the novel are
meaning and life, and thus the essential and the temporal, separated; one
can almost say that the whole inner action of a novel is nothing else
but a struggle against the power of time.'[1] As a genre that emerged
when the potency of myth and the authority of traditional storytellers
were declining, the novel, in contrast to myth and folk tale with which
it shares narrative features, whether set in the past, present, or future,
cannot break away from historical time. Though some novels, *Crime
and Punishment*, for example, point forwards teleologically or to an
alternative time,[2] most are confined to their particular temporal setting.
In 'The Storyteller: Reflections on the Works of Nicolai Lenski', Walter
Benjamin points to how the novel's conception of time and collective
memory radically distinguishes its genre and its approach to human
experience and the 'meaning of life' from myth and fable. 'Memory
creates the chain of tradition which passes a happening on from generation to generation', he writes, and it is memory that secures traditional
learning from the onslaughts of novelty.[3] Memory preserves the past
of human experience, and thus offers a consoling respite from the per-
petual human encounter with the new. The conceptions of time in myth,
legend and traditional story create the narratological focus of the genres
in which they come down to us, whether fairy tale, fable, epic, myth,

1.   Trans. Anna Bostock; Cambridge, MA: MIT Press, 1971.
2.   See Michael Holquist, 'Puzzle and Mystery, the Narrative Poles of Knowing:
Crime and Punishment', in *idem*, *Dostoevsky and the Novel* (Princeton, NJ:
Princeton University Press, 1977), pp. 75-101.
3.   Walter Benjamin, 'The Storyteller: Reflections on the Works of Nicolai
Lenski', in Hannah Arendt (ed.), *Illuminations: Essays and Reflections* (New York:
Schocken Books, 1988), p. 98.

legend, or gospel. But the way that time is conceived and developed in
these forms, though not laid out discursively or analytically, is multi-
dimensional with many chronologies existing simultaneously and each
in its turn directing the meaning conveyed by the narrative. In the 'Once
Upon a Time' world of fairy tale, we are confronted with ageless time,
eternal through equivocal learning, and certainty that the past endures,
the present continues, and the future will exist. The fairy tale delves into
the psyche, explores the harsh realities of life—parental loss, poverty,
cruelty, tyranny—and with its happy ending promises that the world
still makes sense, while reminding us of the role of the story in syn-
thesizing the complexity of human life. Legend records the past and
makes it present by representing history. It explores the eternal in the
inner life of the patterned journey of its hero by pointing beyond the
specific case, and it shows how to encounter the 'transcendental home'
in the timeless future that continues the timeless past. Myths proclaim
their symbolic understanding of the encyclopedia of human culture with
claims to absolute certainty, while telling stories from the beginning of
time and establishing customs, beliefs and codes of behavior that are to
survive for ever. In myth usually the narrative follows in sequences
rather than in chronology. As Hans Blumenberg wrote, myth is 'something that lies very far back, but in the meantime has not been contradicted or pushed aside', for it possesses an 'assumption of trustwor-
thiness on its side'.[4] With urgency, myths recite their claims about
inflexible truths, but they take form in narrative genres that make
their truths ambiguous and open-ended.

In the novel, as in *Don Quixote* or *Crime and Punishment*, for example, individual heroes must work out the 'meaning of life' for themselves, a quest that takes them both on a horizontal and vertical path.[5]
But in myth and traditional story, we are invited to be less interested
in an individual's development and experiences as conceived along a
time-bound passage that ends in the certainty of death. On the contrary, in addition to representing ordinary chronology, the story also
exists on a symbolic level that even defies the power of chronological
time, except in so far as it connects itself to all time, from the very
beginning. Mythological writing remembers the past as normative for
its own time, for the present and for the future. Thus time is removed

---

4.   Hans Blumenberg, *Work on Myth* (trans. Robert M. Wallace; Cambridge, MA:
MIT Press, 1985), p. 126.
5.   Holquist, *Dostoevsky and the Novel*, pp. 75-101.

from the individual chronology of a person's life, for the person's life is important only in so far as it belongs to the history of a people, it records an interlude when 'God' interrupted ordinary time, or it belongs to all time. Myth is narrated according to the cosmic time that absorbs the micro histories of persons and the macro histories of nations and empires, while at the same time making a conceptual 'eternity' the measure of the present. Time and narrative in a mythological text overlap as they convey the orientation towards the world proclaimed in its words. The temporality in a mythological text unfolds what it means to tell us about how to live in the world now, before, in the future and for all time. Its eternal temporal perspective rises over all the actions and actors bound by the past, present, and future and in doing so shows how these actions can be viewed from this alternative time.

As more democratic forms making use of the popular idiom and common experiences, the literary prose genres that emerged in the early modern period share much in common with the Gospels. But the various uses of time in the Gospel narratives radically distinguish them from these later forms, because in contrast to the novel's focus on its narrative time, the events told in the Gospels are only important in so far as they belong simultaneously to the present, to history and to eternity. In the Gospel of Mark, time is the perspective through which the author constructs the Gospel. He shows how the story of the mission and death of Jesus connects to his own Hebraic history. His narrative probes the meaning of this story to his own present, some thirty to forty years after Jesus' death,[6] and to the future readers whom he addresses. Even more importantly, because of their relationship to the cosmic horizon, the events in the Gospel unfold in the context of eternity. Throughout this study I use Gérard Genette's distinction between *story* and *narrative*,[7] the former the essential Jesus story, which, with some important variations (birth and childhood narratives; post resurrection

6. The Gospel is dated sometime between 64 CE and 75 CE. See Paul J. Achtemeier, *Mark* (Philadelphia: Fortress Press, 1980), pp. 1-10; Werner Georg Kümmel, *Introduction to the New Testament* (trans. Howard C. Kee; Nashville: Abingdon Press, 1973), pp. 97-98; E.E. Ellis, 'The Date and Provenance of Mark's Gospel', in F. Van Segbroeck, C.M. Tuckett, G. Van Belle, and J. Verheyden (eds.), *The Four Gospels 1992: Festschrift Frans Neirynck* (Leuven: Leuven University Press, 1992), II, pp. 801-15 argues for the late fifties and Caesaria as the Gospel's earliest date and place of composition.

7. Gérard Genette, *Narrative Discourse: An Essay in Method* (trans. Jane E. Lewin; Ithaca, NY: Cornell University Press, 1980).

sightings) is more or less parallel in all four Gospels. The *narrative* is
the particular shape the Gospel writer gives this story through his narratological interpretation. Mark's immediate and urgent tone makes the
crisis story continually present, but it is a present that follows a coher-
ent past and that is always becoming the future. Mark does not confer
specific chronological cues (dates and times) on the crisis time narrative
but his setting is inescapably the contemporary milieu of first-century
Palestine, a time and place within memory.

Paul Ricoeur's theories about time and narrative will be evident in
this study, for I take as a starting point precisely his idea that it is
through narrative that various concepts of time are conceived. For Ricoeur, 'the world unfolded by every narrative work is always a temporal world'[8] since it is through narratives, whether 'history and fiction',
that time is imagined. In addition, I refer to many of his terms throughout, including 'historical', 'ordinary', 'ritual' and 'mythic' time, which
I adapt for my own purposes. Historical time is a schematized arrangement of time often with 'famous' or 'infamous' primary actors and
major events. Ordinary time is the historical day-to-day reality in which
humans live. Both of these are also mortal time. Mythic and ritual time
take us outside these ordinary time experiences. All these words for
time actually describe the narrative mode that brings the series of events
into focus.

By repeating continuous and long-standing celebrations of originating events with symbolic meaning outside day-to-day living, ritual
time, like mythic time, takes humans out of ordinary and historical time
into a broader concept of time. Mythic time is a concept that envelops
all reality and minimizes the importance of historical or ordinary time
by making it a microcosm of a larger universal understanding of human
experience viewed against divine and eternal boundaries. Other time
words I will use include 'suspended' or interrupted time, the term I use
to describe the narratives that halt the central narrative and temporarily interrupt it; 'crisis time', Mieke Bal's phrase for a narrative
that takes place in 'a short span of time into which the events have been
compressed' is the term I use for the series of events composing Jesus'
public mission and career.[9]

8.   Paul Ricoeur, *Time and Narrative* (trans. Kathleen McLaughlin and David
Pellauer; Chicago: University of Chicago Press, 1984), I, p. 3.
9.   Mieke Bal, *Narratology: Introduction to the Theory of Narrative* (trans.
Christine van Boheemen; Toronto: University of Toronto Press, 1985), p. 38.

Another important term is 'duration', or the time the story or the narrative takes to happen. Often story time is completely different from narrative time.[10] The narrative may distort or re-arrange the order of events and therefore the time when they occurred in the story. The one outstanding instance of such an anachrony in the Gospel of Mark is the John the Baptist novella, but because Mark appears uninterested in specific chronologies, and only in immediacy (immediately, then, and after, for example), the events as they unfold in the narrative follow rapidly one after the other, emphasizing their accumulative power. Another aspect of 'duration' is the difference between the time an event actually took to happen and the time it takes to be narrated; often the latter may be briefer or far longer than the actual event, leading Gérard Genette to talk about the 'pseudo-time' of the narrative.[11] The duration of the parables, for example, takes the same narrative time as the performance itself. However, the series of events within the parables can take a season (Parable of the Sower) or many years (Parable of the Vineyard). On the other hand, although time signatures are provided, the passion narrative telescopes the actual time for the events.

The kinds of temporality expressed in the Markan Gospel convey the 'aporias' of time, the impossibility of measuring time and its simultaneous open-endedness,[12] yet the narrative offers a way of dealing with the inconclusiveness of time. Different kinds of time intersect and overlap throughout the narrative. But the Gospel presents a hierarchy of time that shows how chronological time itself can be overcome, for time can be measured by 'how close or how far a given experience approaches or moves away from the pole of eternity'.[13] While the Gospel never negates the central importance of the historical moment, nonetheless, the experience of this dynamic confrontation between the moment and eternity, between ordinary/historical time and mythic time[14] is the

10. Genette, *Narrative Discourse*, pp. 86-88.

11. Genette, *Narrative Discourse*, p. 35, pp. 86-112.

12. Ricoeur, *Time and Narrative* I.

13. Ricoeur, *Time and Narrative* I, p. 28, in Ricoeur's discussion of Augustine's concepts of time.

14. This idea goes much further than Oscar Cullmann's *Christ and Time: The Primitive Christian Conception of Time and History* (trans. Floyd V. Filson; Philadelphia: Westminster Press, 1964), originally published in Germany in 1945, which used the New Testament as a single document to define the Christian concept of time. Arguing against those who saw the New Testament as 'consistently eschatological',

crossover point that makes it possible to conquer human time and all the fears that accompany it.

he pointed out that it has a 'consistently historical method of revelation' (p. 60). Adopting a too radical opposition between Hellenic and Hebraic ideas of time, Cullmann took as his starting point the idea that primitive Christianity makes the time distinction between 'Formerly and Now and Then' rather than the spatial distinction between 'Here and Beyond' (p. 37). His position was countered by James Barr, *Biblical Words for Time* (London: SCM Press, 1962), who approached the question philologically and insisted on the polysemy in biblical words, arguing that it was not possible to develop a 'concept' from the words καιρός or χρόνος (p. 51). Barr also correctly criticized the contrast Cullmann made between Hebraic and Hellenic thought (pp. 78-81). Identifying Greek thought with 'abstractness' and Hebraic with 'concreteness' led Cullmann to distinguish Hellenic interest in 'timelessness' from Hebraic and New Testament linear time (Cullmann, *Christ and Time*, pp. 51-68).

ABBREVIATIONS

AJT	*American Journal of Theology*
ANRW	Hildegard Temporini and Wolfgang Haase (eds.), *Aufstieg und Niedergang der römischen Welt: Geschichte und Kultur Roms im Spiegel der neueren Forschung* (Berlin: W. de Gruyter, 1972–)
Bib	*Biblica*
BJRL	*Bulletin of the John Rylands University Library of Manchester*
CCSL	*Corpus Christianorum Series Latina*
CSEL	*Corpus scriptorum Ecclesiasticorum Latinorum*
Int	*Interpretation*
JBL	*Journal of Biblical Literature*
JSNTSup	*Journal for the Study of the New Testament*, Supplement Series
JTS	*Journal of Theological Studies*
NovT	*Novum Testamentum*
NovTSup	*Novum Testamentum*, Supplements
SBLDS	SBL Dissertation Series
SC	*Sources Chrétiennes*

INTRODUCTION:
SIGNALLING TIME IN MARK

'πεπλήρωται ὁ καιρὸς'

'The time has arrived'. The first words spoken by Jesus in the Gospel of Mark (1.15) signal the start and the end of the Gospel in time. Mark is unique in putting in Jesus' mouth these claims for time. Elsewhere, the time has not yet come (Jn 7.8), it is close (Rev. 1.3; 22.10), or it has not yet arrived (1 Thess. 5.1).[1] As Paul Ricoeur has written, the dichotomy between the concept of time in the biblical texts (καιρός) and the Hellenic χρόνος has given rise to enormous debate. Scholars have argued that the Hebrew concept of time was historic whereas the Greek was cyclical, a distinction leading to the conclusion that Hebraic experience rendered the 'ear' and 'hearing' central whereas the eye and vision took precedence for the Greeks.[2]

Mark's καιρός is the eschatological moment, the turning point in history orchestrated by God, and it has arrived.[3] The Gospel proclaims a present arrived time of great significance at the beginning of Jesus'

---

1. Werner Kelber, *The Kingdom in Mark: A New Place and a New Time* (Philadelphia: Fortress Press, 1974), pp. 9-10.

2. Paul Ricoeur, 'Biblical Time', in Mark I. Wallace (ed.), *Figuring the Sacred: Religion, Narrative, and Imagination* (trans. David Pellauer; Minneapolis: Fortress Press, 1995), pp. 167-80. Cullmann, *Christ and Time*; Barr, *Biblical Words for Time*.

3. Willi Marxsen, *Mark the Evangelist: Studies in the Redaction History of the Gospel* (trans. James Boyce, Donald Juel, William Poehlmann, with Roy A. Harrisville; Nashville: Abingdon Press, 1969; originally *Der Evangelist Markus: Studien zur Redaktiongeschichte des Evangeliums* [Göttingen, Germany: Vandenhoeck & Ruprecht, 1956]), p. 134. Barr points out that the word καιρός can mean 'right or decisive time' or plain 'time', referring to a period 'without any element of decisiveness' (*Biblical Words for Time*, p. 51). In 1.15, he argues, it means the former (p. 42).

public career. This eschatological revelation[4] occurs in the busy, teeming squares, country fields and remote areas, and crowded city streets of the contemporary world of first-century Palestine.[5] Also, the major historical figures of this current time (Pontius Pilate, Herod and Herodias, or the High Priest) and contemporary political history (the Herodian tetrarchy and the Roman occupation of Palestine) determine the fates of the main characters, John the Baptist and Jesus. It tells a crisis time story in which every step of its main character and those around him in the central narrative moves towards the imminent end-time of Jesus' death. Yet its author reaches back to the sacred traditions of the Hebrew people to remember revered laws, prophetic utterances and promises of redeemed histories.[6] The crisis time narrative connects ordinary or real living local time with 'universal' or mythic time because the narrative has both a historical reality and a symbolic reality that undergird the mythic time of the Gospel and make claims for all-time eternal truth. Thus, though the Gospel makes the καιρός its central temporal concept, it nonetheless follows Hebraic temporal traditions. As Paul Ricoeur wrote of time in the Hebrew Scriptures, 'the model of biblical time rests on the polarity between narrative and hymn and on the mediation brought about between telling and praising, by the law and its temporal anteriority, prophecy and its eschatological time, and by wisdom in its immemorial time'.[7] In recalling his sacred wisdom traditions and reaffirming the law through allusion and direct reference, Mark follows these traditions, but he brings the sacred horizon to the present to show how the present must be understood in terms of the past, the future and eternity.

From the moment the Gospel opens with its heraldic announcement, recalling Isaiah and Malachi and promising the 'coming of the Lord', the narrative's apocalyptic tone declares its temporal setting 'in crisis'.

---

4.   Fusing structuralist and post-structuralist theoretical approaches, Daniel Otto Via examines apocalyptic time—Jesus' life and career as both beginning and end time in the Gospel of Mark—and connects it to the ethics proclaimed in Mk 10. See *The Ethics of Mark's Gospel—in the Middle of Time* (Philadelphia: Fortress Press, 1985).

5.   Elizabeth Struthers Malbon, *Narrative Space and Mythic Meaning* (San Francisco: Harper & Row, 1986), analyzes the use of space in Mark's Gospel.

6.   This is the concept of time elaborated by Cullmann, *Christ and Time*.

7.   'Biblical Time', p. 180.

The first words spoken by Jesus parallel this apocalyptic, critical beginning (1.15). Before he speaks, only two voices are heard: John the Baptist's, foretelling his coming (1.7), and the voice from heaven conferring divine status on him (1.11).

καιρός (1.15), a word used uniquely by Mark in this context (not in the other Synoptic Gospels) describes the event initiating Jesus' public ministry. καιρός means a critical moment in time, the period when the kingdom of God, μετάνοια, faith and Jesus' public ministry intersect.[8] The Jesus narrative moves forward temporally from this moment on through the series of events, the 'crisis time', prior to and including his passion and death. Despite the fact that we do not know how old Jesus is when he enters the narrative or how long the events of the narrative endured, we are nonetheless made aware that the events are invoked with temporal urgency. Two features distinguish the 'crisis time' narrative from a narrative that develops a story chronologically. First, only brief periods 'from the life of the actor are presented'. Secondly, the crisis is central to understanding all the other actions, actors and their relationships in the narrative.[9]

While ordinary time, in the sense of day-to-day chronology, is not represented in the Gospel, many different versions of contemporary reality are. Ordinary time in which humans live as historical, mortal beings includes the setting of the Gospel in a historical moment; everyday ordinary people act, talk and concern themselves with the reality of day-to-day living. People work as fishermen, carpenters, farmers and tax-collectors. People live in families and parents love their children. People get hungry and sick and they also die; rituals must be followed, and people are expected to live up to the cultural and religious codes. Secondly, the Gospel relies on actual historical characters and events. Thirdly, the time of Jesus' career, from his emergence in the public arena to his ignominious public death and private burial, is yet another present time narrative in the Gospel. Noting these events with special cues, such as proclamations, prophecies and voices from heaven, dramatizes them as parts of a crisis time narrative. The crisis narration puts ordinary time and ordinary people in the same world as prophets and charismatic leaders who talk about extraordinary time and extraordinary realities. Common people will come to experience uncommon

8. Marxsen, *Mark the Evangelist*, pp. 133-34; Kelber, *The Kingdom in Mark*, pp. 9-11, 13, 100.
9. Bal, *Narratology*, pp. 38-42.

events as the world of ordinary time intersects with the extraordinary time. Sacred time's distance and exclusiveness enter contemporary time and common space. This shocking disjunction disrupts the customary comfort associated with the known, the repeated and the ritualized. Never for one moment in the narrative does the Gospel writer allow his audience to become a passive witness to events; rather the events unfold in apocalyptic tones that force the audience to recognize the narrative as a crisis story, the import of which is critical for all who hear it.

Beginning *in medias res,* the Gospel, despite the writer's omniscient knowledge about all the events associated with the crisis narrative, does not follow a biographical chronology because it leaves out Jesus' early life (birth, upbringing, parentage, education, and so on) except that he is Mary's son (6.3). This exclusion focuses the Gospel on the crisis time in the central character's career. In Mark's crisis time narrative, we never find out how much chronological time the story takes; we do not know how old Jesus was, how long his public ministry lasted, or how many years he spent teaching and working miracles before his journey to Jerusalem. Except in the case of the passion narrative, the narrator suppresses these specific time clues about the story and the narrative duration.

Lacking any specific chronological signatures that would place the Gospel historically, unlike the Gospel of Luke, for example, the crisis narrative nonetheless does convey temporal sequences and moods. Moving forward through juxtaposition, parallelism and trebling, the journey of the main character provides narrative unity that substitutes for temporal details. In seemingly unrelated paratactic sequences of prose joined repeatedly by accumulative temporal clues (καὶ or καὶ πάλιν), the Gospel reveals what its teller knows, whether public or private, about the good news of Jesus, the anointed one, in a plotted journey in which each sequence of discourse comments on a previous or forthcoming sequence.

The 'crisis' time begins with Jesus' announcement that the 'time has arrived'. It escalates with a series of pivotal actions, including the calling of the disciples (1.16-20; 2.14; 3.13-19); demonstration of his won-der-working skills through a series of miracles (1.21–2.12); and his series of conflicts.[10] This sets the stage for his eventual demise and

---

10. See Joanna Dewey, *Markan Public Debate: Literary Technique, Concentric Structure, and Theology 2.1–3.6* (Chico, CA: Scholars Press, 1977) and Arland J.

shows him disputing over central teachings with the conventional authorities, whether Pharisee, Herodian, or his own family (2.15–3.35). At 4.1, a suspension of action ensues as Jesus demonstrates a unique characteristic of his teaching style in his first parable. This is the first of many suspensions of time in the Gospel, when the crisis narrative comes to a halt and another narrative takes over. These intercalated narratives often become more important to the primary narrative (the Jesus story) as interpretation or commentary on it than the 'crisis' narrative itself.

Active verbs are the vehicle to convey the movement in the crisis time in the Gospel as Jesus journeys forward. Alone or with others, he enters, goes, drives or is driven out, comes, returns, leaves, is on the road, drives out, immediately and again (εὐθὺς and πάλιν): 1.9, 12, 14, 21, 29, 35, 39; 2.1, 13; 3.1, 7, 13; 5.1, 21; 6.1, 7, 32, 53; 7.24, 31; 8.22, 27; 9.2, 14, 30, 33; 10.1, 17, 32, 46; 11.1, 11, 15, 27. This movement describes the nature of the temporal action, while giving unity and immediacy to the episodes that develop the crisis time of the Gospel. For example, the word ἐκβάλλειν describes Jesus' movement into the desert. Mark had connected John to the wilderness (1.4), but Jesus had to be driven there brusquely by the spirit (1.12), where he would sojourn with angels and the temptations of Satan (1.12-13) for a specific forty days. ἐκβάλλειν usually functions as exorcism terminology.[11] Here its use invites us to believe that this was not Jesus' first choice. Jesus' stay is brief, bound by time, although he returns to this arid place for prayer and tranquility (1.35), but John's, like Isaiah's ministry, is tied to the wilderness. Jesus' successful struggle against the devil contrasts with forthcoming conflicts in the cities when the civil powers will conclude both prophets' missions. Further, Jesus' initiation in the wilderness is juxtaposed with the abrupt announcement of John's arrest (1.14), in a tragic foreboding of Jesus' own later arrest. This makes the wilderness seem a peaceful, tranquil place, ordered by the natural-spirit powers and is the temporal and spatial backdrop with which Mark initiates Jesus' public career, in contrast to the cities where vicious motives rule. In the first use of the verb ἐκβάλλειν, the spirit drives Jesus, but from this point on, it is Jesus who takes on the role of the spirit as he

Hultgren, *Jesus and his Adversaries* (Minneapolis: Augsburg, 1979), pp. 39-64, for a description of the generic characteristics of conflict stories.

11. See Edwin K. Broadhead, *Teaching with Authority: Miracles and Christology in the Gospel of Mark* (JSNTSup, 74; Sheffield: Sheffield Academic Press, 1992), p. 171.

drives out devils and disease (1.34, 39, 43; 3.22, 23; 5.40; 6.13; 7.26; 9.18, 28, 38) or confers these powers on his disciples (3.15). When Jesus drives the traffickers in money from the temple (11.15), ἐκβάλλειν connects his earlier forceful retreat with his later expulsion of corruption from the temple cult, showing the critical, almost compulsory, nature of both actions, with the later action of Jesus mimicking the spirit's in the first. Both testify to the καιρός, the momentous gravity in the actions, with the earlier occurrences functioning as anticipation[12] of the later. This accumulation of verbs of coming and going continues until the arrival in Jerusalem when the journey is over. Only two references to the act of coming or going to places occur after the third entrance to Jerusalem, one to the Mount of Olives (14.26) and the other to the Garden of Gethsemane (14.32).

This journey narrative, as in the book of Genesis,[13] facilitates the temporal sequencing and intercalation of discrete narratives in which a number of seemingly unrelated plots intersect. The road, a common feature of novelistic discourse, provides the circumstances for encounters with the other characters the author includes in the story. It permits apparently random encounters, where all kinds of people (rich, poor, Jew, non-Jew, Roman, Pharisee, Sadducee, old, young, men, women, outcasts, and so on) pass. Those who normally would not mix because of social, religious, economic or political barriers accidentally meet or collide on roads. Thus the journey mediates the social milieu and collapses social distances. The journey substitutes for specific time clues because it holds together what happens before and afterwards.

The use of prepositions, temporal nouns and adverbs provides repeated generic time clues about Jesus' journey and emphasizes the apocalyptic nature of the 'crisis narrative'. πάλιν and εὐθὺς ('again' and 'immediately')[14] are most frequent; but other time indicators are ὀπίσω ('after', 1.7); τεσσεράκοντα ('forty', 1.13); καιρὸς ('critical time', 1.15); πρωῒ ἔννυχα λίαν ('early next morning', 1.35); ὀψίας δὲ

---

12. 'Anticipation', is Mieke Bal's word for foreboding or flash-forward (*Narratology*, p. 54).

13. Hermann Gunkel, *The Legends of Genesis* (New York: Schocken Books, 1964), p. 81.

14. A most useful and thorough work on the frequency of isolated redactional features in the gospel is David Barrett Peabody's *Mark as Composer* (Macon, GA: Mercer University Press, 1987). εὐθὺς is used approximately 42 times in the Gospel and πάλιν an approximately equal number.

γενομένης ('when evening came', 1.32, 4.35); ὅτε ἔδυ ὁ ἥλιος ('when the sun set', 1.32); variations of 'on the Sabbath' (2.23), or γενομένου σαββάτου, ('sabbath came' 6.2); μετὰ ἡμέρας ('six days', 9.2). However, these times designate a temporal space or crisis time rather than historical or specific chronological time. They situate the action in time but the time is not part of a chronological sequence; they link the separated discourses and do not emphasize duration but the immediacy in the momentous events. The time designations, provided with numbers possessing allegorical or typological significance, forty days in the desert and the six days preparatory to the transfiguration on the mountain, remove the events from any specific historical time categories. Mark's use of time signatures vividly contrasts with Luke's, who situates his story within the historical framework of the political events of his times (Lk. 1.5, 26; 2.1-3, 41-42; 3.1, for example).[15] In Mark, time invariably indicates sequential motion rather than chronology, that is, spatial movement rather than historical time. Such a distinction emphasizes the urgency of the events and the imminence of the crisis they recount.

For example, both John and Jesus enter the Gospel with parallel phrasing, ἐγένετο ('it happened') a narrative signature characteristic of Hebraic scripture that appears to move the story forward. It heralds the event as happening in time but without designating any particular time or even sequence. As a paratactic vehicle to accumulate events, it disregards temporal relationships, connecting the careers of the two prophets, while understating the grandeur of the incident: two prophets, the spirit and the ominous voice from heaven do not simply *happen*. Associating the three prophets, Isaiah, John and Jesus creates ironic anticipation, as it makes the present an ominous foreshadowing of a future that will repeat the past.

The expression ὀπίσω μου ('after me'), another time signal, with which John announces Jesus' coming designates more than temporality and sequence of action. When John the Baptist announces ἔρχεται ὁ ἰσχυρότερός μου ὀπίσω μου ('After me comes one who is mightier') (1.7), the audience/reader is informed of the sequence in which the actions took place, though not the actual time or the length of time that John's ministry endured. But the 'afterwardness' builds the narrative crescendo, for it points to a more important actor and event coming

15. David Aune, 'Luke–Acts and Ancient Historiography', in *idem, The New Testament and its Literary Environment* (Philadelphia: Westminster Press, 1987), pp. 77-115.

after this one. In addition, the prophecied after time has a symbolic meaning because if the audience were acquainted with the fate of John, through tradition, it must instantly recognize the irony in this statement: will the greater one who follows experience the same fate? When Jesus calls his four fishermen, the phrase ὀπίσω μου (1.17; 1.20) is repeated. Again, the surface statement seems clear, 'after me', but in each case, coming after involves far more than chronological sequence or narrative duration. Does 'coming after' mean the same vocation, the same suffering, the same death for John, Jesus and disciples? The ironic repetition creates narrative anticipation, connecting the narrative segments, prompting these questions and connecting events from different times as patterns of repetition. Also, Mark's use of the word παραδοθῆναι (1.14) for John's arrest anticipates its repetition in one form or another by Jesus about his own arrest (9.31; 10.33), thus confirming the fateful parallels between the two prophets. Thus Mark's use of the time signature ὀπίσω conveys the sequence of events, but this is not its primary purpose. Because of its repetition, it dramatizes the parallelism between the public careers of the central actors in the Gospel and reveals the urgency in the impending crisis narrative.

Similarly, the trebling, about which many commentators on the Gospel have remarked,[16] functions as a 'focalizor', one of the most powerful means of directing and controlling an audience. 'Focalization', a term used by narrative theorists, is the relation between the vision and that which is seen or perceived. 'Vision' is the way in which elements of the story are presented and 'focalization' is the relationship between this presentation, the reader, and what he or she sees in the act of reading.[17] 'Focalizors' pull the critical events into the temporal foreground. In addition to Pesch's overall triadic structure for the Gospel, we find significantly, for example, at three critical moments, Jesus is called the son of God: the baptism (1.11), the transfiguration (9.7) and the crucifixion (15.39), twice by a voice from heaven, and

16. Werner Kelber, *The Oral and the Written Gospel* (Philadelphia: Fortress Press, 1983), p. 66; Gert Lüderitz, 'Rhetorik, Poetik, Kompositionstechnik', in Hubert Cancik (ed.), *Markus Philologie* (Tübingen: J.C.B. Mohr, 1984), pp. 186-88 (165-203); Rudolph Pesch, *Das Markus-Evangelium*.I. *Mark 1.1–8.26* (2 vols.; Freiburg: Herder, 1976); *Das Markus-Evangelium*.II.*8.27–16.20* (2 vols.; Freiburg: Herder, 1977).

17. Bal, *Narratology*, pp. 100-18. Genette, *Narrative Discourse*, pp. 189-98.

once by a Roman centurion, a man of a different race, creed and political affiliation; three disciples witness the transfiguration (9.2) when three holy men converse together, Moses, Elijah and Jesus (9.4); three times Jesus predicts his death and resurrection (8.31; 9.31; 10.33-34); thrice after these predictions, his disciples display their crude understanding of Jesus' mission (8.32-33; 9.33-34;10.35-38);[18] Jesus enters Jerusalem three times (11.11, 15, 27); taking three disciples with him, three times Jesus exhorts them to stay awake as he prays in Gethsemane (14.34, 37, 40-41), and finds them sleeping; three times Peter denies Jesus (14.68, 70, 71), three die by crucifixion, and three women find the tomb empty (16.1-8). During the trial, the chief priests or high priest try three times to find evidence against Jesus (14.56-64); three times Pilate asks the crowd to decide on Jesus' fate (15.9-14), and the crucifixion follows its grim appointments every three hours (15.25, 33, 34).[19] Triadic structure and trebling are synchronic components of folk and oral literature,[20] but in Mark, their number and significant placement forcefully argues that the trebles occur precisely at the crisis moments in the Gospel, thus functioning as 'focalizors'. They draw the narrative events out from their context and setting to communicate their place in the temporal urgency of the narrative, and thus make the events axiomatic.

In contrast to these narratival devices that connect events temporally or substitute for concrete information about temporal duration, specific chronological time signatures are everywhere in the final stage of the journey: ἦν δὲ τὸ πάσχα καὶ τὰ ἄζυμα μετὰ δύο ἡμέρας ('The festival of Passover and unleavened bread was only two days off', 14.1); καὶ τῇ πρώτῃ ἡμέρᾳ τῶν ἀζύμων ('on the first day of unleavened bread', 14.12); σήμερον ταύτῃ τῇ νυκτὶ πρὶν ἢ δὶς ἀλέκτορα φωνῆσαι ('this night, before the cock crows twice', 14.30); οὐκ ἴσχυσας μίαν ὥραν γρηγορῆσαι ('not able to stay awake one hour?', 14.37); ἦν δὲ ὥρα τρίτη καὶ ἐσταύρωσαν αὐτόν ('it was the third hour in the morning when they crucified him', 15.25); καὶ γενομένης ὥρας ἕκτης σκότος ἐγένετο ('and in the sixth hour it became dark', 15.33); καὶ τῇ ἐνάτῃ

18. F.J. Matera, 'The Incomprehension of the Disciples and Peter's Confession (Mark 6.14–8.30)', *Bib* 70 (1989), pp. 153-72.

19. Kelber, *The Oral and the Written Gospel*, p. 66.

20. This was pointed out by Vladimir Propp in *Morphology of the Folktale* (Austin, TX: University of Texas Press, 1968 [1928]), p. 74; Alfred Lord, *The Singer of Tales* (Cambridge, MA: Harvard University Press, 1960).

ὥρᾳ ('and in the ninth hour', 15.34); καὶ ἤδη ὀψίας γενομένης ('and when evening came', 15.42); καὶ διαγενομένου τοῦ σαββάτου ('and when the sabbath was over', 16.1). Although many of these time tokens find parallels in Matthew and Luke, Mark has more. In this last segment of the Gospel, the emphasis on the chronological time of events situates the passion (the Last Supper, Jesus' trial, crucifixion and resurrection), as action begun and ended within chronological time. This emphatic reference to human chronological time in the central crisis of the Gospel, emphasizes that this is a one-time only event, and that the sacrifice is not a model subject to repetition. On the contrary, unlike other sacrificial scapegoats, Jesus has taken the place of all other victims.[21] The quote from Psalms as the lament on the cross, ἐλωι, ἐλωι λεμα σαβαχθανι, expresses the anguish of human temporality and limitation, connecting the Jesus narrative typologically to Hebrew Scriptures and shifting the narrative from the mythologically timeless road trodden by the prophets of old (1.2-3) to the contemporary reality of human history.[22] The symbolic or generic character of the time cues up to the passion narrative when chronological time takes over moves the crisis narrative from the typological pattern to historical reality.

Besides the crisis narrative with its generic time cues and the passion story's specific chronology, the Gospel has an alternative narrative duration. The second, the series of intercalations, anachronies and parables break up the linearity and progress of the primary narrative and suspend its duration. I call these interruptions, which have been variously labelled, suspended time narratives. These secondary or suspended time narratives in which Jesus may or may not be the prime actor overtake the primary crisis narrative. They point both to their interrelationship with the central series of events and away from them to critical implications reaching beyond the historical moment to the future and to the creation of the living present community formed by the series of original events.

This second group includes all the stories about others that punctuate the sequence created by the series of events in the primary narrative: the Parable of the Sower, Mustard Seed and Vineyard; the

21. René Girard, *The Scapegoat* (trans. Yvonne Freccero; Baltimore: The Johns Hopkins University Press, 1986), p. 200.
22. A.C. Charity, 'The Way of Jesus', in Harold Bloom (ed.), *The Gospels* (New York: Chelsea House, 1988), pp. 17-23.

Gerasene demoniac, Jairus's daughter, the bleeding woman, Syrophoenicean woman, the death of John the Baptist, cursing of the fig-tree, and Peter's denial. Both the crisis and suspended time narratives develop three paradoxical but parallel paths: the mission of Jesus, the development of the disciples and the education of the community of the faithful.[23] The primary Jesus narrative and the education of the disciples occupy the crisis time, but the suspended time narratives often interpret the primary narrative or function to educate the community of observers within the Gospel, and the audience or readers outside. They are stories set in ordinary time that represent possible ways of being open to everyone who hears the Gospel and responds in faith at any time. As parables, they are also interpretations of the central narrative, harboring implications about the crisis story that have meaning in other times—perhaps the present, that is, the time when the Gospel was written, and the future it addresses.

In addition to these two narrative durations, the symbolism in the historical crisis-time narrative points to an implied time, a 'mythic time' that speaks for all time and all reality.[24] This symbolic narrative interprets the central events as a liminal time, a break with contemporary life as usual, that makes it possible to scrutinize and evaluate all the structures and codes ruling ordinary time. The liminal time comes to an end with the death of Jesus, but this interlude serves to present a model of how to be in the world in mythic or universal time, that is, according to the terms of eternity rather than according to the pleasures, pressures, strains and coercions of the ordinary time. This is one of the most fascinating aspects of the Gospel of Mark. Although the narrative setting is well within human memory it possesses many synchronic features of mythic narratives and it proclaims a mythic uncontingent reality,[25] summoning all humans to its demands. Not set in a time before time as most myths, not even in a long time ago history, this uncontingent mythic narrative reveals itself in a recognizable world, a contemporary reality that this exceptional story interrupts. But Mark never negates the real world of historical-ordinary living. On

23. Herman C. Waetjen (*A Reordering of Power: A Socio-Political Reading of Mark's Gospel* [Minneapolis: Fortress Press, 1989]) shows how these dimensions of the Gospel convey its social teaching.

24. Paul Ricoeur, *Time and Narrative* (trans. Kathleen Blamey and David Pellauer; Chicago: University of Chicago Press, 1988), III, p. 105.

25. Blumenberg, *Work on Myth*, p. 126.

the contrary, mythic and historical time intersect to open up the possibility for both individual and historical redemption. This aspect of
Markan temporality, found also in the other Christian Gospels, characterizes other Christian literature. A similar multiple temporality
occurs also in Augustine's *Confessions*, Dante's *Divina Commedia*, and
Langland's *Piers Plowman*, for example. When the central character as
a historical person becomes an allegory (parable or typology), the character's personal story is played out against his own time, the past (as
history and as typology) the historical future and against eternity. The
person's life, or immediate experience as unfolded in the narrative
simultaneously involves his or her own time and all time.

Because the present is interpreted according to the past with which
it is in continuity in the Gospel of Mark, allusions direct the audience
to see human life in broader terms than day-to-day ordinary time or
immediate historical event time. These allusions include the memory
of the past, whether of teachings, stories, or promises that still resonate
in the present and that possess meaning precisely because of their continuing importance in the present. The Gospel also remembers the
'ritual times'[26] when Jesus and his followers experienced spontaneous
community.

This study comprises five extended discussions of kinds of time in the
Gospel and of how time directs the focus of the narrative. In Chapter
1, I explore the Gospel's contemporary setting and what this has to do
with its genre and its relationship to other generic models from the
Greco–Roman world and its own Hebraic traditions. Its genre and contemporary setting reveal its social purposes, the audience for whom it
is intended and the socio-cultural world from which it emerged. Chapter 2 takes up the recomposition of Hebraic fragments and typologies
to remake the past into the present by remembering and recalling past
teachings, prophecies and histories that have meaning and power in
the present. This remembering re-enforces the connection between the
present story and the continuing narrative of Hebraic history and experience. Chapter 3 deals with the suspended time narratives, that is, all
the interruptions to the central framing events, including Jesus' parables and the intercalations that suspend the crisis narrative. The actors
in these narratives are themselves often in suspended time because of
their status as outsiders due to illness, ethnicity, gender and self-chosen
exile. In Chapter 4, I examine how all the symbolic cues in the Gospel

---

26. Ricoeur, *Time and Narrative*, III, p. 105.

build it as a mythic narrative that takes place in a liminal interruption of ordinary time. But this mythic possibility presents a way of being in the world that shows the liminal experience as the way to live in ordinary time according to the axis of eternity. In the final chapter, I discuss how the 'ritual time' puts the Gospel narrative in a broader time than its own historical setting. On the one hand, the ritual experiences overcome the time distinctions between the past and the future, or between ordinary and mythic time, making all time eternally present. The last supper ritual memorializes a parodoxical event that disrupted community but continues as a living tradition that is still relevant in the present and the future. The ritual, in fact, repeats the meditation on time suggested by the original series of events and by their framing in the Gospel narratives.

The Gospel writer refers to Hebrew Scripture to connect the story he tells to the past, but his apocalyptic interpretation of the events recounted makes them significant for the present of the Gospel and the imminent future. This constant interweaving of past, present and future with frequent suspensions of time and anachronies, pointing outside of time, allows the Markan author to connect his crisis story with the continuity of sacred and ordinary history. His narrative unravels the dead-endedness of the crisis story by symbolically taking it outside time, and he revives the past by making it part of the living present and future. With the institution of the new ritual in the Gospel initiated at a Passover dinner, itself a ritual recapitulation of historical events, he ties the new event to that history and simultaneously takes it outside ordinary time as it becomes the means to remember and to connect to the past in an ongoing repeated ritual that will continue in the future. Thus, though crisis is imminent, continuity prevails.

Chapter 1

MARKAN PRESENT TIME:
THE GOSPEL AS PICARESQUE NOVELLA*

A central feature of the narrative of the Gospel of Mark is its setting in the world of contemporary first-century Palestine. Mark imitates the paratactic style of the Hebrew Bible and the immediacy of the apocalyptic tradition, but he simultaneously draws the sacred horizon into the ordinary time of his own world. This contemporaneity serves to mediate between traditional religious and present time, and therefore to connect the historical world of then and the people who acted in it with the present world of now and with the people who experience the narrative.[1] Like picaresque, which presents a main character experiencing a contemporary world chaotically charged with social dissonance, the Gospel of Mark constructs a comparably familiar world, that is closer to his audience's experience and to contemporary history than any other literary genres represented in his immediate cultural milieu. But, no matter to what degree events in first-century Palestine or Rome may have been ethically neutral, the precise purpose of the Gospel writer, in keeping with his Hebraic models, is to load these worlds with value. Mark weaves his Hebraic literary heritage into how he tells about the world of the dynamic present where the important social, political, ethical and religious questions of the time are dramatically enacted. In doing so, he revolutionizes the traditional sacred timeless narrative, transforming it into a narrative model for picaresque. In this chapter, I will focus on Mark's genre as one means to examine how the present time is represented in the Gospel.

Picaresque is an anachronistic term when applied to the Gospels because it did not exist as a generic category in the ancient world. Nonetheless, the dominant features of what was later labelled picaresque

---

*   A version of this chapter will appear in *Genre* (1998).
1.   Ricoeur, *Time and Narrative* III, pp. 104-26.

do appear in a number of ancient works. The style of the Gospel of Mark in terms of language, subject, plot and character turns the contemporary world upside down, so that all conventional value temporarily ceases, while the marginalized hero and the companions he picks up along the way occupy the main road, and so expose this world to a sustained investigation. This is a narrative pattern common in picaresque novels. What does the first Gospel[2] have in common with picaresque? First, both are short prose episodic narrative works. The narrative moves forward by juxtaposing a collection of narratives with little or no hypotactic intervention. In the Gospel, as in picaresque, the main character, a trickster or underdog, without social, political, or financial power, bursts upon the contemporary scene. He undertakes a journey with an unclear destination, although the unplanned journey makes random encounters and adventures the occasions for developing the narrative. The main character's subversive political and social orientation pits his behavior and attitudes against those having conventional merit or acceptance. This character has no close love relationships and despite his social orientation, he often chooses to be alone. The main character serves to unify the novella's episodes. The narrator recounts the events, no matter how fantastic, in a journalistic tone most akin to the style of realism, while characters, who are usually ordinary people,

---

2.   Christian Hermann Weisse, *Die evangelienfrage in ihrem gegenwartigen Stadium* (Leipzig: Breitkopf and Hartel, 1856); Christian Hermann Weisse, *Die evangelische Geschichte kritisch und philosophisch bearbeitet* (2 vols.; Leipzig: Breitkopf and Hartel, 1838). The argument for the priority of Mark was a long struggle beginning with G.S. Storr's (1790) thesis that Mark was a source for Matthew and Luke (Bernard Orchard and Thomas R.W. Longstaff [eds.], *J.J. Griesbach: Synoptic and Text-critical Studies 1776–1976* [Cambridge: Cambridge University Press, 1978]). This contradicted a fourteen-hundred-year tradition upheld since Augustine's 'Marcus eum subsecutus tamquam pedisequus et breviator eius videtur'. *De consensu evangelistarum*, CSEL 43, 1.2. Augustine's position was so powerful that despite the eighteenth- and nineteenth-century scholarship systematically contradicting it, the Biblical Commission affirmed the traditional authorship, date of composition, and historical character of the Gospel of Matthew by official decree on 19 June 1911. (Arthur J. Belinzoni, Jr [ed.], *The Two-Source Hypothesis: An Appraisal* [Macon, GA: Mercer University Press, 1985], pp. 101-102); for cases for and against Markan priority, see *idem*, 'The Case for the Priority of Mark', pp. 21-93; *idem*, 'The Case Against the Priority of Mark', pp. 97-217 in *The Two-Source Hypothesis*. Arguments against the two-source theory are made in William O. Walker, Jr, *The Relationships among the Gospels: An Interdisciplinary Dialogue* (San Antonio, TX: Trinity University Press, 1978).

speak in a colloquial language about personal concerns or contemporary issues. The scenes in which the narratives are enacted are often socially charged. The society depicted appears chaotic because many conflicting groups and contradictory ideologies are represented. Despite the social critique often implicit in picaresque, it exhibits little or no discursive writing. Narratives or conversations communicate matters of social and religious importance. Finally, the genre in which these events and their main character's actions are narrated is controversial.

A closer look at the Markan narration, I will argue, reveals it has more in common with picaresque than any other literary models. Picaresque, as it emerged in Spanish literature in the sixteenth century, is usually written by a member of the newly-emerged middle social class, addresses a broad readership, is in an autobiographical or biographical form, is concerned with the real lives of ordinary people, and most importantly, is ideologically, socially or politically subversive. The picaresque hero, a trickster personality, takes a random journey whose course plunges him into many different environments (country, city, road, outside, inside, mountain, plain, church, and so on) where he encounters all sorts, conditions, and classes of human beings. The main character inhabits a social-political world he exposes to ironic, critical scrutiny.[3] Despite the obvious parallels between the Gospel's features and picaresque, it is surprising that no scholar of the genre has suggested a relationship. A somewhat comparable ancient picaresque

---

3. As pointed out in all studies of picaresque, see, for example, Mikhail Bakhtin, *Rabelais and his World* (trans. Helene Iswolsky; Cambridge, MA: MIT Press, 1968); Stuart Miller, *The Picaresque Novel* (Cleveland: Case Western Reserve University Press, 1967); Alexander A. Parker, *Literature and the Delinquent: The Picaresque Novel in Spain and Europe 1599–1753* (Edinburgh: Edinburgh University Press, 1967); Richard Bjornson, *The Picaresque Hero in European Fiction* (Madison: University of Wisconsin Press, 1977); Fernando Fernán-Gómez, *Historias de la picaresca* (Barcelona: Editorial Planeta, 1989); Ulrich Wicks, *Picaresque Narrative, Picaresque Fictions: A Theory and Research Guide* (New York: Greenwood Press, 1989); Robert Alter, *Rogue's Progress: Studies in the Picaresque Novel* (Cambridge, MA: Harvard University Press, 1964); Christine J. Whitbourn (ed.), *Knaves and Swindlers: Essays on the Picaresque Novel in Europe* (University of Hull Publications; London: Oxford University Press, 1974); Gustavo Pellón and Julio Rodríguez-Luis (eds.), *Upstarts, Wanderers or Swindlers: Anatomy of the Picaro, A Critical Anthology* (Amsterdam: Rodopi, 1986); Robert Alter, *The Art of Biblical Narrative* (New York: Basic Books, 1981).

equivalent that scholars have noted is Petronius's *Satyricon*, which appeared in Rome in 67 CE,[4] probably during the same period as the Gospel of Mark.[5] Petronius's generic model is the Homeric epic which he parodies.[6]

Both the *Satyricon* and the Gospel of Mark recount journeys of less than financially and socially reputable characters and their encounter with all social types of people in chance meetings on the streets of Rome or ancient Palestine, and both use their main characters' journeys to censure their own societies. As in picaresque, in the Gospel of Mark, the main character takes himself onto the roads of first-century Palestine, where he wanders from place to place, meeting personalities from all social classes, whom he confronts in argument or agreement, ministers to, dismisses, or brings into his communal action. The characters encountered in the Gospel (Simon, James, John, Levi, the hemorrhaging woman, Jairus, the blind, deaf, dumb, crippled, officials and onlookers) are the socially and linguistically mixed types one might expect to meet in the town market-place (7.4), around the synagogue (1.21, 29) which appears to be the parallel place to the *agora* of Hellenism, or around the temple in Jerusalem in the first century. Incidents, events, arguments, or conversations occur in this social arena that provides the circumstances for debating and highlighting the central political and social questions of the times. The people the main character meets are concerned about contemporary political, moral and social issues, including sickness; infirmities of ordinary people as well as street people (1.34, 40; 3.10); trafficking with the socially and morally suspect like tax-gatherers and others (2.15); rites and customs (1.45; 2.18–3.5; 7.1-4; 10.1–12); religious beliefs about the afterlife (12.18-27); and God's commandments (12.28-34). Market-place or town-square topics include the Jewish political relationship to the Romans (12.13-17) and who has teaching authority (3.22; 11.19, 27-33), yet another question that pits Jesus against the authorities, whether Sadducees or Pharisees (12.38-40). The questions and problems probed pit the main character against the dominant political and social values and those who uphold them.

---

4. Wicks, *Picaresque Narrative*, pp. 13, 28, 312-15; P.G. Walsh, ' "Nachleben": The Roman Novel and the Rebirth of Picaresque', in *The Roman Novel: The 'Satyricon' of Petronius and the 'Metamorphoses' of Apuleius* (Cambridge: Cambridge University Press, 1970), pp. 224-43.

5. Ellis, 'The Date and Provenance of Mark's Gospel', pp. 801-15.

6. P.G. Walsh, 'The Literary Texture', in *idem*, *The Roman Novel*, pp. 32-66.

Like picaresque, the Gospel's socially ordinary hero and followers in fact link its story and the genre through which the story comes to us to popular sources. Recent studies suggest that early Christianity was a religion which appealed to many levels of society, rather than to the downtrodden as has often been asserted.[7] This mixture of people also characterizes the social world of the Markan Gospel, and one might extrapolate from it a description of Mark's audience, and as a consequence the appropriate genre for such a community. Some scholars have argued that the Greek language in Mark and the other Gospels is the language of the lower classes, or that it is similar to the Jewish Greek spoken by translators of the Greek *Septuagint* (from the Hebrew Scriptures), or a 'ghetto' language common to the early Christian minority. Many of the Gospel's so-called 'semiticisms' (i.e. Hebrew and Aramaic idioms awkwardly expressed in Greek) do appear in Greek popular literature.[8] The Gospel, like Matthew and John (though not

7.   Despite the consensus of recent years, a great diversity of opinion characterizes earlier discussions of the social status of early Christians. These are represented by the work of E.A. Judge, *The Social Pattern of Christian Groups in the First Century* (London: Tyndale, 1960); Adolf Deissmann (*Light from the Ancient East* [trans. Lionel R.M. Stracham; Grand Rapids: Baker Book House, 4th edn, 1965]) took the most extreme position, identifying the members of the movement 'among the weary and heavy-laden, men without power and position. . .' (p. 466). The work of Abraham J. Malherbe modified Deissman's position, based on what he called a 'new consensus' among biblical scholars that 'the social status of early Christians may be higher than Deissmann had supposed' (*Social Aspects of Early Christianity* [Philadelphia: Fortress Press, 2nd edn, 1983], p. 31). Since Malherbe's book, a number of outstanding studies on the social world of the first century have appeared including John H. Elliott, *Home for the Homeless* (Philadelphia: Fortress Press, 1981); Gerd Theissen, *Social Reality and the Early Christians: Theology, Ethics, and the World of the New Testament* (trans. Margaret Kohl; Minneapolis: Fortress Press, 1992); Wayne Meeks, *The First Urban Christians: The Social World of the Apostle Paul* (New Haven: Yale University Press, 1983); John E. Stambaugh, and David L. Balch, *The New Testament in its Social Environment* (Philadelphia: Westminster Press, 1986). Notwithstanding the fragmentariness of the evidence about the social status of early Christians in the Pauline communities, Meeks shows that while the middle level of society is markedly present in Paul's social milieu, the very rich and marginal are absent. See also Waetjen, *A Reordering of Power*.

8.   For Mark's language and its connection to popular literary style, see Aune, *New Testament in its Literary Environment*, p. 47; J.W. Voelz, 'The Language of the New Testament', *ANRW* 25.2 (1984), pp. 893-977; more recently, Christopher Bryan, *A Preface to Mark:. Notes on the Gospel and its Literary and Cultural Settings* (Oxford: Oxford University Press, 1993), pp. 54-56, concludes that Mark's

Luke which follows many of the conventions of ancient history),[9] breaks with antecedent literary conventions in a number of ways, and actually sets the agenda for later 'christian' literature because of its stylistic characteristics. These include the mixture of a common or low-style with high import issues which the author proclaims have apocalyptic significance.[10] The setting is contemporary for timeless concerns. The narrative focuses on the non-conformity, humility and simplicity of the Gospel's main character, Jesus of Nazareth, who survives by making use of his unique personal traits. In other words, his humble birth, lack of social privilege and economic status force him to support his journey with his wit and considerable personal talents. His journey and therefore the focus of the narrative leads to a temporary suspension of hierarchies of rank and status, as the Gospel shows us the tragedy of this extraordinary common man. The end of his moral debate occurs with the action of the state and religious authorities against the subversiveness of Jesus' talk and action on the streets. Jesus was rejected and punished precisely because of his seditious confrontation with the authorities and not because he was reversing 'Israel's' religious traditions or its moral convictions. Jesus attacks those who possess religious authority, whether chief priests, scribes, lawyers, Pharisees, Sadducees, and others, but not the tenets of the Hebrew religion they claim to uphold. Jesus' conflict begins with his transgression of the intellectual and social boundaries of the town-square where his actions and ideas challenge authorities rather than merely debate with them; it ends with his violation of the temple. His crucifixion as the 'King of the Jews', ironically restores the established political, religious and social power structures. Up to the time of Jesus' arrest (with the exception of the intercalated story of John the Baptist's death, 6.14-29), we witness a temporary suspension of the conventions of social and political hierarchy in the narrative, even if not ultimately understood by his followers.

Greek is not worse than Secundus's, a fact he uses to support his theory that Mark is writing a Hellenistic-style life (p. 56); see also J.K. Elliott (ed.), *The Language and Style of the Gospel of Mark: An edition of C.H. Turner's 'Notes on Marcan Usage'. Together with other Comparable Studies* (NovTSup, 81; Leiden: E.J. Brill, 1993).

9.   Aune, 'Luke–Acts and Ancient Historiography'.

10.   Erich Auerbach, *Mimesis* (trans. Willard Trask; Garden City, NY: Doubleday, 1957), pp. 35-43; *idem, Literary Language and its Public in Late Latin Antiquity and in the Middle Ages* (trans. Ralph Manheim; New York: Pantheon Books, 1965).

Assuming, as Abraham J. Malherbe has argued, that the literary genre is a clue to the social environment of the work,[11] in my discussion of the genre of the Gospel of Mark, I will be discussing the Gospel as popular literature, and like picaresque, linked to 'low' or 'folk culture'. The Jesus movement as presented in Mark is not quite the 'folk culture' characteristic of picaresque, although it shares many features with it. I am aware that the use of the term 'folk culture' is problematic for a first-century Palestinian/Greco-Roman setting, which was territory occupied by the Romans, who held ultimate authority over everyone, and who had come after the Hellenistic invasions which had successfully impressed many features of Hellenistic culture on Judaism.[12] But the term is intended to designate the culture of those people who are excluded from political, economic, social and religious power, status or authority. In contrast to epics and tragic drama, or the legends of the Hebrew Bible (both mythical and legendary but nonetheless fixed in past time) popular literature is often set in the contemporary world of real people, with real concerns for the present moment or the near future. This present world is uncertain as it moves steadily but unwittingly into the future, even though the more imminent the future, the more intangible and inconclusive it becomes. These popular literature traits characterize the Gospel of Mark, the style of which is closer to what later has been classified as picaresque than to any fixed ancient models, although many ancient forms share features with picaresque.

In the Gospel of Mark, the Palestinian Jesus story begins and ends as a mixed status movement, including the poor and marginalized, artisans (Jesus, a carpenter, 6.3), property owners (John and James, the sons of Zebedee, 1.19-20, the wealthy Jairus, 5.22-24, and Joseph of Arimathea, 15.43), women (5.23–5.43; 15.40-41; 16.1-8), and tax collectors (2.15), all of whom share in the communal charismatic interlude. Such a social environment for the Gospel combined with the 'low' linguistic and prose style suggests a comparable environment for its audience. Within the Jewish community itself there were hierarchies of

11. Malherbe, *Social Aspects of Early Christianity*, pp. 29-59.
12. Arnaldo Momigliano, *On Pagans, Jews, and Christians* (Middletown, CO: Wesleyan University Press, 1987); Saul Lieberman, *Hellenism in Jewish Palestine: Studies in the Literary Transmission, Beliefs and Manners in Palestine in the I Century BCE–IV Century CE* (New York: Jewish Theological Seminary of America, 1950).

power, represented by the temple priesthood in Jerusalem, the Sadducees and the Pharisees. Besides these powerful groups there was also
the Herodian tetrarchy and the presence of the Roman government,
represented in the Gospel of Mark by Pontius Pilate and according to
Josephus, the latest in a long line of vicious Roman governors. In the
first century, there were numerous strands of social, religious and political status and power shared unequally among these diverse groups.[13]
Jesus, according to the Gospel of Mark, was a carpenter (6.3), and his
immediate followers represented diverse political positions (3.19,
Simon, a member of the Zealot party) and social-economic status.
Simon's and Andrew's financial status is specifically contrasted with
James' and John's, the former fishing from the shore, while the latter
have their own boat, as well as hired men (1.16-20).

As with folk culture as represented in picaresque, the Jesus story
arose from the outsiders of the social spectrum, from those excluded
from cultural, social, or political power. In forming an alternative
community, the Jesus movement is in direct confrontation with the
privileged and powerful, the Pharisees, Sadducees, Herodians and the
Roman authorities (2.24; 3.1-2, 6; 7.1-3; 11.27-33; 12.13-27, 34-37;
14.43, 53-64; 15.6-15). Further, the narrative questions the standards
and expectations of the empowered, particularly its authoritarianism
and rules, as related to ritual purity and cleanliness (7.2, 18-23); its
social, ethnic and gender taboos, as Jesus chooses to eat with 'tax gath-
erers and others' (2.14-15), traffics with the marginalized, including
women (5.25-43; 15.40-41), the mad (5.1-20), and other social depen-
dents or outsiders (1.32-34; 2.4; 7.32-35); he rejects the prejudices and
taboos about religious blasphemy, ignores food, gender, ethnic, and
other socio-religious prohibitions (2.6-7, 18-19, 23-28). Flouting religious piety for its own sake, but not the moral convictions that lie
behind it, Jesus rejects individual egoism while, in the tradition of
Daniel, in his proclamation of the coming kingdom of God, (1.15; 9.35-
37; 13.10-11), he asserts a universal message representing all the people.[14] His emphasis is on the material against the ritualized, for his

13. Even though Josephus is not an entirely reliable source because of his own
complicity with the Romans, his description of Pontius Pilate shows him as a cruel
and vindictive governor. Pontius Pilate was appointed by Sejanus, an infamous anti-
semite, during Tiberius's reign. See Josephus, *The Jewish War*, 1–3, 4–7.

14. Momigliano, 'The Origins of Universal History', in *idem, Pagans, Jews, and
Christians*, pp. 31-57.

actions confront the physical reality of those he encounters. The Gospel emphasizes Jesus' miraculous cures, but these are all dramatic transformations of the body from illness and physical debility, whether it be deafness, blindness, lameness, hemorrhages, or even death, to health. These actions show how the Gospel writer translates the abstract, ideal and elevated to the material, thus rejoining the body, the earth and the spiritual and emphasizing their unity.[15] Thus Mark is interested in material reality, the body of the woman who bled for twelve years, the Gerasene demoniac's uncontrollable physical furor, the blind, deaf, dumb, and crippled—all the physically defective and the hungry—who are cured or fed, and thus brought into a universal egalitarian community (2.5; 4.40; 5.34; 6.6; 9.23-25; 13.11).

Besides the focus on the physical reality of the characters, another aspect of picaresque literature and the folk culture generating its energy is the style of 'grotesque realism', a literary feature often appearing in wonder tales, ancient myths and legends. Grotesque realism focuses on sheer corporeality, and because of the enormous number of miracle stories in the Markan Gospel in contrast to the other Gospels, we see numerous examples of this physicality. For example, the specific medical condition of the hemorrhaging woman (5.25); the grossly perverted dinner ritual which serves up the head of John the Baptist (6.27-28); the crippled, blind, deaf; the question of eating food with unclean hands (7.2), or slicing off the ear of the High Priest's servant (14.47), all emphasize the physical reality of humans. Mark does not sanitize any of these disturbing conditions or events; rather he exposes them in all their troubling rawness.

Like other picaresque literature that scrutinizes the 'contemporary' world outside of the conventions that rule social, political and economic power hierarchies, the Gospel of Mark proclaims a radical questioning of 'normal' behavior and value as it examines established criteria for moral and social life and those responsible for their preservation. The Gospel, like picaresque, examines convention, taboo and habit. At the same time, 'Israel's' laws undergird these debates. Like the Hebrew Bible's prophetic mode of writing, the Gospel is ready to stand outside power in order to undermine or probe received traditions.[16]

15. As Bakhtin describes the picaresque project in *Rabelais and his World*, pp. 19-20.

16. Herbert Schneidau, *Sacred Discontent* (Berkeley: University of California Press, 1976), p. 265.

Choosing a genre is one of the means the author has at his or her disposal to communicate with his or her audience. Identifying a literary work's genre is critical to understanding it, because the choice reflects how the work relates to similar writing in the genre and distinguishes the work from related texts. Through the classification of a written text, we can usually identify it with a social and cultural community. Authors' genre choices declare the literary tradition they identify themselves with, the social-literary milieu within which they write, and even the work's geographical location. The form of a literary work identifies it with a time (past and present), a place and a community. At the same time that every text assumes a shape prompted by the literary community from whence it emerges, it also absorbs and revises earlier texts whether through imitation, re-construction, or other transforming activities. Boundaries between genres are also fluid as writers tend to adapt forms to their personal literary aims.[17]

The purpose of discussing the Gospel's genre is not to define or classify it, but, by identifying it, to characterize its communication because such a literary activity helps us to 'interpret the exemplar'. The genre of a work informs the audience about the author's intentions because genre is identified with specific convictions, revealing the cultural climate from which the author emerges as well as the social environment for which the text is intended. To give an ancient example, Virgil's choice of epic for his story of the founding and future of Rome and its leaders was intended to revive the epic form and to connect his subject to the esteemed tradition of heroic epic, the form whose subject (war, monumental human action, and heroic values) and ideologies conformed with or could be adapted to those of his wealthy and powerful audience in the first century BCE. In Virgil's case, he flattered his patron Augustus Caesar by writing about his political ancestor Aeneas, the founder of Rome, in the same genre as the great Homeric epics. As a rule, the subjects, concerns, and characters of a genre are compatible with the interests of its intended audiences although author and audience's points of view inevitably diverge.

17. Jonathan Culler, *Structuralist Poetics: Structuralism, Linguistics, and the Study of Literature* (London: Routledge & Kegan Paul, 1975); Mikhail Bakhtin, *The Dialogic Imagination: Four Essays* (ed. Michael Holquist; trans. Caryl Emerson and Michael Holquist; Austin, TX: University of Texas Press, 1981); Alastair Fowler, *Kinds of Literature: An Introduction to the Theory of Genres and Modes* (Cambridge, MA: Harvard University Press, 1982).

Genres emerge at specific times, are selected deliberately by authors, and are regulated by defined conventions. They belong to specific historical moments, as epics, for example, belong to an idealized past time that is valued precisely because of its fixity in the past. This same point can be made about much of the literature of the classical world (tragedy, elegy, and so on) which was set in this imagined past, divorced from the fluctuations of contemporary temporality, even though at the time of its creation it may have expressed and discussed current social, political and intellectual concerns. This revered high literature is conserved as the project of the learned and endowed, and its forms are preserved by imitation, adaptation and correction, identifying its writers with this fixed tradition and the social and cultural privilege that accompanies it.

In the ancient world, what choices a writer had as he or she selected a genre might be regulated by the social status of the writer and the audience for whom he or she intended the work; the nature of the subject and the requirements that such a subject might impose because of literary convention; and the actual choices available. These choices were further regulated by other factors including such material concerns as availability and accessibility of the means of production. An obvious example will suffice here—letter-writing, if it exists as an option, is a genre that becomes accessible to everyone once literacy has spread and paper or other materials are available because it is compact and the means of production and distribution are democratized.[18] It was, therefore, a frequently chosen genre, particularly by early Christian writers, which even those excluded from higher education, wealth and status could enjoy in the ancient world.[19] The availability of writing materials and the means to deliver the letter facilitated Paul's choice of letter-writing to communicate to his audience. After writing has established itself as a dominant medium for literary activity, even if a person had the intellectual capacity and literary background to write an epic, such an enterprise would be restricted by the available means for production and distribution of the work, as well as by contemporary tastes and the audience an author intended to address. Clearly,

18. Stanley K. Stowers, *Letter-Writing in Greco-Roman Antiquity* (Philadelphia: Westminster Press, 1986).

19. Aune, 'Letters in the Ancient World', pp. 158-82 and 'Early Christian Letters and Homilies', pp. 183-225, in *idem*, *New Testament and its Literary Environment*.

it was the genre of the upper social strata for whom patronage was an established means of supporting literary activity. The kinds of books we are used to, the codex composed of sheets of paper bound together, appeared at the time of the Roman Empire. First it was only used to produce compact editions of very long works. Up to that time, books were rolls of papyrus that were both fragile and awkward to hold.[20] It was not until the modern period, for example, after the printing press and widespread literacy, when novels could be serialized in newspapers, making them accessible to large numbers of people, that the novel became a serious as well as popular genre even though there had been a number of successful and popular novels in earlier periods. In the early centuries of Christianity, the codex made collections of written materials less unwieldy, and also, more importantly, made distribution of written works easier. Both of these features facilitated more widespread access to written materials, a fact appreciated by early Christians who chose writing from Paul on as a primary medium for communication among the dispersed Christian communities.

Concerns with the literary character of the Gospel are essential to understanding it, and they help to bring us closer to identifying the generic family of the work, which is also an important clue to its interpretation. The Gospel's literary features associate it with other narratives that reveal their messages with the same or similar claims on timeless sacred language but contemporary setting. The combination of narrative and 'sacred language', in fact, links the Gospel with the author's own Hebraic past more specifically than do the formal features that have led commentators to other generic labels.

Because of the general consensus since 1838 that Mark was the first of the four Gospels, scholars have argued that Mark created the Gospel genre for his unique purposes and that Luke's and Matthew's versions are imitations. This theory has been problematic because it has been hard to explain how John, whose Gospel developed as a separate tradition, 'invented' the same genre or how it is that the apocryphal gospels share features with the canonical Gospels. In fact, Mark and John share so many features (Mark and John begin their stories with John the Baptist and the baptism of Jesus; both have a dramatic structure that parallels Greek tragedy; both ignore the early childhood of Jesus)

---

20. H.I. Marrou, *A History of Education in Antiquity* (trans. George Lamb; New York: Sheed & Ward, 1964), pp. 154-55.

that it seems likely they were writing at least within parallel traditions and in a literary form sharing common features.[21]

Identifying the genre of the New Testament Gospels has been one of the most intense 'form' debates by biblical scholars of the last two centuries.[22] In fact, the Gospels have no specific generic companions in the ancient world, except, of course, the non-canonical gospels. The Gospel of Mark has many of the generic features of Hebraic literary models, but sōme of Mark's adaptations of the style of the Hebrew Bible are so radical that it is difficult to see the parallels. These Hebraic features include using paratactic diction and giving apocalyptic religious significance to events and to characters he portrays as historical. But while Mark adopts the style of his Hebraic literary tradition, he breaks with it by presenting a contemporary environment, making the central character a humble man and writing in a 'low style'. As a consequence, despite the fact that the genre of a work usually indicates the work's intended audience and its social-literary culture, the Gospel of Mark has eluded any easy identification. In the last one hundred and fifty years, it has been identified with a number of ancient forms including memorabilia,[23] biography,[24] aretalogy,[25] history,[26] parable,[27] tragedy,[28]

21. For the range of opinions on the gospel form, see Martin Dibelius, *From Tradition to Gospel* (trans. and rev. edn Bertram Lee Woolf; Cambridge: James Clarke & Co. Ltd, 1971); Charles H. Talbert, *What is a Gospel?: The Genre of the Canonical Gospels* (Philadelphia: Fortress Press, 1977); Aune, *New Testament in its Literary Environment*; Richard A. Burridge, *What Are the Gospels? A Comparison with Graeco-Roman Biography* (Cambridge: Cambridge University Press, 1992); Christopher Bryan, *A Preface to Mark*.

22. See Mary Ann Tolbert, 'Text-Specific Requirements: Genre', in *idem*, *Sowing the Gospel: Mark's World in Literary Historical Perspective* (Minneapolis: Fortress Press, 1989), pp. 48-79 for an overview of these discussions and her conclusion that as an example of Hellenistic popular literature it has links to 'aretalogy, biography, and memorabilia and the ancient novel' (p. 78).

23. Vernon Robbins, *Jesus the Teacher: A Socio-Rhetorical Interpretation of Mark* (Philadelphia: Fortress Press, 1984).

24. Aune, *New Testament and its Literary Environment*; Ernest Renan, *Vie de Jésus* (Paris: Michel Levy, 1863); Clyde Weber Votaw, 'The Gospels and Contemporary Biographies', *AJT* 19 (1915), pp. 45-73, 217-49; Talbert, *What is a Gospel?*; Adela Yarbro Collins, *Is Mark's Gospel a Life of Jesus? The Question of Genre* (Milwaukee, WI: Marquette University Press, 1990); Burridge, *What Are the Gospels?*; Christopher Bryan, 'Mark as Hellenistic Life', in *idem*, *A Preface to Mark*, pp. 32-64.

25. Moses Hadas and Morton Smith, *Heroes and Gods: Spiritual Biographies in*

comedy,[29] popular novel[30] and sacred narrative.[31]

Despite the consistency with which genre tends to indicate both its original and subsequent audiences, the Gospel of Mark, as the first in its genre, and as in so many aspects of its revelation, has eluded specific nomenclature. Most of the scholarly arguments about the gospel's genre inevitably encounter a facet of the Gospel that contradicts the usual requirement for the particular genre. For example, if biography is suggested, we must be aware of the fact that both Mark and John only tell part of a life, leaving out some details that other ancient writers, including the other Gospel writers, find essential to a biography (as birth, parentage, upbringing, and so on). In terms of history, the setting is certainly historical, but the subject of the Gospel is not strictly history. And it breaks one of the most common conventions of sacred narrative because its concerns and events are within memory, and its setting is contemporary. The communities within the Gospel, that is, the audience and participants in the cult-hero's journey range across status, occupation and class lines in sharp contrast to sacred narrative, conventional Greco-Roman histories and biographies. Likewise, the language of the Gospel, κοινε Greek, links its genre to popular forms and contemporary culture rather than to high literature, which would exclude Greco-Roman tragedy and history.[32]

Originally identified as ἀπομνημονευματα (memoirs) of Peter by Papias,[33] this designation still holds some adherents. However, for at

Antiquity (New York: Harper & Row, 1965).

26. James M. Robinson, *The Problem of History in Mark and Other Marcan Studies* (Philadelphia: Fortress Press, 1982).

27. Frank Kermode, *The Genesis of Secrecy* (Cambridge, MA: Harvard University Press, 1979); James G. Williams, *Gospel Against Parable: Mark's Language of Mystery* (Sheffield: Almond Press, 1985).

28. Gilbert Bilezikian, *The Liberated Gospel: The Gospel of Mark Compared with Greek Tragedy* (Grand Rapids: Baker Book House, 1977).

29. Daniel Otto Via, *Kerygma and Comedy in the New Testament: A Structuralist Approach to Hermeneutic* (Philadelphia: Fortress Press, 1975).

30. Tolbert, *Sowing the Gospel*, pp. 48-79; Mary Ann Tolbert, 'The Gospel in Greco-Roman Culture', in Regina Schwartz (ed.), *The Book and the Text: The Bible and Literary Theory* (Oxford: Basil Blackwell, 1990), pp. 258-75.

31. Ernest Best, *Mark: The Gospel as Story* (Edinburgh: T. & T. Clark, 1983).

32. See nn. 24 and 28.

33. As quoted in Eusebius of Caesarea, *Eccl. Hist.* 3.39.15.

least a century, one branch of biblical scholars has tried to show that
the Gospel writers were biographers using the ancient genre of the
βίος. Like ancient biography,[34] the Gospel debates with the contemporary world; its interests are in the present moment and the imminent future. Thus the Gospel can be seen as world-affirming like the
Greco-Roman biographies, but not affirming of conventional worldly
values like wealth and status. Further, if we examine the Gospel's literary characteristics rather than proceeding from assumptions about
its religious function, important as it happens to be, different conclu-
sions might emerge. While there can be no doubt about the apocalyptic language of Mark, the story is impressed with the contemporary
world of first-century Palestine. Written in an 'unlettered' literary
style, with no doubt a popular audience in mind, the Gospel employs
what has been called 'sacred language', with its directive, revealing,
or evangelical character. The Gospel's assertions have a claim to
urgency, and the theoretical or practical view that does not fit with
them is 'outrageous'.[35] Further, its announcements, particularly in the
parables and Jesus' sayings, claim to stand outside of time.

Choices in genre throughout time have not been made arbitrarily.
In *Kinds of Literature*, Fowler shows that an author's selection of a
genre, like the canon itself, is ruled by a number of criteria. One of
these certainly is fashion , but according to Fowler this may not be as
important as is sometimes assumed.[36] Frank Kermode, in *Forms of
Attention*, identifies literary and aesthetic canons with canons of taste
which are mutable.[37] In the larger cultural context of Mark's times,
authorial choices included epic, pastoral, elegiac, satiric, lyric, comic
and tragic. Roman and Greek literature of the period has bountiful
examples of all of these, the works of which form the canons of literature to this day (Homer, Virgil, Ovid, Horace, and so on). An
examination of the canons of genre current in the Latin *hochliteratur*
of the first century will show us very quickly that Mark was not
writing in such a literary tradition:

34. Patricia Cox, *Biography in Late Antiquity* (Berkeley: University of California
Press, 1983).

35. Ernesto Grassi, *Rhetoric as Philosophy* (University Park: Pennsylvania State
University Press, 1980), pp. 103-104.

36. *Kinds of Literature*, p. 213.

37. *Forms of Attention* (Chicago & London: University of Chicago Press, 1985).

Paradigm of Main Genres

Cicero	Tragic, comic, epic, melic, dithyrambic
Horace	Epic, elegiac, iambic, lyric, comic, tragic, satyric
Quintilian	Epic, pastoral, elegiac, satiric, iambic, lyric, comic, tragic.[38]

These are poetic genres, showing the stylistic preference for poetry among elite readers in the first century. Even though the epics and dramas of ancient Greece were popular genres in their own time periods, they were preserved as the literary artifacts of the privileged. By the first century, these were the genres of the privileged social groups that had been educated at least to secondary school. Since Greco-Roman education was dominated by the rhetorical schools, study of the great writers of the past began early, but continued throughout higher education.[39] Mark's syntactic and grammatical usage and literary expression declare an absence of the influence of such an education. Scholarly arguments in favor of tragedy and comedy respectively are not satisfactory precisely because the cultural context of the Gospel cannot fit such Aristotelian or Horatian categories.

Connecting the Gospel to popular Greco-Roman genres has proved more fruitful. The canons of popular forms for the period include biography, romances and novels, with history a kind of intermediary form between 'high' and 'low' culture. Mark's style shows his affiliation with the popular culture which would have offered such choices as Greco-Roman biography, history and the popular novel, whether written by Palestinian, Alexandrian or other diaspora Jews, Romans, or Greeks.[40] Richard Burridge's recent, *What Are the Gospels?*, David Aune's *The New Testament in its Literary Environment*, and Christopher Bryan's *A Preface to Mark*, following the lead from Renan's *Vie de Jésus* explore the similarities between the literary features of the various New Testament documents and those of other popular genres in the biblical era. They show convincingly that the Gospels share many characteristics with the popular biographies of the period, concluding that although the Gospels have no *exact* literary analogues in

---

38. Fowler, *Kinds of Literature*, p. 220.
39. Marrou, *A History of Education in Antiquity*, pp. 210-26, 266-81.
40. David L. Dungan and David R. Cartlidge (eds.), *Documents for the Study of the Gospels* (Minneapolis: Fortress Press, 1994); see also Burridge, *What are the Gospels?*

antiquity, nevertheless in terms of formal features, the Gospels parallel Greco-Roman popular biographies.[41] Maintaining that this type of biography occurs rarely in Judaism (*Lives of the Prophets*, Philo, *Life of Moses*, *On Abraham*, and *On Joseph*), Aune argues that Greco-Roman biographies focused on the rich, the powerful and famous (kings, military commanders, philosophers, poets, and so on) while Israelite–Jewish biographical writing 'emphasized charismatic leaders, kings, and prophets'.[42] These biographies formed the tradition for conceptualizing the literary treatment of Jesus, but the Gospels reflect the popular literary culture of the lower strata of society. Aune makes his argument based on a number of factors including the language used in the Gospel as well as comparable contemporary literary genres.

Examples of popular biographical literature include the Jewish *Lives of the Prophets*, *Life of Homer*, *Life of Euripides*, *Life of Pindar*, *Life of Aristophanes*, *Life of Aeschylus*, and *Life of Sophocles*. Burridge also discusses Tacitus's *Agricola*, Plutarch's *Cato Minor*, Suetonius's *Lives of the Caesars*, Lucian's *Demonax* and Philostratus's *Apollonius of Tyana* as βίοι that have comparable generic features to the Gospels.[43] Using empirically established data to generate the essential character- istics of these works, Burridge shows how the generic features of the Gospels conform to these works. The Greek poets' lives also share generic features with the Gospel of Mark in the sense that they are written in a common style, are almost journalistic in their brevity and they attempt to cover only the main details (by following conventional rhetorical treatises they include ancestry, birth, upbringing and edu- cation, special events, entrance into the adult world, public career, family, virtues, and death) (Hermogenes' *Progymnasmata*), but in con- trast to Mark, they narrate the lives of the poets from birth to death. Further, not only are they much shorter and lacking in the apocalyptic resonances, they also lack the dynamic, often rebellious, picaresque qualities and the interest in contemporary reality I have identified as central to the style of the Gospel of Mark.

The Gospel version of the life of Jesus offers a radical critique of society as it is and the life of Jesus is the vehicle for exploring this world; these popular biographies are more concerned with praising

41. Aune, pp. 17-76; Burridge, pp. 154-217; Bryan, pp. 22-31.

42. Aune, *The New Testament in its Literary Environment*, pp. 47-54.

43. Burridge, *What are the Gospels?*, pp. 154-90; see also Bryan, *A Preface to Mark*, pp. 9-64.

ancient authors than in exposing the societies to which they belonged. They focus on established revered figures rather than on someone recently dead. The setting of the Gospel of Mark and Jesus' movement through the various environments his journey leads him into disrupt the strictly biographical narrative,[44] for the Gospel leads us to consider what this contentious contemporary world has to do with the story being unfolded. Mark's environment sets up the spatial and temporal oppositions in the Gospel that move its concerns from history and the present to the eternal. Like the Hebrew Scriptures, standing as a model behind it, the Gospel puts the historical and biographical events in the context of the 'sacred horizon'. Burridge's cursory treatment of 'Setting' in the Gospel is precisely what leads him to conclude that the Gospels are βίοι: 'This personal focus of the work's settings on an individual, rather than a place or topic, is also a feature of βίοι literature'.[45] Any argument about the influence of generic models must contend with the possibility that the Gospel authors might not have encountered these forms. Burridge's argument assumes that the gospel writer would be familiar with these Greek and Roman works, which would have to be demonstrated rather than assumed. Consistently scholars interested in the genre of the Gospels look to the Greco-Roman world, despite the fact that the authors (Mark, Matthew and John) are Jews, who may be only superficially hellenized, rather than to the Hebrew scriptures that offer the most likely literary resource, particularly for Mark. Nonetheless, one of the most attractive aspects of Aune's and Burridge's argument about the genre of the Gospel, is its attempt to connect the genre to the social environment and historical-cultural milieu of the Gospel's performance. Other generic suggestions, as for example, Greek drama (Bilezikian), neglect the social environment. Ancient Greek drama was outside the immediate experience of the masses of people in the empire. Certainly the Gospel writer himself did not exhibit any formal literary knowledge.

Another recent suggestion is that the Gospel shares features with the Greco-Roman popular novel. Both are prose forms, written in the colloquial language, and intended for a large audience. Only five complete examples of these ancient novels are extant at the moment (Chariton's *Chaereas and Callirhoe*, Xenophon's *An Ephesian Tale*, Longus's *Daphnis and Chloe*, Helidorus's *An Ethiopian Tale*, and Achilles

---

44. Malbon, *Narrative Space and Mythic Meaning*.
45. Burridge, *What are the Gospels?*, pp. 206-207.

Tatius's *Leucippe and Clitophon*). These erotic popular novels include
the mixture of historiographic and dramatic features, and an amalgam
of earlier genres like biography, memorabilia of a sage, aretalogy and
apocalypse; the plot is episodic with minimal introduction, turning
point and final recognition scene. The grammar is crude, and the style
is repetitious and conventionalized.[46] If we examine these observations
about the features of the Gospel, every one of these could also be used
to describe a number of stories in the Hebrew Bible or in their
Septuagint versions. It is not necessary to look as far afield as the
popular novel of the Greco-Roman world because Mark had literary
resources within his own cultural traditions; the sacred narrative tradition of Israel provided him with models of history, apocalypse, saga,
biography or novella.

A comparison of Greco-Roman and Hebraic-Jewish literature might
seem inappropriate, but it is important because it so readily exposes
the very complex and different literary and cultural matrix out of
which Mark was writing. Literary scholars of our own times are often
working in the same *hochliteratur* tradition and tend to apply its terms
to a literature that is alien to its context. Greco-Roman literary culture
did indeed have distinct canons of genres, with the epic at the top of
the hierarchy for *hochliteratur*. It also had a distinct division between
popular and high literary forms, with the former catering to the
ordinary reader and the latter patronized by the highest levels of the
society.

But the Hebraic situation is completely different, for 'high' literature also happens to be 'sacred' literature. The Bible is neither *klein*
nor *hoch* literature, though it has characteristics of both; its language,
literary traditions and intended audiences include all social levels, as it
addresses all the members of a specific group. Though much of the
Hebrew Testament compilation was patronized, it nonetheless was
addressed to all 'members of the tribe'. The Gospel of Mark is not a
patronized literary effort in this way, but like its Hebraic literary
precursors, it addresses all potential members of a present or future
community of believers, and thus was never exclusive to narrow literary and social salons.

Within the Palestinian and Greco-Roman Jewish milieu, the *Septuagint* or texts of the Hebrew Bible provided models of history, biography and short biographical narrative incidents, folk tales, saga,

46. Tolbert, 'The Gospel in Greco-Roman Culture', pp. 262-65.

debates, apocalypse, and novella (the Abraham saga, Joseph novella, Moses' life, Jonah, Esther, and the lives of the kings, for example).[47] Mark would have known these both orally and as written models.

The author also had oral formulaic stories, of which we have no written models dating from the period other than those which we find in the New Testament and other non-canonical Gospels in the form of parables,[48] miracle stories,[49] and so on. Some have suggested that the Gospel is a parable (Kermode, Williams), a word the Markan author uses for the first time in 4.2, telling his audience simply that Jesus taught in parables, a word he equates with mystery (4.11). Mk 4.1-34 which includes Jesus' first parable and several others on the nature of the kingdom of God, expresses in story form the Markan theory of parable. This section explains what parable is by giving several examples, suggests its method of interpretation, reveals its literary form, and the audience for whom it is intended. Parable is a narrative form (4.3-8), requiring interpretation, and its meaning is open to those who listen (4.9, 13-20, 22-24). In 4.1-34, Mark comes close to revealing his theory of story and its interpretation for the entire Gospel. The parable and explanation show us that the author relies on parabolic story-telling to convey the good news of Jesus: a sacred history unfolds through metaphor, allegory, and symbolism.

That Mark's Gospel shares many features with the parable genre cannot be denied, but this does not resolve the question of genre. Rather it merely describes a literary characteristic of the genre employed. Though both parables and the Gospel of Mark are set in a contemporary time world close to the audience who heard or read the story, and both are paradoxical, a central feature of the parable,[50] unlike parable, the narrative resources of the Gospel of Mark are not primarily timeless actions that are allegorized to point to a specific though many-dimensioned meaning. The Gospel writer names historic people, describes one-time only actions, and fills the Gospel with people who

47. Norman K. Gottwald, *The Hebrew Bible: A Socio-Literary Introduction* (Philadelphia: Fortress Press, 1985).

48. Joachim Jeremias, *The Parables of Jesus* (trans. S.H. Hooke; New York: Charles Scribner's Sons, repr. 1972 [1954]).

49. Gerd Theissen, *Miracle Stories of Early Christian Tradition* (ed. John Riches and trans. Francis McDonagh; Edinburgh: T. & T. Clark, 1983).

50. John Dominic Crossan, *Cliffs of Fall: Paradox and Polyvalence in the Parables of Jesus* (New York: Seabury Press, 1980).

debate urgent and contested current issues. Therefore, 'parable' is un-
satisfactory as a generic category for the entire work, because it applies
the part to the whole, when the whole is composed of many different
kinds of parts (parables, miracle stories, conflict stories, history, the
John the Baptist novella, among others).

Mark no doubt had oral resources, including scriptural refrains, the
sayings source, short narratives which were themselves interpretations
of biblical stories, miracle stories, parables, and the passion narrative.
When we consider the question of Mark's genre, we must be alert to
the complexity of the cultural situation of the author, writing about
the life and significance of a Jewish charismatic figure to a Greco-
Roman audience. A genre chosen from *hochliteratur* would have been
inappropriate for the universalist claims of the Gospel. He rejected the
letter and the apocalypse, although the Gospel contains hints of both
genres. (1.1 with the introduction of the word εὐαγγέλιον is sugges-
tive of a letter, and the Gospel includes a small apocalypse, ch. 13, as
well as the many promises of the coming Kingdom [1.15; 9.1; 14.25]).
The Gospel, though it has characteristics of parable, apocalypse, and
letter is none of these generically. Genres strictly from the Palestinian
and Jewish experience, as exemplified by oral traditions and Hebrew
Scripture sacred writings[51] as his literary heritage of form, content
and style, surely must have inspired the writer, although his adaptations of these forms for his own purposes have contributed to the
creation of an unrecognizable genre.

Since the Greco-Roman *hochliteratur* genres would have appealed
more specifically to a highly educated audience, such choices were
contrary to the author's aim and purpose, as well as outside his educa-
tional and intellectual experience. His choices, therefore, were much
narrower than might at first appear. He selected a type of literature
which was compatible with his own cultural heritage and with his material constraints. Though he adopted a recognizable style associated with
Hebraic forms, nonetheless he adapted it to his particular rhetorical
purposes. While he imitated the paratactic sentence level style of his
Hebraic models, he rejected the chronological remoteness of their settings and the historically established authority of their main characters.

Having eliminated all the high and low genre choices available to
Mark in the first century milieu, only history, biography and sacred

---

51. Hermann Gunkel, *The Legends of Genesis* (New York: Schocken Books,
1964).

narrative remain. Hebraic sacred narratives, whether in their Greek, Hebrew, or Aramaic forms show their imprint on the Gospel. The brevity and parsimony of literary expression, attention to special events in the hero's life, and focus on a central trickster-underdog character (a persistent type-character in Hebraic literature),[52] whose actions direct the sequence of events in the narrative: all these figure in Hebraic sacred narrative whether in sagas like those of the Patriarchs or Moses, or novellas as in the case of Joseph and Esther.[53] An important difference between these and the Gospel of Mark, however, is the time and setting, critical features of sacred narrative. The distant, heroic world of the Hebraic past contrasts with Mark's current time frame, popular setting and contemporary reality.

The Gospel shares traits with popular ancient biography, although the author deviates from the genre on a number of counts. First, he is writing about someone who is only recently dead, not a figure who has reached heroic stature because of many centuries of admiration, like the ancient Greek poets or Moses or the prophets. Secondly, the Gospel writer has introduced apocalyptic universalism in the style of Daniel,[54] an element not to be found in other ancient biographies. The style he adopted deviates from the conventions of *hochliteratur* historical biography. In contrast to Greco-Roman and Hebraic histories, Mark provides no genealogy, no important blood ancestors and no important priestly or political connections for his main character; just the contrary, he divests these conventional categories of social power and status of their significance, advancing in their stead universalist claims for his main character.

The Gospel also shares traits with history, but it is history in the style of 1 Maccabees or the Abraham saga.[55] The kind of history Mark wrote is unlike other ancient histories. We cannot find precise parallels in ancient Greece or Rome, for Herodotus, Thucydides, Tacitus, Suetonius or Josephus, whose literary tradition is Greek rather than

52. Susan Niditch, *Underdogs and Tricksters: A Prelude to Biblical Folklore* (San Francisco: Harper & Row, 1987).

53. Gottwald uses the term novella for the Joseph story (*The Hebrew Bible*, p. 100).

54. Momigliano, 'Origins of Universal History', pp. 31-57.

55. Ernest Best, *Following Jesus: Discipleship in the Gospel of Mark* (JSNTSup, 4; Sheffield: JSOT Press, 1981), pp. 141-43.

Hebraic, are concerned with specifying dates, times, places, circumstances, causes and consequences. Their primary interest, which they have in common with the bulk of post-Renaissance historians, is to establish facts about the past and develop a philosophy of history; though their histories are not developed separately from the conditions and assumptions of reading and writing, these authors' primary concern is the factual or empirical data about the past and what it tells us about human history. Ancient Greek critical historiography is the root of modern European histories, indeed the model for history writing. Van Seters's *In Search of History* attempts to show that the histories of the Hebrew Bible are histories because they share common themes with Herodotus: 'divine providence, of retribution or salvation, and the use of the past as a mirror for the present and future events in order to deal with the problem of change'.[56] His working definition of history, 'the intellectual form in which a civilization renders account to itself of its past', is a definition which works compatibly with classical critical history and its idealist structure, but puts him in the defensive position of proving that ancient biblical history fits within its definition. But what distinguishes the histories of the Hebrew Scriptures is their authors' absolute conviction about divine purpose in their tribal history unfolded in a catena of texts interpreting the meaning and purposes of their past, directing the present, and informing the future.[57]

The ancient histories of Greece and Rome that we still study were recognized as exemplary in the times when they were written, finding themselves in literary canons often within the lifetime of the writer. Their writers usually recorded the events of the immediate past (as for example, Herodotus the Persian wars and Thucydides the Peloponnesian wars) and more importantly, their subjects tended to be wars or revolutions involving many states and empires (rather than individual cities or states), which were believed to be the main cause of historical change. Historians were chroniclers of this change and interpreters of its meaning.[58] The most significant aspect of these histories,

56. John van Seters, *In Search of History: Historiography in the Ancient World and the Origins of Biblical History* (New Haven: Yale University Press, 1983), p. 52.
57. Meir Sternberg, *The Poetics of Biblical Narrative, Ideological Literature and the Drama of Reading* (Bloomington, IN: Indiana University Press, 1985).
58. Momigliano, 'Tradition and the Classical Historian', pp. 161-77.

besides the historians' study of empirical data, for this study, is that they dwelt on wars, revolutions and the leaders who held political power under these conditions. They dealt with the issues of macro-history, the great events that would bring about change, rather than with day-to-day living.

The Greek historians, followed by the Romans, adopted an ancient form of the historical-critical method, even though, in fact, they told stories, interpreted events, and passed moral judgment on the people and situations they described. Despite claims to accuracy and factual knowledge, these historians also 'emplotted' their narratives, framing their literary and poetic insight with the pretense of 'scientific history'.[59] The difference between Hebraic histories, which are Mark's models, and others, is the narrator's deference to divine authority and the required personal and tribal changes mandated by this absolute claim. In the Christian Bible, the Gospel of Luke comes closest to the 'scientific' brand of history, and in fact, the Lukan author's introduction identifies his storytelling method with the Greco-Roman genre of history. Investigating objective data was not the goal of the Markan author. In contrast to Luke, he does not establish his credentials by explaining his method and sources; nor did he expect to persuade his audience with an accumulation of eye-witness testimonies like Luke (1.1-4). Rather, the Markan author chose proclamation (1.1).

For Greco-Roman historians, the claim to empirical truth regulates their approach to their literary activity. Hebraic histories, certainly more than Greco-Roman or modern histories, do not claim to be 'factual reality'; rather they emphasize God's guiding role in human history, thus taking possession of their own literary brand of history. Mark is not an objective, empirically-driven historian, but a member of the community that is developing as he narrates his history. What this means is that the author not only has commitment to the task of telling the story, but also is yoked to the meaning of the story, and to persuading others about the events, their significance, and his interpretation of them.

The same story underlies all four Gospels: a charismatic, miracle-working rabbi with close followers who came in conflict with the

59. Hayden White, 'Interpretation in History' in *idem, Tropics of Discourse* (Baltimore: The Johns Hopkins University Press, 1978), pp. 66-67; Hayden White, *The Content of the Form: Narrative Discourse and Historical Representation* (Baltimore: The Johns Hopkins University Press, 1987).

authorities, who challenged custom and taboo, modelled an intimate relationship with a loving Father–God, rejected home and family, empathized with the poor and marginalized, confronted the civil and religious powers in Jerusalem, and who was arrested, tried, executed, and buried, and whose resurrection was attested to. But each Gospel writer has 'emplotted' the story differently. The Gospel of Mark is a history directed forward on two planes of experience, a quotidian historical reality bound by contemporary time, and its opposite, an apocalyptic once-only reality whose eschatology is infinite. It is, as Daniel O. Via has written 'in the middle of time', neither past nor future but in the space between beginning and end.[60] The contemporary atmosphere features those who possess social power or are possessed by it, those who reject the prophetic call to reform, the marginal and powerless, and those who heed the message and respond in faith to form an alternative community that exiles itself from the conventional social values of wealth, power and status.

Mark has not chronicled the events of Jesus' public life, but he has interpreted the meaning of the events, pointing to the changes open to his audience once they have heard the Gospel's words. Unlike ancient historians, he is less interested in concrete and factual data, but as in the ancient histories of his own Hebraic tradition, the author does dwell on the all-time meaning of the events at hand. He transcends macrohistory or the affairs of Romans, Palestinians and others, and instead, in the tradition of Hebraic sacred narrative, he elevates the activities of his socially humble or humiliated subject (whether underdog person or people, or exiled nation) into a cosmic history. In so doing he makes the concerns of ancient historians appear to be a micro-history in contrast to the grand scheme in which Mark delivers his version of the Jesus story, just as in the Hebrew Bible the power of all ancient empires is insignificant in contrast to God's universal power. Within the Gospel, this new social time overturns convention momentarily, for the rich are poor, the poor are rich, the powerful powerless, the powerless powerful, the sick healthy, the marginal central, the alive dead, and the dead alive. Outside the Gospel, the audience is invited to redesign the social and political city mentally and spiritually, and to envision a world where change, reversal—μετάνοια—whether personal or social, now has both human and cosmic significance and the

60. *The Ethics of Mark's Gospel*, pp. 60-66.

landscape of human affairs is merely a part of the universe of God's affairs.

Biography as a category of history, has always been a more popular genre than history from the time of its emergence in the fourth and fifth centuries of ancient Greece. The ancient Greeks did not consider biography a kind of history, because history dealt with politics, wars, and relationships between states, whereas biography dealt only with the life of a single man from birth to death. By the fourth century in ancient Greece interest in biography and autobiography permeated all aspects of literature.

The major distinction between the style of historians and biographers was apparent by the fourth century, and this aspect characterizes biography from this point on. While histories dealt with major political events (war and revolution) in a style requiring attention to fact, biography, which dealt with the lives of important people (poets, philosophers, powerful families), permitted greater license. Already in the fifth century, the Socratics had experimented with biography, choosing to describe the possibilities in an individual's life rather than the true facts, but by the fourth century biography had blurred the difference between fact and fiction.[61] Biography, therefore, from its beginnings in Greek literature was a more specifically rhetorical activity whereas history's origins were more empirical.

Like Hebraic history, Hebraic biography, as for example the Joseph novella, the Jacob saga, or the Esther novella, is written in a style congenial to a mixed audience, since it does not require skilled literary habits to appreciate its message or its story. Furthermore, its diction matches the expectations one could assume of the less educated members of society. Its emphasis is interpretation and meaning of a person's life to Israel's history, rather than the change occuring in society due to a war or revolution. But in contrast to its Hebraic models, the Gospel has a contemporary context and focuses on ordinary people. Mark's use of this genre is quite different to other ancient classical biographies. The person he writes about, Jesus of Nazareth, is not an ancient prophet, poet, or legendary-historical figure; rather he is only recently dead. Also, ancient biographies invariably include the birth, childhood, and early adulthood of their subjects. But, as if without biological or cultural roots, Jesus arrives on the scene full-grown.

61. Arnaldo Momigliano, *The Development of Greek Biography* (Cambridge, MA: Harvard University Press, 1971), p. 56.

Furthermore, the writer, while placing the events in contemporary
reality, gives their meaning universal significance. He foregrounds the
adult life of this humble but special carpenter against the major political, religious and social crises of first-century Palestine, and by implication first-century Rome. Although this political background ultimately controls the fate of both John the Baptist and Jesus of Nazareth
within the Gospel framework, the apocalyptic claims of the Gospel
minimize the affairs of the Romans, Herodians and high priests in
eschatological time.

This chapter surveys the literary characteristics of Mark's genre,
arguing that it modifies the traditions of sacred Hebraic texts, employ-
ing the resources of oral and literary forms from the author's own
Hebraic environment. I would suggest that in primarily following Hebraic literary traditions, he was consciously or unconsciously revealing
his cultural and religious affiliation with the past, but more importantly drawing an essential connection between the events in Jesus' life
and God's actions in 'Israel's' history. For Mark, this story was the
latest in a long history of texts of suffering which nonetheless promised
God's redemptive presence. His literary gesture was bold, for he
adopted the generic features and style from his own valued sacred
literary traditions, whose setting and time removed them from contemporary political and social fluctuations. Nevertheless he claimed
these same literary features for a narrative set in his own time, lend-
ing the reverence for the heroic remote past setting of Hebrew sacred
narrative to these events of the recent past, thus culturally validating
the narrative. I have also attempted to show that in adopting a popular
genre, the author showed his affiliation with the contemporary popular culture, presenting an interpretation of the life of Jesus that
aligned his sacred cultural heritage with subversive activities and apocalyptic and universalist claims.

Mark's Gospel dramatizes the events in the life of its main
character, an 'underdog', nonetheless called 'my beloved Son' by a
voice from heaven, who laments his desertion by God at his moment
of death. The failed disciples, the virtual absence of God throughout
the Passion (except for the tearing of the Temple curtain), and the
empty tomb together testify to an unpretentious version of the story,
paradoxically called the 'good news of Jesus, the anointed'. As in picaresque, in this Gospel story of a common man, Mark presents a temporary suspension of hierarchies of political and religious rank, and

of social, political and religious order. In the upside-down world of his life of Jesus, the author transgresses these conventions and points to an egalitarian message for the 'family of man' (3.32-35) and 'the children of God'. The author displaces hierarchical systems with a charismatic overture reaching out to everyone who hears or reads his story. He adapted traditional forms to his unique social and religious purposes. Thus the Gospel is a popular and contemporary form of a 'sacred' narrative using the resources of Hebraic history, fiction, apocalypse and biography. Mark aligns his genre choice with his ideological intentions. In his version of Jesus, he presents a wonder-working wandering teacher, who violates contemporary social, religious, and political habits and behavior, until his death when order is restored. In this narrative world of ordinary time, Mark subjects the present to critical scrutiny.

Chapter 2

NARRATIVE AS MEMORY: GOSPEL AS FRAGMENTS

ὁ σπείρων τὸν λόγον σπείρει
Mk 4.14

In the last chapter, I argued that Mark's original contribution to Jewish literary traditions was to tell a contemporary story in the style of the sacred narrative traditions. He conferred on his contemporary character's life and death the same revered style and language as the timeless ancient scripture. In this chapter, I will discuss the relationship of the Gospel to the past, Mark's narrative as memory. For, in citing texts or making allusions to the Hebrew scriptures, the Gospel writer attempts to make the past present. He works to make connections between the present and the past in order to retrieve and remember the past. Thus, another important dimension of Markan time is the Gospel writer's effort to retrieve the fragments of his own historic tradition and to interpret his narrative in the context of the values, stories, and Laws of Israel. In other words, the Gospel writer presents an understanding of his own narrative according to the terms of past traditions and convictions. He makes the past an essential feature of the living present.

One of the most debated areas of biblical studies is the relationship of the Christian to the Hebrew Bible. The Gospel and letter writers of the New Testament make copious use of the sacred texts of Judaism. The relationship between the Christian texts and antecedent religious traditions, in fact, caused controversy from the beginning of Christianity as a religious movement with a textual tradition. In the patristic period, discussions turned into heresies as early Church figures deliberated on how the Christian Gospels connected to the Hebrew texts. Marcion eliminated the Hebrew Bible and included Luke with

Paul minus all Judaicisms in his Christian Bible.[1] These debates led to the development of interpretive methods that would help accommodate the Christian texts to their antecedent traditions. For example, Origen's threefold methodology (literal, historical and spiritual) made it possible to allegorize the Hebrew Bible so that it could be reconciled with the teachings of the Christian texts.[2] Such a reading system also invited the creation of typologies that could be seen in a pattern across the combined Hebrew and Christian Bibles. Augustine's interpretative method, undergirded by his conviction that the Bible (Hebrew and Christian combined) must teach love of God and love of neighbor, likewise invited readers to construct patterns of relationships through allegories or typologies throughout the entire corpus of texts.[3] From the earliest period of the Christian religion, authoritative readers have sought to establish a reading method that would relate the Hebrew textual tradition to the Christian texts.

Intertextuality, the citing or re-phrasing of earlier texts in later literary works, or the re-making of earlier generic models used as patterns for later literary works, has been the focus of theoretical discussions among biblical and literary scholars in the last forty years. One position is represented by biblical theologians and Christian scholars for whom 'fulfillment' is the word used to describe the relationship of the more recent text to the former.[4] These writers read canonically, that is, *through* the canon as the 'Word of God', to make all the words consistent. They depend on typological and structural parallels to undergird their arguments that connect the Hebrew and Christian Bibles. For Harold Bloom, Christians, as typified by Northrop Frye have made the Hebrew Bible the 'captive prize of the Gentiles'.[5] Such a position does not seem far-fetched when we remember that the Christian Bible was canonized at the Council of Carthage and included

1.   Tertullian, *Adversus Marcionem.*
2.   Origen, *De Principiis* in SC 252-53; 268-69; 312.
3.   Augustine, 'De Doctrina Christiana' CCSL 32.
4.   James M. Robinson, *The Problem of History in Mark and Other Marcan Studies.*
5.   *The Book of J* (trans. David Rosenberg and interpreted by Harold Bloom; New York: Grove Weidenfeld, 1990), p. 14.

the Hebrew Bible and the New Testament texts. Furthermore, when this text was interpreted with the idea of 'fulfillment' to explain textual references, and narrative patterns were made typological, the Hebrew textual tradition was relegated to its status as *Old* Testament, the source for the *New* Testament. Harold Bloom represents one extreme position, that a rupture or chasm exists between a writer and his forebears, as the writer, in this case representing a new religion, sets out to establish his or her own literary territory. The writer also seeks to efface the integrity, if not the existence of the original.[6]

However, following an ancient pattern in the Hebrew tradition in which earlier scriptural texts were woven into later ones, the quoting of earlier texts was common in the texts of the first century.[7] Michael Fishbane, calling this habit 'inner biblical exegesis', a term for intertextuality in Hebrew texts,[8] has argued persuasively that it arises out of a 'practical crisis of some sort', and the tradition therefore 'sets the agenda', taking the form of 'textual annotation, literary allusion, and types of analogical or synthetic reasoning' and transformation of textual content.[9]

Other writers have considered the relationship between one text and its forebears, or newer writers and the tradition they follow. For example, Gérard Genette, seeking to characterize the literary rather than the sociological or psychological nature of the relationship between

6.   Harold Bloom, *Anxiety of Influence* (New York: Oxford University Press, 1973).

7.   See Michael Fishbane, *The Garments of Torah: Essays in Biblical Hermeneutics* (Bloomington: Indiana University Press, 1989); Jacob Neusner, *Canon and Connection: Intertextuality in Judaism* (Lanham, MD: University Press of America, 1987), pp. 6-13; D.A. Carson and H.G.M. Williamson (eds.), *It is Written: Scripture Citing Scripture. Essays in Honour of Barnabus Lindars* (Cambridge: Cambridge University Press, 1988). *It is Written* includes essays on the Old Testament in the Old Testament, the Old Testament in the intertestamental documents, as well as the Old Testament in the New Testament. Dale Miller and Patricia Miller, *The Gospel of Mark as Midrash on Earlier Jewish and New Testament Literature* (Lewiston: Edwin Mellen Press, 1990) evaluates the Gospel as midrashic commentary on earlier Jewish texts; Danna Nolan Fewell (ed.), *Reading Between Texts: Intertextuality and the Hebrew Bible* (Louisville, KY: Westminster/John Knox, 1992) is a recent collection of essays on intertextuality in the Hebrew Bible.

8.   *The Garments of Torah*, pp. 3-18. See also *idem, Biblical Interpretation in Ancient Israel* (Oxford: Oxford University Press, 1985) for a thorough study of intertextuality in Hebraic scriptures.

9.   *The Garments of Torah*, pp. 16-17.

texts, used the term 'transtextualité', or everything that puts one text, manifestly or secretly, in a relationship with other texts.[10] For Michel Foucault and Jacques Derrida, such intertexts and the works in which they are re-made recreate the original text, serving as a 'supplement' to the original.[11]

But these theories, whether traditional 'fulfillment' notions, Frye's typologies, Bloom's anxiety of influence, Derrida's trace or Foucault's version of a 'supplement' have a similar deficiency in common. They all make the 'present' the central time for the literary act. Despite the range in their attitudes, in essence, they assume writers are in a contest with the past and that the present act of writing is the supreme moment—whether it be for fulfillment, parallelism, affiliation, patricide, play or pleasure. But, in fact, the relationship a writer, and in this case, a biblical writer, sets up with his or her literary relatives may be based on memory or fear of loss of connection and continuity. In other words, rather than patricide, it may be ancestor worship. Literary allusion, echo[12] or reference may indeed be an attempt to remember and retrieve the past. For in the case of the Hebrew experience, to lose this history could cause irretrievable cultural and religious damage. The threat of this loss stands always in the background of the Markan text, whether it be the failure of memory of recent events leading to Jesus' death or the abandonment of a textual tradition through which this narrative could be interpreted. In fact the narrative cannot resolve this dilemma—it does not make, as Paul Ricoeur says about Aristotle's theory of narrative—order triumph over disorder.[13] On the contrary,

10. Gérard Genette, *Palimpsestes: La littérature au second degré* (Paris: Editions du Seuil, 1982), p. 7.

11. Michel Foucault, 'The Prose of the World', in *The Order of Things: An Archaeology of the Human Sciences* (New York: Vintage Books, 1973), pp. 17-45; 'Supplement' is Jacques Derrida's term for commentaries; see Derrida, 'From/Of the Supplement to the Source: The Theory of Writing', in *Of Grammatology* (trans. Gayatri Chakravorty Spivak; Baltimore: The Johns Hopkins University Press, 1974), pp. 269-316.

12. John Hollander's theory of 'echoing' in literature (*The Figure of Echo: A Mode of Allusion in Milton and After* [Berkeley: University of California, 1981]) has been adopted by Richard B. Hayes for biblical interpretation in *Echoes of Scripture in the Letters of Paul* (New Haven: Yale University Press, 1989).

13. See 'Emplotment: A Reading of Aristotle's *Poetics*', in *Time and Narrative*, I, pp. 31-51.

it thrusts before us its own temporality—with the immediate and paradoxical past of Jesus' career, the remote past that remains only as scattered fragments of ancient stories, sayings, and teachings, and the present, with the close disciples scattered and martyred and the destruction of the temple looming—all intertwined in the hope of some future triumph that remains only a promise. The Gospel invites us to view these disorderly events that lack resolution in two affiliated time spans: one connects all the events of the present with the past and the other proclaims the continuity of historical time with a future moving into eternity.[14] The past is thus made a necessary component of this coming future.

Mark's allusions to this revered past include direct citations or more obvious references like unidentified quotations as well as rephrased citations and parallel word choice or refrains. In fact, the narrative is composed of and interpreted by these scattered references from the Hebrew Bible, the sacred past of Hebrew experience. On one level Mark certainly uses some of his textual references to convey the idea of prophecy fulfilled (1.2; 7.6; 9.12; 11.17; 12.10, 36; 14.49).[15] The verb πληρόω (fill, fulfill, accomplish), however, occurs only once in the Gospel of Mark in relationship to scripture when Jesus says at the time of his arrest, ἀλλ᾽ ἵνα πληρωθῶσιν αἱ γραφαί. καὶ ἀφέντες αὐτὸν ἔφυγον πάντες ('Let the scriptures be fulfilled. Then the disciples all deserted him and ran away', Mk 14.49-50). The only other undisputed occasion when Mark uses this verb is at the beginning of Jesus' public ministry (Mk 1.15) as Jesus says ὅτι πεπλήρωται ὁ καιρὸς ('The time is fulfilled'), but this use is not textually connected to scriptural prophecy. Nevertheless, theologians and biblical exegetes have relied heavily on the 'fulfillment' concept to understand the pattern of textual citation in the Christian Bible. Such a position may be appropriate on occasion, more particularly in Matthew who quotes Hebrew texts in Greek translation with regularity and authority, in contrast to the other Gospel writers. Mark assembled these fragments of his literary-religious tradition to support the story he claimed was 'the good news'. They frequently serve as reminders of 'Israel's' sacred laws and of a history in which God interceded on behalf of his 'exiled' people.

14. Ricoeur, discussing Augustine's theory of time in *Time and Narrative*, I, p. 28.
15. Robinson, *The Problem of History in Mark*, p. 105.

The triumphalism expressed by the concept of textual 'fulfillment' is misleading in Mark's case because it establishes a fundamentalist and one-dimensional relationship between the later text and its predecessor. It interprets the first text as a commentary on the later text, denying the integrity of its original communication and the many possible relationships between the first and second citation. It precludes the possibility that the second text is a multi-layered commentary on the first. It reduces the first text to mere prediction, and when prophecy is reduced to prediction, it works to dismiss the real meaning of the original utterance, culturally severing it from the present. It reduces the complexity of time in the narrative by forcing it into a one-dimensional track from past to present to future. It fails to see the ways in which the past, present and future are intermingled through this textual continuity, the means by a which a people renders account of itself to itself.[16] It defies the idea of what Brian Stock, Jacob Neusner and others have called 'communities of texts' that are in continuity with each other.[17] It gives the second text transcendence by erasing the context of the first text's message and appropriating it to a new context, that is the writer's, interpreter's and redactor's understanding of its meaning in its new location. From a theoretical viewpoint, it makes a fundamentalist reading through which the new text supplants the older text as the source of social norms, ethical values and historical lore. This seems to deny what is in fact happening as the writer incorporates, echoes, or cites earlier texts. Writers may be connecting their work to a literary past, to a canon with which they remain socially, religiously and culturally affiliated. They may be contrasting the current social/historical situation in which they cite the passage with its original situation. Conversely, they may be recalling the former text as commentary on the present situation. In a historically minded culture like Judaism, time is certainly linear, but it moves back and forth in historical linearity rather than steadfastly focusing on the present.[18]

16. See my article, 'A Blind Promise: Mark's Retrieval of Esther', *Poetics Today* 15.1 (1994), pp. 115-31.

17. See Brian Stock, *The Implications of Literacy: Written Language and Models of Interpretation in the Eleventh and Twelfth Centuries* (Princeton, NJ: Princeton University Press, 1983), pp. 90-91, 522-31; Neusner, *Canon and Connection*, pp. 147-59.

18. See Danna Nolan Fewell, 'Introduction: Writing, Reading, and Relating', in

The selections writers make proscribe their textual community as they connect with a past and establish continuity with it, for the act of incorporating earlier texts into later ones, in fact, retrieves a canon of readings that pertain culturally and literarily as well as historically to the time when the later writer composes. In contrast, the 'anxiety' and 'fulfillment' positions about textual references deny this cultural continuity and propose a severe difference or rupture between authors, texts and their models. This can be healed only through a new act of interpretation or creation by which the newer text usurps the original meaning of the older. But the 'anxiety' theory likewise condones the 'strong' misreading, for it accepts the same chasm between the Christian and Hebrew Bible and fails to recognize that the majority of the writers of the Christian Bible are Jews, who, like many of the rabbis of the first century, are reconsidering and remembering long-held religious practices and beliefs.

While the Christian writers, it is true, distinguish themselves from these other Jewish sects, they are interrogating their own antecedent traditions. This was not an act of appropriation or theft, but an effort to retain cultural continuity with this past. 'Listening' is therefore a central feature of this effort to reclaim and retain the past, a word the Markan author uses to connect the Gospel to a religio-historical-literary past. This connection between past, present and future is made quite explicitly by Mark when Jesus cites Isa. 6.9-10 to alert his audience to listen because hearing and understanding the message of his communication is the means to conversion:

> βλέποντες βλέπωσιν καὶ μὴ ἴδωσιν,
> καὶ ἀκούοντες ἀκούωσιν καὶ μὴ συνιῶσιν,
> μήποτε ἐπιστρέψωσιν καὶ αφεθῇ αὐτοῖς
>
> That seeing they may see/And not perceive
> And listening they may listen/And not understand
> Lest they might turn again/And might be forgiven (Mk 4.12).

By using this passage from Isaiah, Mark ties Jesus to the prophetic tradition, and also ties listening to this continuing tradition of understanding and conversion, that is, to an interwoven past, present and future time. Emphasizing the centrality of the message, the reference recalls a critical communication, that understanding or 'interpretation'

idem, *Reading Between Texts*, pp. 11-20 for a discussion of this trait of Hebrew Scriptures.

is coterminous with a transformation, a conversion of the self from one way of being to another. The invocation to 'heed' recalls the historic covenant between God and his people, and thus aligns the teaching of old with the contemporary rendition about to unfold in the public ministry of the main character.[19] In the remainder of this chapter I will specifically explore how Mark's work uses direct citations, rephrased citations, unidentified quotations, or allusions to the Hebrew Bible or its *Septuagint* versions to remember, recall and save the past as an essential feature of the present and the future.

Mark's Gospel emerged in the post-resurrection world of early Christianity, when the Romans laid siege to Jerusalem and the destruction of the temple and dispersal of the Jewish people was imminent. The *second coming* had not occurred, Peter and Paul had argued and divided their missions among themselves, the one adopting the Gospel for the Jews and the other the Gospel for the Gentiles. Roman rule was triumphant, and the original witnesses to the life of Jesus were dead or dying. Between 65 and 70 CE, the Neronian persecution, the deaths of Peter and Paul, the catastrophe of Palestinian Judaism, the split between the church of the Gentiles and the church of the Jews, together with the transition to the second generation of the religious movement, all created a new beginning for the Christian movement.[20]

When Mark set out to write the Gospel, the devastation of the Jerusalem temple, the ancient cultural center of the Hebrew people, together with the Roman humiliation of the Jewish people loomed in the very near future. This was not a climate for a self-immersed writer intent on undermining and dismantling the past, severing the stranglehold of oppressive traditions, or appropriating the past to a triumphant present. Nor was it an age of ebullient optimism about the future of a church which saw itself as the fulfillment of prophecy embedded in the Hebraic tradition. The hegemony of the Christian church was some three centuries into the future, the time when the post-Constantinian Church would conspire against its charismatic beginnings and systematically reassess Hebraic, Roman, and Greek cultures while taking their political and civic structures, as well as their

19. For a recent dissertation on the role of Isaiah in the Gospel of Mark, see Richard Schneck, S.J., *Isaiah in the Gospel of Mark I–VIII* (Vallejo, CA: BIBAL Press, 1994).

20. See Leonhard Goppelt, *Apostolic and Post-Apostolic Times* (trans. Robert A. Guelich; Grand Rapids: Baker Book House, 1977).

texts and methods for interpreting them to itself. In Mark's period, the religious climate was one of earnest desire and fretful hope that these fragments of a disappearing past could be preserved, that they could be reassembled, and that together these scattered words might become a mosaic of broken pieces transformed into the 'good news'. Despite the ostensible sacredness both of the ancient Hebrew texts and of sayings, stories and legends of Jesus, the boundary between these 'holy' words and those of others was less intractable than with many secular texts of the same period. Appropriating others' words, even those revered because of their religio-historic status, was common because neither canonicity nor property rights had been assigned to them. Texts were composed from the filaments of other texts with commitment to a literary practice that applauded a writer's capacity to draw on tradition and to connect the present to this revered past. Other extant Jewish texts of the period also followed the same or a similar practice.[21] In fact, scriptural allusions are not just glosses or interpolations but are often central to the author's literary purpose.[22] In other words, the allusions are one of the means the author uses to unfold his interpretation of the Jesus story.

This emerging religion that was an offshoot of Judaism did not have a textual tradition of its own, since the words, sayings and deeds of Jesus had existed primarily as an oral tradition for the previous forty years.[23] The greatest single influence in the formation of New Testament theology is the First Testament. The Bible of early Christianity was largely the *Septuagint* which the Jews renounced after the destruction of the temple in 70 CE in a rabbinic effort to consolidate the textual traditions of what was emerging as normative Judaism.[24] The 'supposed' Rabbinic Assembly of Jamnia in 90 CE had closed the canon of Hebrew Scriptures.

In addition, the synagogue, or place of assembly was a firmly established institution by the time of Jesus, with a tendency towards a regularized liturgy and lectionary. The reading of the law was a main

21. Geza Vermes, *The Dead Sea Scrolls in English* (Harmondsworth: Penguin Books, 1962). See particularly the section titled 'Biblical Interpretation', pp. 214-49.

22. Jacob Neusner, *Early Rabbinic Judaism: Historical Studies in Religion, Literature, and Art* (Leiden: E.J. Brill, 1975), pp. 115-36.

23. Werner Kelber, 'Mark's Oral Legacy', pp. 44-89; Dibelius, *From Tradition to Gospel*.

24. Gottwald, *The Hebrew Bible*, p. 122.

feature of synagogue worship.[25] The Jewish liturgy in the first half of the first century included public readings from scripture and singing of psalms.[26] Mark's acquaintance with biblical quotations could quite easily have been through Jewish liturgical services as well as cate-chetical memorization, specifically of the laws, which every Jewish male heard regularly. The liturgy and celebration of regular holy days (Passover and Purim, for example) as well as the Pharisaic-rabbinic house-discussions about the law would have provided Mark with a combination of oral formulations from prophets, psalms, writings, and laws in either Greek (in the diaspora) or Hebrew–Aramaic (in Palestine). Biblical texts in Greek or Hebrew are also not out of the question as potential sources.

Mark was probably also working with a collection of Jesus-related oral stories and sayings, which he transformed for his own theological and literary purposes as he wrote the Gospel. The Q document was another of Mark's possible sources.[27] Because form and source arguments remain hypothetical and do not deal with texts that can be examined, I have excluded them from this discussion.

The fact that the author has chosen to *write* a narrative of the Jesus kerygma-event to show its connection to Hebraic tradition establishes the significance he places in the act of writing itself as an essential mechanism for recording, preserving and understanding it. It also shows the author's desire to retain cultural continuity with Jesus' Hebraic past, an accomplishment to some degree dependent on the act of writing itself.[28] The fact that the Gospels and letters were written down, whether they were read aloud or even recited in an oral or secondarily oral environment,[29] incontrovertibly shows that the Christian

25. Asher Finkel, *The Pharisees and the Teacher of Nazareth: A Study of their Background, their Halachic, Midrashic Teachings, the Similarities and Differences* (Leiden: E.J. Brill, 1974), pp. 143-44.

26. Gregory Dix, *The Shape of the Liturgy* (London: Dacre Press, 1945), p. 37.

27. See Dieter Lührmann ('The Gospel of Mark and the Sayings Collection Q', *JBL* 108 [Spring, 1989], pp. 51-71) for a recent discussion of the influence of Q on Mark.

28. Kelber, *The Oral and the Written Gospel*, raises this issue in his discussion of the orality-literacy of the Gospel of Mark; Bryan, *A Preface to Mark*.

29. A secondary oral environment is Fr. Walter Ong's term for a society in which one level of society may be highly literate but other layers may have little or no literacy, thus replicating a primary oral society although still possessing some characteristics of a literate society (*Orality and Literacy* [London: Methuen, 1982]).

writers were engaged in a recording-remembering-fixing literary
activity achieved through the act of writing. In fact, it could be argued
that with the expectation of a political, social and cultural exile from
'Israel', and lacking a written record, they feared the loss of the memory of the kerygma-event and its connection to the Hebraic tradition.[30]
The integration of textual resources from the Hebraic tradition,
whether from written or oral sources,[31] emphasizes the author's interest in and commitment to cultural continuity to be achieved through a
textual tradition. The author's selection, retrieval and restatement of
particular textual allusions, in fact, constitutes his creation of a canon
of precursor readings to which he attaches his own narrative. By select-
ing specific texts, he is establishing continuity with the past through
showing deference to its most revered textual resources. Nevertheless,
though this selection of texts serves as his canon that he relates to his
own work, his use of the texts shows his liberty to control and rede-
ploy the references for his own rhetorical purposes. In this respect,
the author's literary activities are precisely those which had characterized the scribal traditions practiced with the Hebrew biblical texts.[32]

In the Gospel of Mark, the author's textual references include his
transformation of oral sources, particularly the sayings ($\chi\rho\varepsilon\iota\alpha$) of
Jesus, miracle stories and parables; his deployment of translated direct
or indirect refrains and quotations from the Hebrew scriptures or
their *Septuagint* versions; and the reappropriation of vocabulary of the
first Testament and formulae that occur in other Greco-Roman texts.
Some of these are exact quotations, or quotations with one or two
words altered; others are single words or phrases used with specific
emphasis or for special occasions; a third variety suggests a reminiscence of its source, recollecting events in Hebrew history that highlight human courage or divine intervention. Some of the quotations
are in the mouth of Jesus, from a heavenly voice, provided by the omniscient narrator, or spoken by characters in the Gospel.

Mark's sorting, rearranging, adoption and recrafting of his numerous scattered sources were an act of hope that through his writing the
history he recounted could be preserved and connected to a long-es-
teemed tradition, and thus remembered. The subtexts in the Gospel,

30. See Goppelt, *Apostolic and Post-Apostolic Times*.
31. Bryan argues persuasively for the oral character of Mark's textual references
('Oral Characteristics of Mark's Appeal to Scripture', pp. 136-51).
32. On this topic, see Fishbane, *Garments of Torah*.

gathered from the diverse strands of Hebrew textual and oral history, are allied with its apocalyptic predictions. Through these constant allusions to the past, Mark presents time horizontally, with religious movement from a salvific former time into a promised future; such a temporality distinguishes Mark from the mystery religions of the Greco-Roman world where movement was within or vertically, outside of time. In his act of restitution, Mark was restoring the past to the present in an effort to communicate to both present and future listening believers about the salvific connection between the events of past, present and future. The allusions reflect the related theological and rhetorical concerns of the author and serve his rhetorical strategy. His selection of texts or of discourse traditions shows his self-conscious creation of a literary-religious past to which he connects the present events. Though the references are primarily from Hebraic texts in κοινή Greek, his choices represent a selection, a process of sorting, reducing and focusing on particular strands of the Hebraic past. Though they do not replace their original source, for, on the contrary, they often remind the audience of their source, by reassigning the original, they simultaneously reinterpret it. By assigning specific allusions to Jesus, for example, Mark also confers authority on the reinterpreted quotation. In general, the allusions focus the audience's attention on moral and social laws, on the issue of political liberation, on the universalism of the gospel message, on the unique relationship between the voice of the heavens and Jesus and on the moral and social responsibilities of the people of God.

Markan intertextuality, this chapter will show, reflects political, religious and cultural crises both during the time of Jesus' public career and when Mark wrote the Gospel. Mark's use of texts from the law emphasizes the field of his legal interests, his references to the writings connect the historical-political context of his own times with earlier events in Hebrew history, and his citations from psalms and prophets interweave the psychological, emotional and poetic themes they develop with the events and characters of the present. As commentary formed from the continuous textual tradition of Israel, together these references create Mark's criteria for understanding and interpreting his contemporary cultural-religio-political world as represented in the narrative of the Gospel.

Mark's subtexts, whether direct or indirect references from both oral and written sources, are selected primarily from the Pentateuch,

Psalms and the Prophets, with a few additional references to Kings, Chronicles, Daniel, Esther and Judith. This breakdown of sources shows the heterogeneity of Mark's claims on his textual heritage because he includes moral and cultic laws, chronological and apocalyptic history, prophecy and poetry. This selection includes a timespan from the beginnings of Hebraic culture up to 200 BCE.[33] Mark's sources also reveal his specific interests in the traditional laws; the historic promises to the Hebrew people; Jewish messianic hopes, which took the form of expectation for both a human monarchical redemption as well as apocalyptic salvation; and in prophecy. The quotations from the psalms attributed to Jesus link the prophet's lyric outbursts with the poetic tradition of Israel. Mark's intertwining of these fragments of his own Hebraic tradition in his Gospel rendition serve to interpret the current events in the terms of the past. They memorialize the present events by associating and understanding them according to the teachings and stories of the past. Mark's narrative vivifies the past in the disordered present to make sense out of the murky present times by remembering central teachings, former suffering and salvation, and historic promises.

The Law: Pentateuchal Texts

The timeless laws of Israel—absolute then, now and in the future—are recalled in the Gospel of Mark as teachings from the past that will not be revoked. However, because Jesus, according to the Gospel of Mark, was executed on the grounds that he violated the law, any discussion of the law in the Gospel must first consider its possible dangers. In the immediate past to the writing of the Gospel, both the original leader and followers of this new religious movement were in violent disputes with both civil and religious authorities, conflicts that resulted in their executions. Jesus, according to Mark (and Matthew) was condemned

---

33. The Hebrew Bible includes oral traditions that began to take written form around 1200 BCE as Israel's national-religious writings, becoming the sacred-religious writings in the period between 400 BCE and 90 CE. Separate literary units (oral and written) formed from 1200 BCE to 100 BCE. Between 400 BCE and 90 CE, the Hebrew Bible became an authoritative collection including the Law, Prophets, and the Writings. Gottwald, *The Hebrew Bible*, p. 93. See also Brevard S. Childs, *Old Testament Theology in a Canonical Context* (Philadelphia: Fortress Press, 1986), for a discussion of the relationship among the texts of the Hebrew Bible from a canonical perspective.

on the basis of a specific Pentateuchal law: ἠκούσατε τῆς βλασφημίας ('You have heard the blasphemy', Mk 14.64), the high priest says; οἱ δὲ πάντες κατέκριναν αὐτὸν ἔνοχον εἶναι θανάτου ('Their judgment was unanimous, that he was guilty and should be put to death', Mk 14.64), a punishment required for blasphemous naming of the Lord: 'Whoever utters the name of the Lord shall be put to death: all the community shall stone him…' (Lev. 24.16).[34] Mark's literary attention to the assignment of a Pentateuchal punishment for blasphemy to Jesus, however, irrevocably exposes the law, demonstrating in the most striking way its potential for abuse.

Jesus nevertheless makes a number of seemingly absolute statements about the traditional laws and practices associated with them. Because of his own condemnation on the grounds of religious legal violation, the discussion of the law throughout the Gospel must be viewed as less absolute and more ambiguous or contingent, in the sense that the pronouncements are appropriate for the immediate circumstances of their utterance, rather than all time and all circumstance dogmatic utterances.

The Pentateuchal references Mark assigns to Jesus either affirm laws and cultic or social practice or adjust them. They appear in the form of questions posed to Jesus or are stated by Jesus as confirmations of teachings,[35] thus connecting Jesus to the respected ancient laws and to contemporary Palestinian Pharisaic practices and beliefs. From the vast corpus of laws in the Pentateuch, Mark and the Jesus he presents to us, emphasize only a select few. Marriage, re-marriage and divorce form one set of concerns; sabbath practices and priestly certification of cures (Mk 1.44 and Lev. 14.2-32) are also at issue. Jesus restates certain of the Hebrew laws of moral-social behavior, while adjusting or adding to their essential teachings. However, on the vast collection of cultic law and practice, both Mark and Jesus remain almost silent. The

34. See E.P. Sanders, *Jewish Law from Jesus to the Mishnah* (Philadelphia: Trinity Press International, 1990), pp. 60-65, for a discussion of whether Jesus actually commits blasphemy in this scene. Whether historically he did or did not, it seems to me, remains a moot point, for the narrative shows that was the accusation against him. As Sanders proposes, the scene suggests a Christian composition of the events to reflect the Markan interpretation.

35. According to Jacob Neusner the conflict sayings are very similar to Pharisaic legal debates, with Jesus accorded the first and last *lemma* as in the House of Shammai debate form. The opposition gets one chance to argue back, and then is proved wrong. See Neusner, *Early Rabbinic Judaism*, pp. 115-16.

interpretation of certain miracle narratives does however suggest the
Gospel writer's position on many cultic practices.

The book of Leviticus comprises the two largest collections of purity
laws or accepted norms of religious behavior. Chapters 1–16 include
manuals of practice directed at priests, and part 2, chs. 17–27 are
priestly teachings addressed to the Israelite people. The two codes work
to define the behavior required of the people of God, and therefore of
the Hebrew people themselves, and the consequences to them if they
violate the boundaries set by the codes.[36]

According to some anthropologists, purity laws are not designed as
absurd codes to restrict individual freedom but as one of the primary
means to distinguish one group of people from others.[37] In Mary
Douglas's interpretation of Leviticus, God's holiness consists in creation as well as in God himself. As a consequence of this premise, the
concept of purity expresses the wholeness of God's creation; thus it is
essential for those things presented at the temple or persons attending
to possess this 'physical perfection'.[38] Furthermore, if it is true, as
Mary Douglas argues, that the human body is a symbol for the society
in which it sojourns and body boundaries actually stand for social
boundaries, then a breach in the purity system is an assault on the
'wholeness', that is, on the cultural, ethnic and gender integrity as defined by the group.[39] Any adaptation, reform, or transgression against
the purity codes, therefore, would be an assault against tribal identity
and the coded behavior that the tribe mandates by coercion, edict, or
silent consent and cooperation.

The marriage and remarriage question comes up three times in the
Gospel, in connection with Herod's remarriage (Mk 6.18), when Jesus
is asked about the circumstances which would allow divorce (10.4),
and in the Sadducee question about which husband a woman would
belong to in heaven, if a woman had been taken as wife by a series of
brothers-in-law (Mk 12.19). The last is designed to trick Jesus and to

36. *The JPS Torah Commentary: Leviticus* (Commentary Baruch A. Levine;
Philadelphia: Jewish Publication Society of America, 1989). See introduction, pp. xi-
xvii.

37. Mary Douglas, *Purity and Danger: An Analysis of Concepts of Pollution and
Taboo* (New York: Frederick A. Praeger, 1966); Meeks, *First Urban Christians*,
p. 97.

38. *Purity and Danger*, pp. 41-57.

39. *Purity and Danger*, pp. 114-15.

show the preposterousness of beliefs in the after-life upheld by the Pharisees and by Jesus. The problem of marriage to a sister-in-law is specifically raised in the John the Baptist story as John is alleged to have chastised Herod for his marriage to Herodias, his sister-in-law. The legal justification for this refers back to Lev. 18.16, where such a rule is imposed: 'You shall not have intercourse with your brother's wife; that is to bring shame upon him.'

The narrator informs his audience that John the Baptist indicted Herod for ignoring Levitical prohibitions against incest: οὐκ ἔξεστίν σοι ἔχειν τὴν γυναῖκα τοῦ ἀδελφοῦ σου ('You have no right to your brother's wife', 6.18). The edicts against incest (Lev. 18.6-18) are multiple and cover the most clear-cut cases, as blood relationships (i.e. intercourse with a member of the immediate family) and other non-biologically connected family connections:

> You shall not bring shame upon your father's brother by approaching his wife: she is your aunt. You shall not have intercourse with your daughter-in-law: she is your son's wife; you shall not bring shame upon her. You shall not have intercourse with your brother's wife: that is to bring shame upon him. You shall not have intercourse with both a woman and her daughter, nor shall you take her son's daughter or her daughter's daughter to have intercourse with them: they are her blood relations, and such conduct is lewdness. You shall not take a woman who is your wife's sister to make her a rival-wife, and to have intercourse with her during her sister's lifetime (Lev. 18.14-18).

These strict Jewish regulations identifying intercourse with in-laws as incest were in conflict with Roman laws. Though Roman law defined incest more broadly than today's laws, it was a crime, nonetheless, to marry those biologically connected by a direct line of descendancy, which would include first cousins and uncles and nieces.[40] In-law marriages are not covered by the prohibitions. Despite the strong indictment of Herodias and Herod for violation of the Levitical code of incest, Mark implies that the 'incest' violation was actually a token of the corruption of the court. It drew attention to Herod's abandonment of Israel and its revered laws for his own pleasure and power. Mark's Jesus upholds the inviolability of the marriage contract and the John story upholds the incest law.

40. Aline Rousselle, *Porneia: On Desire and the Body in Antiquity* (trans. Felicia Pheasant; Oxford: Basil Blackwell, 1983), p. 79.

In contrast to the focus on punishment for sexual liberty in the John story, Mark's Jesus (10.6) expressly contradicts Deut. 24.1-3, which gave husbands the right to divorce wives in the case of 'shameful behavior', by prohibiting divorce under any circumstances. When an unnamed interlocutor questions Jesus on divorce in Judea, he in fact asks Jesus if it is lawful to divorce a wife: εἰ ἔξεστιν ἀνδρὶ γυναῖκα ἀπολῦσαι ('Is it lawful for a man to divorce his wife?', Mk 10.2). Making use of a variation of Genesis (1.27 and 2.24), Mark's Jesus answers,

> ... but in the beginning, at the creation, God made them male and female. For this reason a man shall leave his father and mother, and be made one with his wife; and the two shall become one flesh. It follows that they are no longer two individuals: they are one flesh. What God has joined together, man must not separate (Mk 10.6-9).

The fact that the question is raised clearly suggests that 'divorce' and the occasions for it are a subject of lively debate in the period. At least in the schools of Shammai and Hillel, according to Countryman, different opinions were argued, none of which would have been definitive.[41] The differences among the Gospels and Paul (1 Cor. 7.10-11) likewise suggests the contradictory contentions in the divorce debate; Paul, who was trained, according to his own testimony by Rabbi Gamaliel, like Mark's Jesus, offers the most conservative opinion: no divorce.

But the fact remains that in the Gospel of Mark, the questioner specifically asked whether a man might divorce his wife (10.3). The opposite possibility, whether a woman might divorce her husband, is not proposed. Furthermore, the interlocutor cites Deut. 24.1, 3 to which he ascribes the authority of Moses, to support his proposition: 'When a man has married a wife, but she does not win his favour because he finds something shameful in her, and he writes her a note of divorce...' Mark's Jesus overturns the proposition, supplanting Moses as authority with a quote that pits God's edicts against Moses'. Giving equal security in marriage to male and female, this logical *tour*

41. L. William Countryman (*Dirt, Greed and Sex: Sexual Ethics in the New Testament and their Implications for Today* [Philadelphia: Fortress Press, 1988]) explains that the Pharisees of the Schools of Shammai and Hillel disagreed on their interpretation of Deut. 24.1 in which divorce is granted if the wife has done anything 'improper'. For the School of Shammai, an improper act is sexual wrongdoing, but for the School of Hillel, the interpretation is broader and includes 'an unseemly thing' (pp. 173-74).

de force is a radical transformation of traditional teachings. Although the argument is presented in formal compliance with standard Pharisaic House-debates,[42] Mark's Jesus has reached back to the time before historic time, Genesis, to impose an absolute and timeless edict that contrasts with the later Deuteronomic teaching.

Because Torah gave divorce rights only to men if they found their wives had done something improper (Deut. 24.1), women, in one sense, never became actual members of their husbands' families. Though there are some objections in the Hebrew Bible about the frequency of male divorces (Mal. 2.13-16), in general the divorce laws and practice supported the patriarchal system that made divorce a male prerogative. In the first century, in the School of Shammai, divorce is permitted for sexual wrongdoing by the wife.[43] In making man and woman equal, Mark's Jesus interprets Gen. 2.24 to make a radical attack on patriarchal rights which he replaces with equality between the sexes, at least in marriage.[44] On the one hand, he reverses the Deuteronomist's patriarchal legal stipulation and replaces it with a conservative interpretation of a text he believed to be older, making God's action take precedence over human laws. The Markan Jesus' conservative position on divorce makes marriage a joint familial as well as a contractual relationship. In making women equal partners in marriage, Jesus takes a modern feminist position, not achieved by women until the twentieth century, although his restriction of divorce under all circumstances undermines the liberty provided for by this equality between the sexes. Whether under Jewish or Roman law, divorces permitted in the first century generally favored men,[45] but Jesus takes a position that is stricter than the actual law.[46] He goes further than equality, and as in his usual program, he favors the victim in the marriage, the one who has been divorced, who would have been the woman in the first-century setting. In his private discussion with his disciples, he explains his

42. Neusner, *Early Rabbinic Judaism*, p. 116.
43. Countryman, *Dirt, Greed and Sex*, pp. 151-52.
44. See Daniel O. Via, *The Ethics of Mark's Gospel*, pp. 102-27.
45. See Sarah B. Pomeroy, *Goddesses, Whores, Wives, and Slaves* (New York: Schocken Books, 1975), who writes that Roman divorce could be initiated by either the husband or the wife, although since Augustus Caesar's family laws made adultery a public offence only when women committed it, divorce was more likely to be initiated by men. In divorce, children remained with their fathers and women returned to their fathers' homes unless they were independently wealthy (pp. 158-59).
46. Sanders, *Jewish Law from Jesus to Mishnah*, p. 91.

position further when questioned by them. In an absolute statement, he rebukes the divorcer, whether male or female, and denies both the right of remarriage, at the same time remaining silent on the person divorced, and thus he implicitly opens up the possibility of remarriage for the person divorced:

ὃς ἂν ἀπολύσῃ τὴν γυναῖκα αὐτοῦ καὶ γαμήσῃ ἄλλην μοιχᾶται ἐπ᾽ αὐτήν, καὶ ἐὰν αὐτὴ ἀπολύσασα τὸν ἄνδρα αὐτῆς γαμήσῃ ἄλλον μοιχᾶται.

Whoever divorces his wife and marries another commits adultery against her: so too, if she divorces her husband and marries another, she commits adultery (10.11).

Another case pertaining to remarriage, the question about which of the woman's seven husbands would claim her in the after-life (Mk 12.19), reveals that the Mosaic law permitted such a remarrying pattern (Gen. 38.8; Deut. 25.5). Mark's Jesus counters this trick question, that took an ancient teaching from its context in order to expose Jesus' teachings, with a syllogism. He quotes from the First Benediction which cites Exodus when God communicated directly with Moses saying, 'I am the God of your forefathers, the God of Abraham, the God of Isaac, and the God of Jacob' (Exod. 3.6, 15, 16). Jesus answers the attack and its problem by affirming that 'God is not the God of the dead but the God of the living', οὐκ ἔστιν θεὸς νεκρῶν ἀλλὰ ζώντων πολὺ πλανᾶσθε (Mk 12.27), a reference inspired by the Second Benediction, which refers to God's eternal power to heal the sick and revive the dead. The Eighteen Benedictions, of which these are the first two were the central daily prayer of the Jewish people at the time of Jesus.[47] The question attempted to pull Jesus into a squabble over an ancient teaching, but Jesus counters it with a recitation about God which removes the discussion from day-to-day historical living and puts it in the context of God's eternal time. Thus Jesus has made time hierarchical, rendering the fixed past historical time less significant than the open-ended eternal time. But he does not stop here. He brings the eternal to the historical present situation so that the present and past can be seen in a new light.

47. David Daube, *Appeasement or Resistance and Other Essays on New Testament Judaism* (Berkeley: University of California Press, 1987), p. 6.

Another Levitical code is raised by the story of the 'bleeding woman'. The conventional interpretations of this passage (5.25-34) have concentrated on how Jesus' action in allowing a 'polluted' woman to be healed, breaks with restrictive purity laws spelled out in Lev. 15.19-28:

> When a woman has a discharge of blood, her impurity shall last for seven days; anyone who touches her shall be unclean till evening. Everything on which she lies or sits during her impurity shall be unclean. Anyone who touches her bed shall wash his clothes, bathe in water and remain unclean till evening. Whoever touches anything on which she sits shall wash his clothes, bathe in water and remain unclean till evening. If he is on the bed or seat where she is sitting, by touching it he shall become unclean till evening. If a man goes so far as to have intercourse with her and any of her discharge gets on him, then he shall be unclean for seven days, and every bed on which he lies down shall be unclean. When a woman has a prolonged discharge of blood not at the time of her menstruation, or when her discharge continues beyond the period of her menstruation, her impurity shall last all the time of her discharge; she shall be unclean as during the period of her menstruation. Any bed on which she lies during the time of her discharge shall be like that which she used during menstruation, and everything on which she sits shall be unclean as in her menstrual uncleanness. Every person who touches them shall be unclean; he shall wash his clothes, bathe in water and remain unclean till evening. If she is cleansed from her discharge, she shall reckon seven days and after that she shall be ritually clean.

Some have argued based on Josephus (*Ant.* 3.9.5) that strict adherence to these laws was widespread during the first century. E.P. Sanders, on the other hand, argues that Josephus's assertion that women were secluded during menstruation is not incontrovertible evidence that they were. Quoting Josephus (*War* 5.227), '...the temple was closed to women during menstruation', he concludes that while this does not prove that women were not secluded during menstruation, it does prove that they were allowed to wander the streets.[48] As in other cultures, Israel's purity codes designate order, consistency and predictability: in defining 'purity', they identify what is outside this order and predictability as 'dirt' or profanation, which threatens to destabilize the community's self-definition.[49] Thus, purity codes, like keeping kosher,

48. Sanders, *Jewish Law from Jesus to the Mishnah*, pp. 157-58.
49. Douglas, *Purity and Danger*, p. 2, 35, 76-93 and Countryman, *Dirt, Greed and Sex*, pp. 12-19.

circumcision and a host of other regulations, functioned to create boundaries setting Jews apart from other people.

But rather than being an example of Jewish restrictions of women on the basis of biology, the bleeding woman story, which I will discuss in the next chapter, emphasizes that Jesus does not respond in horror because some ancient sanction has been violated. In this case at least, memory could be suffering, and both the Gospel writer and his main character choose to obliterate the power of sanctions that inhibit return to health and salvation.

Another apparent conflict with the law is Jesus' reassessment of the nature of work permitted on the Sabbath. However, the way Mark introduces his allusion to the specific law shows how Jesus' actions are a review of how to respect the Sabbath. 2.23–3.6 specifically addresses Sabbath questions, but the section is introduced with a vague reminiscence of Deut. 23.25, which permitted plucking of another man's corn as long as the action was manual and without tools. When challenged about violating the third commandment (Exod. 20.8-10; Deut. 5.12-14) and working on the Sabbath, Jesus counters with a loose reference to 1 Samuel 21, when David, because of need, had eaten the special bread from the temple, a reference to the holy bread reserved only for priests (Lev. 24.5-9). Jesus appropriates David's abrogation of rule to his own compulsory need. Assuming priestly status, Jesus not only suspends traditional teaching, but replaces it with his personal authoritative interpretation, τὸ σάββατον διὰ τὸν ἄνθρωπον ἐγένετο καὶ οὐχ ὁ ἄνθρωπος διὰ τὸ σάββατον ('The Sabbath was made for the sake of man and not man for the Sabbath', Mk 2.27).[50]

The third variety of Pentateuchal references affirms the central Mosaic laws; these are often cited by Jesus to point out the inadequacy of his interrogator or his audience to heed these ancient teachings, as for example Mk 7.10 and 10.19: τίμα τὸν πατέρα σου καὶ τὴν μητέρα σου ('Honour your father and mother' from Exod. 20.12, Deut. 5.16), or 'The man who curses his father and mother must suffer death' from Exod. 21.17, Lev. 20.9. When Jesus tells a stranger that to win eternal life he must follow the commandments, μὴ φονεύσῃς, μὴ μοιχεύσῃς, μὴ κλέψῃς, μὴ ψευδομαρτυρήσῃς ('Do not murder; do

---

50. Sanders concludes that Jesus' behavior, despite this apparent conflict, fell within the range of current debates about the Sabbath (*Jewish Law from Jesus to the Mishnah*, p. 23).

not commit adultery; do not steal; do not give false evidence...', Mk 10.19), he recites Deut. 5.16-20, telling the interrogator that in addition to these ancient laws, he must also sell all he has, give it to the poor, and follow him (Mk 10.21). His method when dealing with the ancient law is to endorse its rules while making his own unique additions. Asked what the first commandment is, Jesus responds by quoting Deut. 6.4-5, in which Yahweh states, 'Hear, O Israel: the Lord our God is the only Lord; love the Lord your God with all your heart, with all your soul, with all your mind, and with all your strength' (Mk 12.29), adding that the second commandment is, ἀγαπήσεις τὸν πλησίον σου ὡς σεαυτόν ('Love your neighbor as yourself', Mk 12.31), a quote from Lev. 19.18. His interrogator, a scribe, responds to this communication by repeating the commandments catechetically (Mk 12.32-33), suggesting this section of the Gospel might have functioned in the early Church as a means to preserve the catechism of basic beliefs.

The confirmations of central teachings of the Law show that this religious movement was not a radical break with the past but a self-conscious continuation of many of its central codes, and Mark's narrative brings this past into the present. It is important to recognize, however, as the conflict and discussion narratives make clear, that these codes were not irrevocably sealed; rather, they were subject to discussion, dispute and reassessment. The choices, additions and adjustments that Jesus makes to them represent a redaction of the Pentateuch which reduces legal and moral codes to a fundamental few. For example, when we consider the huge body of law found in the Pentateuch, the teachings that Mark has Jesus restate, or that he has a character state, restrict the laws to their essence: the ten commandments, the revised recommendation on divorce, love God and love your neighbor. Besides the one reference to priestly certification of cleanliness from leprosy, there are no restatements of dietary, ritual cleanliness, or other cultic practices. On the contrary, when the scribe repeats the basic catechism, Jesus expressly dismisses the value of cultic practice, περισσότερόν ἐστιν πάντων τῶν ὁλοκαντωμάτων καὶ θυσιῶν ('that is far more than any burnt offerings or sacrifices', Mk 12.33). Demonstrating that this rejection of cultic practice was not new in the Jesus movement, this quotation hearkens back to two First Testament passages in which the sacrifices of burnt offerings are rejected in favor of loyalty, obedience and knowledge of God (Hos. 6.6; 1 Sam. 15.22):

Does the Lord desire offerings and sacrifices
    as he desires obedience?
Obedience is better than sacrifice,
    and to listen to him than the fat of rams
                (1 Sam. 15.22).

The Last Supper also represents Jesus as replacing a blood sacrifice with a commemorative celebration recalling the 'blood of the covenant'. Mark's sub-text is Exod. 24.8, 'Moses then took the blood and flung it over the people, saying "This is the blood of the covenant which the Lord has made with you on the terms of this book".' Jesus says, τοῦτό ἐστιν τὸ αἷμά μου τῆς διαθήκης τὸ ἐκχυννόμενον ὑπὲρ πολλῶν ('This is my blood, the blood of the covenant, shed for many', Mk 14.24). The sub-text, which reaches back to an ancient agreement between Yahweh and Moses, and to a time-honored covenant and ritual practice, makes possible the substitution of Jesus' blood for ancient blood custom. It also represents an irreversible rupture with cultic practice, as Jesus' forthcoming death will ritually replace all blood sacrifice. The textual reference therefore serves two purposes: to connect this event to the Hebrew covenant that Mark's Jesus specifically applies to his own sacrifice, and to reject traditional blood sacrifice, to be permanently replaced by commemoration of the Last Supper, a practice already active as Mark wrote his Gospel.[51] Time-honored cultic practices are not overturned but are revised to reflect practices contemporary with the Markan period. An old ritual is not rejected but the object of the sacrifice is replaced with a narrative memory of the one-time only sacrifice of Jesus' body and blood. Memory is at the center of the entire ritual, whether it be memory of the exodus from Egypt, of the change in status from slavery to freedom, of being in exile to being home, or of the re-enactment of these memories at the last supper. The ongoing living ritual commemorates these narrative memories, making the revered past still alive in the present.

Thus Mark's Pentateuchal sub-texts serve to remember and restore the past by restating basic Hebrew laws, which he recapitulates in a highly succinct form, adjusted to the social-religious circumstances of his own times, when ritual and cultic practices were abandoned in favor

51. Robinson, *The Problem of History in Mark*, pp. 130-32. Table fellowship as practiced by the Jewish Christians was also a major feature of Pharisaic and Essene Judaism, although the Christians rendered it a spiritual occasion. See Neusner, *Early Rabbinic Judaism*, pp. 43-46.

of table fellowship and a redefined community with interiorized religious convictions. Finally, Mark's report of a levitical punishment for Jesus' *blasphemy* challenges the efficacy of law for its own sake by ironically exposing its violent and abusive power. This conclusion to the legal debates in the Gospel regulates our interpretation of all the texts that have introduced the law, pointing to the inherent danger of legalism and the capriciousness with which it could be exercised. It also distinguishes between laws for personal advantage and those which affirm altruistic action and construct social communities (Mk 7.10; 10.19; Exod. 20.12; Deut. 5.16-20; Mk 12.28, 31; Deut. 6.4-5; Lev. 19.18). Mark shows Jesus as dismissing the former and thereby elevating the latter.

The Writings

Mark's use of textual references from the Writings considered together with certain refrains from the Prophets point to his interest in history and the political situation of his own times. His artful interweaving of references to the Writings and to prophetic texts dealing with divine 'universalism' allow him to indict contemporary political situations and people and to examine the Roman Empire in terms of the political attitudes preserved in the prophetic tradition.

Mark introduces the traditional themes of universalism and political liberation through his recollection of texts from the Prophets and the Writings. In connecting the universalism of the Gospel message to its Jewish past, Mark disassociates Jesus' social radicalism from the political universalism provided by the ideology of Roman citizenship, which, beginning with the *pax Augusta* in the first century was transcending nation, tribe, sex and social status while simultaneously adopting a posture of religious tolerance.[52] By recalling Hebraic universalist convictions from his own revered sacred canon, Mark contrasts the divinely initiated utopia with the human imagined political utopia. The

---

52. See Everett Ferguson (*Backgrounds of Early Christianity* [Grand Rapids: Eerdmans, 1987, pp. 19-52]) for a summary of the political-legal status of Romans and those living within the Empire. Also, see Klaus Wengst, *Pax Romana and the Peace of Jesus Christ* (trans. John Bowden; Philadelphia: Fortress Press, 1987) for an examination of the claims of the Roman Empire in the first century and the diverse status of early Christians within it.

contrast diminishes human political utopias and elevates God's universal kingdom.

Using a formulaic γέγραπται ('it is written') opening, Mark has Jesus cite Isa. 56.7: ὁ οἶκός μου οἶκος προσευχῆς κληθήσεται πᾶσιν τοῖς ἔθνεσιν ('My house shall be called a house of prayer for all the nations', Mk 11.17). In the Gospel Jesus uses this scriptural reference to attack the religious authorities of his own time who have made the 'house of prayer' a 'robber's cave'. But the Markan rhetorical strategy makes possible reapplying this Jewish prophetic universalism to the contemporary Roman situation, where the οἶκος is open to all people, not just to Roman citizens.

Because the theme of universalism is not uncommon in the First Testament writings, references to this theme in Mark are both allusive and elusive, making it impossible to identify them with one specific source; rather, their allusiveness to several earlier texts simultaneously connects all the references to a single tradition to which Mark's text is a recent addition. The frequency of references to this theme points to the importance Mark places on its message to the meaning of the Gospel. God's universal kingdom opposes all worldly kingdoms. According to Mark, rather than being microcosms of God's kingdom, they are undermining it because of their corruption and secular commitments, whether under Herod as tetrarch or Pontius Pilate as procurator. For example, in the Parable of the Mustard Seed (Mk 4.30-32), Mark quotes Jesus as saying,

> How shall we picture the kingdom of God, or by what parable shall we describe it? It is like the mustard-seed, which is smaller than any seed in the ground at its sowing. But once sown, it springs up and grows taller than any other plant, and forms branches so large that the birds can settle in its shade.

The last part of this alludes to Ezek. 17.23 as well as to Dan. 4.12 and 21. All the lines suggested are from poetic texts describing a great tree, provided by God's plenitude, whose abundance would shelter and support all creatures (Ezek. 17.23-24). Another possible allusion is to Ezek. 31.3-9, recalling that Assyria, the cedar of Lebanon, which overshadowed all others, also came under the universal power of the God of Israel (Ezek. 31.5-9). All assert that human kingdoms, no matter how successful they may appear in dispensing their benefits, do not encompass the universal power and all-embracing transcendence of divine hegemony. These allusions taken together emphasize God's universal sovereignty in contrast to the limited powers of human kingdoms. This divine utopia contrasts with the political world in which Mark situates his story, whether the Herodian tetrarchy or Pontius Pilate's official role in Jerusalem, neither of which are models for secular government. On the contrary, both seem models of all a utopia should not be, for both collude in murder. Again this hierarchy of universals, in which human pretenses at utopian idealism are shown to be inadequate in contrast to God's divine kingdom, set two kinds of time against each other: historical time versus eternity. But this opposition does not dismiss historical time. Rather, in keeping with traditional Hebraic teachings, it requires humans to make the divine kingdom present in history and pit it ideologically at least against the proclaimed utopian universal kingdoms, whether Egyptian, Assyrian, Babylonian or Roman.

The ideal of the Roman Empire, however, which was probably in the imaginations of at least some of Mark's audience, as opposed to the reality, might indeed have seemed to some to mirror the 'universal' sovereignty of God's kingdom. Mark's retrieval of these texts of divine hegemony over all microcosmic utopian political models, infers that all such models are ultimately flawed. Mark's audience would immediately be aware that this included the Roman Empire, no matter where the Gospel was written and read within the Empire. Thus Mark's retrieval of these texts serves as subtle political commentary on the Roman Empire and its claims to universal sovereignty while also contrasting human empires with the eternal kingdom of the God of Israel. Mark brings the sacred texts of the past to bear on the present; he uses the texts with their eternal promises to interpret the contemporary political situation: God's universal kingdom contrasted with the Roman Empire.

The few allusions to Kings (1 Kgs 22.17), Chronicles (2 Chron. 18.16), Judith (Jud. 11.19) and Esther are related because they all comment on the leaderless status of the Jewish nation at the time of Jesus, using the shepherd and sheep metaphor (cf. Ezek. 34.8 and Zech. 10.2-3). The quotation from Esther, however, directly indicts Herod and the Herodian complicity with the Romans, a political malfeasance that contrasts with Esther's selfless sacrifice for her people. Through the quotation 'Israel's' present is juxtaposed with 'Israel's' past, and as a consequence it re-enforces the present usurpation of political and moral authority by Herodian depravity and collusion with the Romans.[53]

53. For a full discussion of the meaning of this reference, see my essay, 'A Blind Promise: Mark's Retrieval of Esther'.

Also, the quotation is a mechanism to juxtapose the immediate political loss with the stable literary, cultural and moral traditions, thus re-enforcing God's continuing presence in Israel's history.

When Herod asks Herodias's daughter what she would like as a reward for her delightful dancing, he swears an oath, ὅ τι ἐάν με αἰτήσῃς δώσω σοι ἕως ἡμίσους τῆς βασιλείας μου ('Whatever you ask I will give you, up to half my kingdom', Mk 6.23), quoting Est. 5.3, when King Ahasuerus is so enchanted with his anonymously Jewish wife Esther, he wants to please her. The ironies in these parallels abound as they point to political and moral turmoil and corruption. Both kings' marriages are socially and morally suspect. In the first case, John the Baptist questioned the moral probity of Herod's marriage to Herodias; in the second, King Ahasuerus has unwittingly transgressed ethnic and religious codes by taking a Jewish wife. Both queens are vulnerable to social and political attacks, and both are assaulted by a third party. In both cases, the kings are sexually entrapped by women, making generous offers that they feel obliged to respect. But here the parallels end. The reference provides the means for the stories to comment on each other; citing the first story provides a commentary on the second, just as it also draws attention to the contrast between the stories.

In the Esther story, we see a strong and courageous woman, who, in an act of selfless generosity for her own people, mesmerizes an enamored and malleable king. Esther uses her beauty and her power over the king to liberate her people in an act of unselfish courage, 'If I have won your majesty's favor', she answers, after the king's second offer to give her anything up to half his kingdom, 'my request is for my life, my petition is for my people. For it has come to my ears that we have been sold, I and my people, to be destroyed, plundered, and enslaved, we and our children, male and female' (Est. 7.3-5). In the Markan story, a young girl, at her mother's instigation, makes a depraved, selfish request that the king honors. The stories contrast female sexual power that can prove both moral and immoral depending on the circumstances. This citation exposes the corruption and cowardice of the feminized Herodian court that is destroying its own people and failing morally and politically, in contrast with the historical model of female courage remembered by the refrain from the Esther story. The reference recalls an incident when fearless, moral personal action had beneficial political consequences, suggesting the impossibility of political solutions in the debased present time of the Herodian tetrarchy.

Mark's opposition of divine universalism to localized political universalism through his many references and allusions to the Writings and related prophetic utterances subtly reveals his own political doubts, showing that the present time (whether Jesus' in Palestine or his own, forty years later) offers little political hope. The references, culled from the revered narratives of the Hebrew experience, suggest that human political structures, whether ideals or realities, contemporary or historical, are flawed and inadequate at their best, and corrupt and depraved at their worst. More importantly, they contrast political models for human organization with the divine macrocosm, directing attention to the flaws and limitations of political solutions. Nevertheless, this divine macrocosm has both social and political consequences, because a rearrangement of worldly order under divine aegis demands changes in political and social values and alliances. In other words, there is not an implicit kind of Manichaean separation between the domain of humans and God recommended here; just the contrary, there is a call for a reappraisal of lines of division with worldly kingdoms losing their boundaries and power within the universal boundaries of the divine kingdom. This is a call to bring the utopian promise from the past and to make it present.

The Prophets and Psalms

The third major source of First Testament texts Mark selects are from the Prophets and Psalms. Again, these are citations, plagiarisms and allusions. In the citations, Mark occasionally identifies the source or uses the introductory formula, γέγραπται, to inform the audience that he is quoting from scripture. All three types attach the major events of the Gospel to the Jewish prophetic tradition, delineate the relationship between Jesus, this tradition and the transcendent divinity, while simultaneously reflecting hope that these fragments of the past can be remembered. They are central vehicles for conveying the author's interpretation of the events he retells. They are the poetry through which he renders the narrative of Jesus' last days. Where Mark places them in the narrative creates the ironic tension in the passion narrative as celebration mixes with hypocrisy and suffering and death replaces triumphant expectation.

The first of these weaves together Exod. 23.20, Mal. 3.1 and Isa. 40.3 in the opening verses of the Gospel which Mark, through the γέγραπται formula, incorrectly attributes to Isaiah as prophecy fulfilled:

Ἰδοὺ ἀποστέλλω τὸν ἄγγελόν μου πρὸ προσώπου σου,
ὃς κατασκευάσει τὴν ὁδόν σου·
φωνὴ βοῶντος ἐν τῇ ἐρήμῳ,
Ἑτοιμάσατε τὴν ὁδὸν κυρίου,
εὐθείας ποιεῖτε τὰς τρίβους αὐτοῦ

Here is my herald whom I send on ahead of you, and he will prepare your way. A voice crying in the wilderness, 'Prepare a way for the Lord; clear a straight path for him' (Mk 1.2-3).

Mark here quotes the Isaiah text and applies it to the John/Jesus occasion. However, his specific alteration of line 5, 'clear a way for our God', to 'clear a way for him' (i.e. Jesus), rewrites the original. The prophet of old cleared the way for God; here John clears the way for Jesus. The Gospel writer has realigned the texts and grafted together First Testament texts as if they were a single citation, and then, with the last word αὐτοῦ, assigned it to the εὐαγγέλιον he relates. But, this triumphant tone of prophecy fulfilled, opening the Gospel belies the forthcoming events when the 'way' will lead messenger and prophet alike to suffering and death. The exultant 'fulfillment' readings of this text, it seems to me, ignore the fragility of the interconnections, a pastiche of tokens which remind us of God's historical covenant with the chosen people (Exod. 23.20) and gift of the promised land, and God's warning against the idolatries of their neighbors. The quotation, in fact, recalls to us the fate of God's prophets (Mal. 3.1; Isa. 40.3). If Mark's audience were acquainted with the fate of John the Baptist, as they must certainly have been with that of Jesus, Peter and Paul, and assuming their knowledge of the textual references, such a reference ironically undermined its own triumphal tone. Just the contrary, the allusion connects an entire history of failure to heed the prophetic voices of 'Israel' to this latest event.

The word ἔρημος (desert) in the quotation functions as a metaphor and connects and distinguishes the stories of John the Baptist and Jesus from each other and from the Hebraic tradition. John the Baptist is a charismatic figure whose mission confines him to the desert. On the other hand, when Jesus withdraws to the ἔρημος (desert/wilderness), it is not to the undefiled wilderness where he is purged of the corruption of the town. Ancient Hebrew prophets identify themselves with the wilderness,[54] a metaphor connoting desolation, aridity, the failure of God's people to heed his prophets, and God's threatened destruction, both real and symbolic (Isa. 1.7; 5.17; 6.11, and especially 40.3; Jer. 2.15; 2.31; 4.11; Ezek. 6.14; 14.8). The metaphor recapitulates the forty-year sojourn when God provided for the Hebrew people while a generation was purged of the defilement of Egyptian culture (Amos 2.10, Jer. 2.6, Ezek. 20.10, 13, 15, 17, 18, 21, 35, 36). Mark's oxymoric opening for the Gospel combines reminiscences of God's promises, human failure, and the fate of prophets.

Referring to the suffering of a 'redeemer' as written in scripture, in a graceful rhetorical and poetical style, full of enigma and ambiguity, Isa. 53.3, 7 (Mk 9.12; 15.4-5) addresses the Lord, with a report of the suffering servant, whose affliction was on account of the iniquities of the speaker/s. Like Zech. 13.7 (Mk 14.27), the speech reports the deliverance of the one who suffered because of their sins. Who this servant was has been the subject of great controversy,[55] and Christian exegetes attach the reference to a prophecy fulfilled in New Testament scriptures with Jesus as the suffering servant and the redeemer. The question remains, how was Mark using them? Before addressing this question, I would also like to examine the use of Zacharias in the Passion context.

In the Passion section of the Markan text, there is one direct citation from Zacharias, perhaps from a *Septuagint* source, and introduced with a ὅτι γέγραπται formula:

πατάξω τὸν ποιμένα
καὶ τὰ πρόβατα διασκορπισθήσονται

I will strike the shepherd down and the sheep shall be scattered (Mk 14.27, Zech. 13.7).

This is said by Jesus as he predicts the σκάνδαλον, telling his disciples, σκανδαλισθήσεσθε ('You will all fall away', 14.27). In addition to this direct quotation, Mark also found many of the themes in Zacharias compatible with his own theological and historical concerns: the suffering of Jerusalem (Zech. 12.11); impending destruction of Jerusalem by Gentiles (Zech. 14.1); the ultimate hegemony and universalism of the Lord of Israel (Zech. 14.9-20).

54. Schneidau, *Sacred Discontent*, pp. 129-30.
55. See Gottwald, *The Hebrew Bible*, pp. 492-502 for an overview of the discussion.

These direct quotations from Isaiah and Zacharias cited with the 'it is written' formula appear to be 'prophecy fulfilled'. But, they are also attempts to align the present events with the past but living textual tradition and to connect the past to the present as parts of a continuous whole. Reading these as Mark's effort to construct continuity and connection rather than as a one dimensional 'fulfillment' does not take away the uniqueness of the Jesus event. Instead it places the event in a long line of texts of suffering, failed expectation, and hope of deliverance, one of the many strands of the Hebraic tradition. The reality of the crucifixion and the scattering of the disciples, in fact, prohibits complaisance about an impending temporal spiritual or political deliverance, making the concept of 'fulfillment' paradoxical at best. Rather, expectation is all.

Direct quotations and indirect allusions to Psalms permeate the Gospel, expressing praise, thanksgiving, lamentation and suffering, and hope. These appear most notably in the Passion section of the Gospel (14–16). The first of these, however, occurs after the transfiguration when Jesus predicts his impending death. This is an allusion to Ps. 22.1-18, the themes of which are reproduced consistently in the Passion, although it is introduced with a γέγραπται formula, implying a citation and that the forthcoming events are prophesied, καὶ πῶς γέγραπται ἐπὶ τὸν υἱὸν τοῦ ἀνθρώπου ἵνα πολλὰ πάθῃ καὶ ἐξουδενηθῇ ('Yet how is it that the scriptures say of the Son of Man that he is to endure great sufferings and to be treated with contempt?', Mk 9.12). Through the allusion, Mark identifies Jesus with suffering Israel, and the lament of afflicted and innocent persons who pray for God's intercession. The second prediction of his impending death, παραδίδοται εἰς χεῖρας ἀνθρώπων ('given up into the power of men', Mk 9.31) also alludes to Isa. 53.6,11, and 12 (παραδιδόν) and to a common expression in the Psalms, 'the hand of sinners'.[56] What these implicit allusions suggest is that the Gospel writer as well as the Jesus he presents had a repertoire of biblical language at his disposal. The author of the Markan text consciously aligns his story and the experiences of the main character with these texts of suffering.

56. André Rose, 'L'influence des psaumes sur les annonces et les récits de la passion et de la résurrection dans les évangiles', in Robert de Langhe (ed.) *Le Psautier: Ses origines. Ses problèmes littéraires. Son influence* (Louvain: Publications Universitaires, 1962), pp. 297-356 (301).

Jesus enters Jerusalem to the crowd's enthusiastic shouting of a refrain from Psalm 118: ὡσαννὰ· εὐλογημένος ὁ ἐρχόμενος ἐν ὀνόματι
κυρίου ('Hosanna! Blessings on him who comes in the name of the
Lord', Mk 11.9). Psalm 118 probably functioned as a chant for a liturgical procession. But assigning a liturgical prayer to a street action in
which the crowd mixes triumph and expectation of a temporal and political deliverance, ironically mocks the prayer and their expectations,
both of which are exposed by the crowd's fickleness as they later reject
the one who came in the name of the Lord (Mk 15.13, 15). Jesus deploys a direct quote from this Psalm, when in a proof-text, following
the Parable of the Vineyard, he reminds his challengers of the Israelite
rejection of prophets:

Λίθον ὃν ἀπεδοκίμασαν οἱ οἰκοδομοῦντες,
οὗτος ἐγενήθη εἰς κεφαλὴν γωνίας·
παρὰ κυρίου ἐγένετο αὕτη
καὶ ἔστιν θαυμαστὴ ἐν ὀφθαλμοῖς ἡμῶν;

The stone which the builders rejected has become the main corner-stone.
This is the Lord's doing, and it is wonderful in our eyes (Mk 12.10-11;
Ps. 118.22-23).

Here he lyrically recalls the psalm to excoriate his enemies, identifying his own present fate with that of other historically 'rejected stones'.

During the Passion (14–16), the Gospel writer uses refrains from
the psalm variety which Hermann Gunkel called anonymous individual
laments (Pss. 41 and 22).[57] This form is addressed by an anonymous
person, who is suffering from political and social oppression, illness,
or personal or psychological distress, to Yahweh, often proclaiming
innocence or asking for help.[58] The speaker, who is persecuted and
mocked, appeals to God to be delivered and vindicated. All the quotations or allusions to psalms in this last section of the Gospel emphasize Jesus' human vulnerability and suffering.

At the Last Supper, the allusion to Psalm 41, a thanksgiving song,
through which Jesus identifies his betrayer as ὁ ἐσθίων μετ' ἐμοῦ
('one who is eating with me', Mk 14.18) poetically exposes Jesus' psychological state: 'Happy the man who has a concern for the helpless!
The Lord will save him in time of trouble' (Ps. 41). The allusion recalls
the entire psalm to expose Jesus' condition and to reveal his emotional

57. Gunkel, *The Psalms*.
58. Gottwald, *The Hebrew Bible*, p. 527.

response to the impending events and those which have preceded the final confrontation. The citation synthesizes the emotions Jesus experiences, including anxiety, fear, expectation and hope, all of which may reflect both his as well as his closest followers' condition. The refrain paradoxically recalls the psalm's conviction about the Lord's protection and restoration of the innocent despite the apparent triumph of enemies. Specifically recalling 'the friend who ate at my table' (41.9), this vulnerable man, Jesus, as he contemplates his own betrayal and death, alludes to a history in which the 'Lord' has interceded for mankind. His foreknowledge of his certain death ironically contradicts the supplication for vindication and liberation expressed by the poem, although the psalm recognizes that the sufferer's innocence unites him to the 'Lord' (41.3).

There are possibly four references to Psalm 22 in the Gospel, the first line of which Jesus quotes in Aramaic as he dies, ἐλωι ἐλωι λεμα σαβαχθανι ('My God, my God, why hast thou forsaken me?') and which Mark translates into Greek for his non-Aramaic speaking audience (15.34).[59] Psalm 22 is both a prayer for deliverance and a prayer of praise for the triumphant God of Israel before whom all nations bow down (Ps. 22.27). Referring to the dividing of clothes (Mk 15.24), Mark takes from the psalm, 'They share out my garments among them/and cast lots for my clothes' (Ps. 22.18), and to the mocking shaking of heads, 'All who see me jeer at me/make mouths at me and wave their heads' (Ps. 22.7; Mk 15.29) as Jesus becomes the archetype of the righteous sufferer before God.[60] As Vernon Robbins points out,

59. Vernon K. Robbins, 'The Reversed Contextualiation of Psalm 22 in the Markan Crucifixion: A Socio-Rhetorical Analysis', in F. Van Segbroeck (ed.), *The Four Gospels 1992: Festschrift Frans Neirynck*, II, pp. 1161-83, is a comprehensive discussion of the use of Psalm 22 in the Markan passion version; see also, Douglas Moo, *The Old Testament in the Gospel Passion Narratives* (Sheffield: Almond Press, 1983), pp. 264-75.

60. Roman law permitted the soldiers to take possession of a condemned criminal's clothes. See N. Sherwin-White, *Roman Society and Roman Law in the New Testament: The Sarum Lectures, 1960–61* (Oxford: Clarendon Press, 1963), p. 46. Here what may have actually happened historically paralleled the typology represented in the psalm, or Mark has presented the story to parallel the typology of the psalm. Robbins makes a persuasive argument based on Dio Chrysostom's Oration 4 that the 'ritual mocking and abuse of a prisoner was a feature of an annual festival in eastern Mediterranean society and culture' ('The Reversed Contextualization of Psalm 22', p. 1163).

the order of events in the Psalm is reversed in the Markan version, rendering the lament from the cross all the more ironic. This lament at his moment of death, with no sense of 'fulfilled' prophecy or spiritual or political liberation, expresses, like the psalmist, his alienation from God and his sense of abandonment: '. . . the sequence of Mk 15 inverts the sequence of Ps. 22, and with this inversion comes a subversion of its rhetoric. The sufferer in the psalm expresses hope to the end; Jesus on the cross expresses the agony of abandonment by everyone including God.'[61]

No amount or kind of exegesis has managed to erase the tragedy in these last words from the cross.[62] The combination of identifying this story as εὐαγγέλιον ('good news'), the isolated and abandoned figure on the cross, and his failure to appear again in the Gospel: together these constitute the central ironic paradoxes of the work. The recall of the psalmist's text reminds us that such suffering is Israel's historic experience.

The expressions, spoken by the heavenly voice, σὺ εἶ ὁ υἱός μου ('Thou art my son', Mk 1.11), repeated as οὗτός ἐστιν ὁ υἱός μου ('This is my son', Mk 9.7) and restated as οὗτος ὁ ἄνθρωπος υἱὸς θεοῦ ἦν ('Truly this man was a son of God') by the centurion (15.39) which identify Jesus as the son of God, find their source in Ps. 2.7:

> I will repeat the Lord's decree:
> 'You are my son', he said;
> 'This day I become your father'.

Appropriating the patriarchal metaphor for the relationship of the divinity to humankind through this royal ceremonial song serves a number of Markan rhetorical purposes. First, the individual address, without reference to the sub-text establishes the uniqueness of the relationship between Jesus and the divinity. Secondly, 'the fatherhood' of God assigns the family metaphor with its universalist overtones, provided by the sub-text, to the human community. Thirdly, having the centurion rephrase the lyric moment from the psalms realigns the ancient metaphor to the contemporary Roman setting when divinizing has become the hallmark of imperial success.[63] The appearance of this

---

61. Robbins, 'The Reversed Contextualization of Psalm 22', p. 1179.

62. The extent of controversy on the meaning of these last words of Jesus testify to their paradoxicality. See Robbins, 'The Reversed Contextualization of Psalm 22'.

63. See the sections on Augustus, Claudius, Vespasian, and Titus in Suetonius,

phrase at the three most critical moments of the Gospel (baptism, transfiguration and crucifixion), the only times when the voice or presence of the heavenly divinity intervenes, draws together the Jewish heritage, Roman politics and the uniqueness of Jesus. It divests imperial Rome of its divine propriety, while simultaneously honoring Jesus' relationship to God, a synecdoche for the human relationship to God, the roots of which have historic precedent in the Jewish textual tradition. Like Mark's use of the ἐγώ εἰμι ('I am', Mk 6.50) revelation formula for a deity found in both 'pagan texts'[64] and the Hebrew Bible (Isa. 6.8, for example), these discreet but nonetheless spotlighted identification tags reflect complex interconnections between pagan, Jewish and the Markan texts. Mark undermines the Roman deification of emperors while making Jesus' connection to the divinity echo the First Testament textual tradition, 'You are my son... I am your father'.

Mark's employment of his textual heritage emphasizes the importance of the past, particularly in interpreting the present and in representing an ideal that can be held up in comparison with the present. In this, like the other Gospel writers, he follows the Judaic tradition as reflected in the Hebrew and Septuagint Bibles, creating an autonomous work that was both connected to the past and a continuation of it. This was the case for the Jesus character he portrays, who quotes freely from ancient Hebrew texts in Greek translation, Mark's revered canon, as well as for himself as he wrote the Gospel. In ancient literature it was memory not knowledge that served as power, so traditions of the past were sacred. For Mark, as for Jesus, it was essential to make message and story reflect ancient traditions, although the political and religious turmoil of the first century raised questions about the efficacy of

The Twelve Caesars. All of these were declared gods. Tacitus refers to Augustus as 'the divine Augustus'. '"Augustus" was an ancient word suggesting the numinous and something more than human. . . ' 'By this epithet Octavian has continued to be known. . . the ruler's name had been C(aius Julius C f) Octavianus. After 27 his official name was Imp(erator) Caesar divi f(ilius) ['son of god', in this case the now deified Julius Caesar] Augustus' (Ferguson, *Backgrounds of Early Christianity*, p. 20). See also, A.-L. Descamps, 'Pour une histoire du titre "Fils de Dieu"' in M. Sabbe (ed.), *L'Evangile selon Marc: Tradition et Rédaction* (Leuven: Leuven University Press, 1988), pp. 529-71.

64. Cox, *Biography in Late Antiquity*, p. 39. Apollonius of Tyana is reported to have used this formula. Jonathan Z. Smith, 'Good News is No News: Aretalogy and Gospel', in Jacob Neusner (ed.), *Christianity, Judaism, and Other Greco-Roman Cults: Studies for Morton Smith at Sixty* (Leiden: E.J. Brill, 1975), I, pp. 21-38.

past and present convictions, and doubt about Israel's future. Such a situation suggested that history had lost its providential meaning and remained only an example of political hopes no longer possible or repeated patterns of suffering (as for example, 'Israel' as 'the sheep without a shepherd'). Mark's recapitulation of the past and selection of texts from this respected history show his consciousness of the historical and cultural processes at work in his own time and represent his reflection on his relationship to this past as shown in his textual heritage. The textual references include direct appropriations, either cited or plagiarized, rephrased references and allusions. These Mark situates in contexts that connect them to the earlier text by restatement (as laws) and by lexical parallelisms that typologically connect the new event with an earlier event (as Jesus is linked to occasions recorded in Psalms, Isaiah and Zacharias; or Herod's oath conjures Esther's story). Also earlier citations are reinterpreted for a new context (as with laws).

Mark's use of a textual heritage, as this chapter tries to show, is far more complex than the unidimensional theories about intertextual relationships suggest. Neither a 'fulfillment' nor an 'anxiety' theory can satisfactorily explain the diversity of the author's references or the varieties of ways in which he handles these textual selections. The author's redaction does, however, show that he is establishing continuity with the textual tradition of 'Israel', that laws, and historical and emotional experiences recorded in that textual tradition still have relevance to the present as commentary, contrast, or hopes both denied or still possible.

To understand the Markan author's textual traditions we must recognize that first-century Palestine was a highly ritualized society in which religion played the central cultural role and where scriptural phrases were commonplaces in the language. Biblical allusion saturated the lexical field in which the Gospel writer and Jesus operated, the rhetoric through which they interpreted and experienced the world. There is little triumphalism in the gathering of the scattered words of this past; rather it is hope that this past be remembered, retrieved, and continued in the present.

Chapter 3

NARRATIVE DURATION:
SUSPENDED TIME

In making a distinction between apparent and symbolic meanings, narrative theorists follow in the long-standing tradition of separating the literal from the allegorical, moral and anagogical. For Paul Ricoeur 'any structure of signification in which a direct, primary meaning designates, in addition, another meaning which is indirect, secondary and figurative, and which can be apprehended only through the first' is symbolic.[1] Though not expressed in the same terms, Ricoeur's point resembles Genette's distinction between 'narrative' and 'narrating', the story and the way it unfolds,[2] or Mieke Bal's 'series of sentences' and 'series of events', the arrangement of which creates an accumulated meaning distinct from the story. Though different in their emphasis, these contemporary approaches to narrative interpretation parallel Origen's, Jerome's and Augustine's division of the biblical text into levels of symbolic meaning.[3] Though the Church fathers had theories of narrative interpretation developed to read the Bible, outside of rhetorical theories about how to create narratives,[4] they did not have

1. 'Existence and Hermeneutics', in Don Ihde (ed.), *The Conflict of Interpretations* (Evanston, IL: Northwestern University Press, 1974), p. 13.
2. Genette, *Narrative Discourse*; Robert W. Funk, *The Poetics of Biblical Narrative* (Sonoma, CA: Polebridge Press, 1988) is a comprehensive application of both Vladimir Propp's and Genette's systematic literary method to biblical narrative.
3. See *De Doctrina Christiana*; Origen's *De Principiis*; and Jerome's *Commentariorum in Hiezechielem* in CCSL 75, XIII, 42, 13-14; Jerome's numerous letters on interpretative matters including, 'Epistula ad Damasum' and 'Ad Pammachium'.
4. See George Kennedy, *The Art of Rhetoric in the Roman World 300 BC–AD*

a theory of narrative per se, even though Augustine clearly did have a complex understanding of narrative as demonstrated in the *Confessions*.[5]

Many different techniques can be used to develop the symbolic dimension in the text—typologies and intertexts, for example, which Mark does use—but one of Mark's primary methods is to disrupt linearity when unfolding the series of events. The Gospel text seems to move forward in a linear pattern to tell its crisis time narrative, but deviations in a strict linearity force the reader to pay attention. Variations in linearity, in fact, make the reader consider other elements besides the storyline. The suspended time narratives interrupt the central narrative by introducing distinct stories that take on a life of their own. These suspended time narratives, almost like narrative asides, are often a critical means to interpret the meaning of the crisis story, or they offer clues about interpretation in general, or they expand the 'message' beyond the immediate narrative to understand it in terms of a larger message. The narratives, themselves outsiders from the central narrative, often are about scapegoats or the weak, and function to redefine outsiders and insiders. Often they also tell of people who are themselves suspended in time due to disease, ethnicity, or other forms of ritual or political exclusion.

Whether in this suspended or the crisis time, Mark's narrative technique dismantles the linearity of the story, forcing the reader to 'focalize'.[6] Focalization, for the reader, involves the narrative segment, the reader or audience, and what he or she creates in response to the narrative segment. Within the work, 'focalization' is the 'point of view' of the character or narrator through whom we experience the narrative, in this case the omniscient but unobtrusive story-teller, who, like a journalist, reports what has happened.

Furthermore, this playing with the sequence of events is not only literary. It focuses the narrative by featuring certain events, incidents,

300 (Princeton, NJ: Princeton University Press, 1972); George Kennedy, *Classical Rhetoric and its Christian and Secular Tradition from Ancient to Modern Times* (Chapel Hill: University of North Carolina Press, 1980); George Kennedy, *A New History of Classical Rhetoric* (Princeton, NJ: Princeton University Press, 1994).

5.   See for example, Brian Stock, *Augustine the Reader: Meditation, Self-knowledge, and the Ethics of Interpretation* (Cambridge, MA: Harvard University Press, 1996).

6.   Bal, *Narratology*, pp. 100-14. Genette, *Narrative Discourse*, pp. 189-98.

structural oppositions and parallelisms, or sayings. In doing so, it presents many ways of looking at or interpreting events and draws out distinctions that may not be readily apparent.[7] These disruptions in the text point to a symbolic meaning that the series of events is intended to unfold. Ignoring or interrupting sequential order is one of the most telling ways for the Gospel to convey its symbolic meanings. The breach in linearity forces us as readers to construct relationships among the sandwiched parts, to ask questions about their connection with the central story and to agree to stop the crisis time narrative while these suspended events take place.

The specific Markan narrative techniques that suspend time, interrupt the reader and force him or her to stop the story and instead to construct the Gospel's hidden meaning and the relationship of the narrative parts to the whole, include the following: 'encasement', that is, the embedding of stories within other stories; 'interlacing' of parallel but discrete narratives; and 'allegorization of narrative',[8] in which the narrative means something other than it appears to mean, its significance being a substitution for the surface, a literary situation created by metaphor, metonymy, and synecdoche. These are all typical Markan narrative characteristics, forcing the audience to experience and perceive contrast, irony, paradox and ambiguity. This irony can result from the difference between Jesus' actions and sayings and the social action he performs or the distance between what he says and the understanding of the persons he addresses.[9] The listener/audience of the text is brought into the text as an active listener, reader and possible member of a Gospel community. I will not discuss every suspended time narrative in the Gospel, but I will focus on a few examples to demonstrate how the narratives break away from the main narrative and take on their own life, while also showing how they interpret, comment on,

7.   Bal, *Narratology*, pp. 52-53.

8.   Eugene Vance, 'Pas de trois: Narrative, Hermeneutics, and Structure in Medieval Poetics', in Mario J. Valdes and Owen J. Miller (eds.), *Interpretation of Narrative* (Toronto: University of Toronto Press, 1978), pp. 118-34 (134).

9.   For a discussion of irony in the Gospel, see Jerry Camery-Hoggatt, *Irony in Mark's Gospel* (Cambridge: Cambridge University Press, 1992), pp. 15-35; Bilezikian (*The Liberated Gospel*) was the first to talk about irony in the Gospel, identifying irony as sarcasm, special language that is clear only to insiders, and reversal. Also, Robert M. Fowler, (*Let the Reader Understand: Reader Response Criticism and the Gospel of Mark* [Minneapolis: Fortress Press, 1991], pp. 11-14 *et passim*) discusses irony as a narrative technique in the Gospel.

develop, or connect to the crisis narrative. It is through the symbolic communication of these suspended time narratives, in particular, that the Gospel educates the community it addresses.

Parables

The parables in the Gospel of Mark, while developing the character and manner of Jesus' public career, nevertheless interrupt the main story line. There have been numerous scholarly discussions of Jesus' parables and the parabolic nature of the Gospel of Mark itself,[10] so I will not be offering fresh interpretations; rather, I will only discuss how the two main parables in the Gospel (Mk 4.3-20, The Sower and 12.1-11, The Vineyard) fit into my analysis of the role of time in the Gospel. As has long been recognized, as synecdoches for the crisis narrative, these parables also interpret or synthesize the central issues, teachings, and events of the Gospel. The first parable, The Sower, synthesizes the narrative action of the first half of the Gospel, Jesus' teaching mission, and the second The Parable of the Vineyard, interprets the occasion, reasons and consequences of the Passion.[11] However, in both

10. See Kermode, *Genesis of Secrecy*; Williams, *Gospel Against Parable*, who writes that the theme and images of the parables in ch. 4 are closely related to the plot of the Gospel (p. 180); John Donahue, *The Gospel in Parable: Metaphor, Narrative and Theology in the Synoptic Gospels* (Philadelphia: Fortress Press, 1988); John Drury, *The Parables in the Gospels: History and Allegory* (New York: Crossroad, 1985); Mary Ann Tolbert, *Perspectives on the Parables: An Approach to Multiple Interpretations* (Philadelphia: Fortress Press, 1979); Mary Ann Tolbert, 'Jesus, the Sower of the Word', in *idem, Sowing the Gospel*, pp. 127-75; Mary Ann Tolbert, 'Jesus, the Heir of the Vineyard', in *idem, Sowing the Gospel*, pp. 231-70; Joachim Jeremias, *Rediscovering the Parables* (New York: Charles Scribner's Sons, 1966); Crossan, *Cliffs of Fall*; John Drury, 'The Sower, the Vineyard, and the Place of Allegory in the Interpretation of Mark's Parables', *JTS* 24 (1973), pp. 367-79; John Dominic Crossan, 'The Parable of the Wicked Husbandmen', *JBL* 90.4 (1971), pp. 451-65; John Dominic Crossan, *In Parables: The Challenge of the Historical Jesus* (New York: Harper & Row, 1973); Birger Gerhardsson, 'The Parable of the Sower and its Interpretation', *NTS* 14 (1968), pp. 165-93.

11. See for example, E. Trocmé, 'Why Parables? A Study of Mark IV', *BJRL* 59 (1977), pp. 458-71; Achtemeier, 'Mark as Interpreter of the Jesus Traditions', pp. 339-52 (351); W.S. Vorster, 'Meaning and Reference: The Parables of Jesus in Mark 4', in B.C. Lategan and W.S. Vorster (eds.), *Text and Reality: Aspects of Reference in Biblical Texts* (Atlanta: Scholars Press, 1985), pp. 27-65; Via, *Ethics of Mark's*

cases, when Jesus tells them, the crisis narrative of his mission and sub-sequent death is interrupted with a living demonstration of his teaching style. Both parables are interpretations of the primary series of events, the first (The Sower) allegorically showing that messages are sown but not necessarily germinated or harvested. The second (The Vineyard) in an even more pointed way reveals that God's messenger is repeatedly rejected and the final messenger is even killed by the recalcitrant tenants the owner allows to care for his vineyard.

The Parable of the Sower uses the symbolic resources of the agricultural world Jesus inhabits. It interprets Jesus' teaching mission, while also defining its own parabolic literary method (4.10-12), and advising its listeners both within and without the Gospel to hear (4.9, 23-25). The disciples do not understand and Jesus must explain it to them. A critical shift takes place between the parable and the explanation, for Jesus tells the story in the past as completed action, even though the characters in it are all anonymous and typed, therefore implying some general or universal meaning in their story. The explanation, how-ever, switches to the present, a time that renders the narrative meaning in more general terms, suggesting that the events are subject to indef-inite repetition.[12] Thus, in order to explain the allegory to his disciples, Jesus takes it from the concrete and specific past completed time (aorist) to the general open-ended and continuous present, but at the same time, he tells the disciples precisely what it means. This time transfer from past to present in the explanation emphasizes that the meaning and narrative conclusion of the parable is still incomplete. Just as the sowing of the seed, its reception is haphazard, for the full results of the sowing are still unsettled. Such a shift in time in the explanation for the parable emphasizes its suspended conclusion—it is yet to come. Anticipation replaces completion.

Gospel, pp. 181-82; Tolbert, *Sowing the Gospel*, pp. 121-26, 127-31, 148-64, 233-39.

12. In κοινή, the present conveys an iterative mood, whereas the aorist conveys the sense of single occurence. I am hesitant to make too much of these tense shifts because the parable may have been translated from Aramaic to κοινή which means that the tenses may have been carried over without concern for the differences in mood conveyed by tense; secondly, Mark is not generally careful with his grammar, so these shifts may be incidental. Nonetheless, both halves of this parable are con-sistent in the use of tenses.

Similarly, the Parable of the Vineyard tells its story in the past time, as completed action, portraying tenants who refuse to pay the vineyard owner his due, and, who, in a series of escalating violent acts, eventually kill the heir to the vineyard. Again, although the ecology is specific, the characters are anonymous and the specific location unidentified, but Jesus concludes it with rhetorical questions that put the story into a different time frame, suggesting that the story is incomplete: 'What will the owner of the vineyard do? He will come and put the tenants to death and give the vineyard to others?' (Mk 12.9). Whether or not this remark is directed at the Hebrew people facing the destruction of their historic homeland by the Romans in 67–70 CE, or a coded story about the futility of armed peasant rebellion, as recently argued,[13] because it is told as an allegory of completed action with an incomplete ending, it removes itself from the immediate historic situation to a projection into the future. Like the Parable of the Sower, its reception is multiple, but the story is pointed enough that some listeners instantly understand it as an allegory of sacred history directed at its audience, who ironically decide to make away with its teller after hearing it (Mk 12.12). Perhaps indeed they interpret is as promoting revolts. Whatever the case, they have understood its veiled meaning as a threat and as Mark insists, they saw that the parable was aimed at them. Emphasizing the accuracy of their characterization as recalcitrant in the parable, they use the threat as their reason for plotting murder (12.12). The most important lesson in the parable is the power it has to promote future action, for it sets a murder plot into motion.

The parables are told as specific examples, with the resources of ordinary time, in ordinary day-to-day places, with ordinary people, but in a recognizable ecological environment. But the anonymous characters and lack of specific locations removes them from ordinary occasions as they point towards their allegorical implications and their timeless truth. Like other suspended narratives, the parables stop the crisis time narrative in order to interpret it, so they are directed outside the Gospel to the community outside the narrative time and outside the crisis events it recounts. Nevertheless, the audience is made aware of the urgency of their message to their own outsider world.

13. See William R. Herzog II, 'Peasant Revolt and the Spiral of Violence', in *idem*, *Parables as Subversive Speech* (Louisville, KY: Westminster/John Knox Press, 1994), pp. 98-113.

Intercalation

'Intercalation', 'interlamination', or what Eugene Vance, writing about medieval narrative technique called 'interlacing of discrete narratives' or 'encasement of narrative',[14] is the embedding of narrative sequences within a larger narrative that is interrupted for the duration of the intercalated story. Markan commentators have identified intercalation as a typically Markan literary device (Mk 3.20-21 [22-30] 31-35; 5.21-24 [25-34] 35-43; 6.7-13 [14-29] 30-31; 11.12-14 [15-19] 20-25; 14.1-2 [3-9] 10-11).[15] The effect of the device is disconcerting, even abrasive, because it interrupts the main narrative and suspends its time while another story is told. The main story line appears aborted for another seemingly unrelated story. The reader-audience, as a consequence, is enticed to reconstruct the relationship among the sequences. This is a device that facilitates the ideological intention of the work, thrusting questions before the audience and requiring the inevitable 'focalizing' response. 'Focalizing' puts the intercalation into the foreground, forcing the reader-audience to try to understand its connection to the story it interrupted. In addition, intercalations compel us to probe their connection in meaning to the immediate literary setting, to some figural

14. Vance, 'Pas de trois', p. 134.

15. Various words have been used to identify this unique Markan technique. Frans Neirynck (*Duality in Mark: Contributions to the Study of Markan Redaction* [Repr; Leuven: Leuven University Press, 1988], p. 133), called the technique 'sandwiching'; David Rhoads and Donald Michie (*Mark as Story: An Introduction to the Narrative of the Gospel* [Philadelphia: Fortress Press, 1982], pp. 51-53) called the device 'framing'; Howard Clark Kee (*Community of the New Age: Studies in Mark's Gospel* [Philadelphia: Westminster, 1977], pp. 54-56), used the term 'intercalation'. Other studies include G. Van Oyen, 'Intercalation and Irony in the Gospel of Mark', in *The Four Gospels 1992: Festschrift Frans Neirynck*, II, pp. 949-74. See also T.A. Burkill, *Mysterious Revelation* (Ithaca, NY: Cornell University Press, 1963), p. 121; T.A. Burkill, *New Light on the Earliest Gospel* (Ithaca, NY: Cornell University Press, 1972), p. 263; John Donahue, *Are You the Christ? The Trial Narrative in the Gospel of Mark* (SBLDS, 10; Missoula, MT: Society of Biblical Literature for the Seminar on Mark, 1973), p. 42; Kermode, *Genesis of Secrecy*, p. 31; James R. Edwards, 'Markan Sandwiches: the Significance of Interpolations in Markan Narratives', *NovT* 31 (1989), pp. 193-216; J. Duncan M. Derrett, 'Mark's Technique: The Haemorrhaging Woman and Jairus' Daughter', *Bib* 63 (1982), pp. 474-505; Tom Shepherd, *Markan Sandwich Stories: Narration, Definition, and Function* (Berrien Springs, MI: Andrews University Press, 1993).

representation, to an interpretation of a sequence of events, or to the entire Gospel. The 'embedded story' may in fact serve as an explanation of the primary story, or as an ironic commentary on it.

Intercalation is one of the devices responsible for creating the tension in the narrative, for making it paradoxical, and for leading its readers to questions about the relationship of the parts to the Gospel's kerygma. They are characteristic of what has been correctly identified as Markan 'textuality', the author's 'transmutation' rather than mere transmission of oral traditions which were associated with or had accreted to the Jesus story.[16]

The intercalated stories particularly singled out by commentators on the gospel are the Cursing of the Fig Tree; the Cure of the Hemorrhaging Woman, and the Recovery of Jairus's Daughter.[17] The Cursing of the Fig Tree, it has been remarked, is the most disturbing action in Jesus' public career because it appears so destructive and cruel, especially since figs were out of season, and his disappointment at the tree's fruitlessness is therefore unwarranted. Jesus' unacceptable action has led to the numerous interpretations that associate the action with the intertwined narrative of the cleansing of the temple in Jerusalem. Although this narratival technique is a way to compel the reader to forego the comforts of traditional fiction,[18] Mark did not have strictly literary ambitions even though his intercalations show his storytelling skill. This is not, however, merely a technique to create fictional tension, but a disconcerting jarring of audience expectation forcing questioning, interpretation, and dialogue between text and audience. It is yet another device to manipulate the audience.[19] In fact, these jarring intercalations cause ruptures in narratival expectation that can be as instructive as the crisis story itself.

Essential to Mark's storytelling, these devices do not direct the reader or the story forward. Rather, they bring it to a halt, or they foreground one scene in the narrative sequences, and together the spotlighted narrative fragments 'embedded' into the larger narrative structure create a new meaning, not apparent in the textual surface. These new relationships require the reader to perceive contradictions,

16. Kelber, *The Oral and the Written Gospel*, pp. 90-139.
17. Frank Kermode, *The Art of Telling: Essays on Fiction* (Cambridge, MA: Harvard University Press, 1983), pp. 196; Achtemeier, *Mark*, pp. 22-30.
18. Kermode, *The Art of Telling*, pp. 197-98.
19. Bal, *Narratology*, p. 116.

antitheses, oppositions and paradoxes that are not easily resolved. Because of these techniques, which frame or disrupt the central narrative, we are forced to read beyond the surface, are moved from the story to perceive another meaning that is sometimes ironic because of the disparity between the narrative we read and its other meaning, hidden and inspired by Mark's storytelling method. Mark creates this other meaning through the arrangement of his material. These literary devices may not be employed in the sophisticated way they are in developed modern fiction, but nevertheless, they are characteristic of conscious, narrative artistry with ideological intentions.[20]

The story of the Gerasene demoniac takes place on the 'other side' (4.35-41).[21] The journey from the land of the Jews to the land of the 'pagans' ('Gentiles') was hazardous, requiring Jesus' mediation between man and nature, the allegorical meaning here implying that the narrator is moving from a known territory to an unknown, perhaps sinister land. Jean Starobinski writes of the 'other side',

> it is the other, in its quality not just an opposing side, but an opposing power. Beyond the shore is an anti-shore; beyond the day is an anti-day; the tombs, sojourn of the dead, are an anti-life; the devils are rebels.[22]

This 'other side' is foreign partly because it is outside the experience of Jesus' group and in an alien land, but also because what they encounter

20. Kermode (*Genesis of Secrecy*, p. 141) found the devices atypical of developed fiction, and noted, '. . . we are jostled from one puzzle to the next. . . as if the purpose of the story were less to establish a comfortable sequence than to pile one crux on another, each instituting an intense thematic opposition. . . they form a sort of aniconic figure for meditative interpretation'. Bal (*Narratology*), on the other hand, shows that 'embedding' is a highly sophisticated narrative technique, a primary means to convey the 'point of view' of the author.

21. For discussions of this story, see Tolbert, *Sowing the Gospel*, pp. 164-72; F.-J. Leenhardt, 'An Exegetical Essay: Mark 5:1-20: "The Madman Reveals the Final Truth" (M. Foucault)', in R. Barthes *et al* (eds.), *Structural Analysis and Biblical Exegesis: Interpretational Essays* (trans. A. Johnson; Pittsburgh: Pickwick Press, 1974), pp. 85-109; J. Starobinski, 'Le démoniaque de Gérasa', in R. Barthes *et al.* (eds.), *Analyse Structurale et Exégèse Biblique* (Neuchatel: Delachaux et Niestle, 1972), pp. 69-70; Jean Starobinski, 'Struggle with Legion: A Literary Analysis of Mark 5:1-20', in Bloom (ed.), *Modern Critical Interpretation*, pp. 35-61.

22. 'C'est l'autre, dans sa qualité non seulement de lieu opposé, mais de puissance opposante. L'outre-rivage est un anti-rivage; l'outre-jour est un anti-jour; les tombeaux, séjour des morts, sont une anti-vie; les démons sont des rebelles.' 'Le démoniaque de Gérasa', pp. 69-70.

there is alien. Just as the Gerasene demoniac narrative interrupts the Jesus narrative by taking Jesus outside his trodden paths, so is the creature Jesus meets living outside any normal time. His life, as the narrative informs us, is suspended, just as is the narrative in which his life comes to us. Mark describes the ferocity and hopelessness of the habitat and behavior of the Gerasene demoniac by accumulating details to accentuate the extremity of the case: he lives among the tombs (5.3); he could not be controlled (5.3-4); even chains were useless; he has often been fettered and chained up, but he had snapped his chains and broken his fetters. No one was strong enough to master him (5.4-5). Further, he bellowed in the place of death, cutting himself (5.5-6). Mark's version is much longer than Matthew's and Luke's, which is not typical of Markan parallels with the other Synoptics, and Mark gives us an exaggerated version of the extreme condition of the demoniac.[23] In this section Mark slides into allegory, without explaining the shift: Jesus crosses to an untamed territory, responding instantly to the extreme suffering of those abroad. Allegorically, Jesus' salvific mission takes him to the Gentiles, to those most disturbed, those marginal people who even the authorities in the alien land cannot tame. The story serves as commentary on the crisis narrative in two important ways. Jesus is experiencing rejection by family and civil and religious authorities. Even his disciples are not close to understanding the meaning of his mission or the reality of the impending final crisis. In the context of the crisis narrative, following as it does an example of the disciples' defects, and preceding two other miracles, the Gerasene demoniac narrative asks us to read prospectively and retrospectively and to contrast the alien madman's instant recognition and acceptance of Jesus with the failure of all those in his 'home' territory. Also the story is an allegory for the possible conversion of those outside Jesus' cultural experience in contrast to the failure of those within it.

While the disciples had been afraid, their faith still inadequate, and still confused about who Jesus is, the Gerasene demoniac, mind and soul obliterated by madness and spiritual deprivation, instantly recognizes Jesus:

Τί ἐμοὶ καὶ σοί, Ἰησοῦ υἱὲ τοῦ θεοῦ τοῦ ὑψίστου;

What do you want with me, Jesus, son of the Most High God? (5.7)

---

23. Starobinski, 'Struggle with Legion', pp. 35-61.

If the community the Gospel addresses has been doubtful about their ability to experience and understand Jesus' teachings because even those closest to him proved ironically obtuse, Mark alleviates those doubts through this suspended time narrative: even the most hopeless case, most distant from Jesus' indigenous social community, most spiritually unhealthy, most apparently incapable of understanding Jesus' mission and teachings, responds instantly to his curative powers. Also, the cured demoniac, while begging to join Jesus, rather, is admonished by Jesus to go to his own οἶκος, a metaphor for community, and there to proclaim (ἀπάγγειλον) and teach (κηρύσσειν) (5.19-20), the same activities he assigns to the disciples (6.7; 6.12).

Like the Gerasene demoniac story, in the Curing of the Hemorrhaging Woman intercalated with the Resurrection of Jairus's Daughter (5.21–5.43), the narrator provides specific details to emphasize the extremity of their conditions. The woman 'had suffered from hemorrhages for twelve years; and in spite of long treatment by many doctors, on which she had spent all she had, there had been no improvement; on the contrary, she had grown worse' (5.25-26). And Jairus's daughter is dead by the time Jesus gets to her (5.35). In all three extraordinary acts, Jesus cures the powerless, the unholy and the marginalized: a demoniac, an old, polluted woman, and an emerging woman, who is a corpse. Specifically tying the bleeding woman and Jairus's daughter together is the repetition of the words θυγάτηρ ('daughter', 5.23; 5.35; 5.34), δώδεκα ('twelve', 5.25; 5.42), and πίστις ('faith', 5.34; 5.36) in both stories. Both these women are daughters, though not biologically. They are daughters in a new definition of family emerging from Mark's understanding of Jesus' message (3.31-35). The emphasis on the role of faith[24] in the healings (5.34; 5.36), an unseen, unknown power which the disciples had lacked as they confronted the first real danger in crossing to the other side (4.40) likewise ties the whole section together.

Commentators on the story of the bleeding woman have primarily focused on what the story tells us about Jesus' or early Christianity's view of menstruation, and how these attitudes might have differed from the prevalent Jewish customs of the times. Attitudes towards menstruation are also connected to issues of women's liberation or enslavement

---

24. See James M. Robinson, *The Problem of History in Mark*, pp. 122-24 on the significance of the word 'faith' in these sequences; also Tolbert, *Sowing the Gospel*, pp. 164-72.

to their biology, and as a consequence, Christian commentaries, whether feminist or not, in particular, create sharp distinctions between Jesus' attitudes and those believed to have been the common Jewish practices of the period.[25]

The Bleeding Woman narrative interrupts the Jairus's Daughter narrative and arrests its progress as attention moves from Jairus's petition to Jesus to the woman's action. At this point, the bleeding woman occupies the central narrative role, the crowd seems to fade into the background, and Jesus becomes an object of her attention. As Mark assumes the role of omniscient narrator, he informs his audience about her condition with the most precise details; there is a remarkable shift here, as this anonymous woman in a huge, oppressive crowd takes over the story, and she becomes the focus of narrative attention. Mark recounts her previous twelve years' experience with her condition, detailing the excessive flow and the failure of all cures (twelve years of flow and long treatment by doctors, Mk 5.25-27), and her medical expenses, all to no avail (Mk 5.26). After this flashback, by which the extreme nature of her condition has been established, the narrator returns to the present to describe her recent decision to seek help from Jesus (5.27), as she literally comes out of the crowd to 'touch his cloak', a phrase that is repeated three times (5.27; 5.28; 5.30). This recapitulation functions to let us know how much of her life has been consumed by seeking cures. Her condition is chronic, she has boldly sought help, used up all her money, yet she has actually grown worse. But she has not given up. The narrator focuses attention on her story here, but actually, just as she has seized control of her own medical problem, despite her suffering (πολλὰ παθοῦσα) (5.26), she takes over the narrative, seizing control over an opportunity and aggressively seeking to eliminate the source of her pain. Moving from retrospection, the narrator shifts to the present, and in contrast to many of the women in the Gospel, as focal point, the bleeding woman also speaks, ἐὰν ἅψωμαι κἂν τῶν ἱματίων αὐτοῦ σωθήσομαι ('If I touch even his clothes, I shall be cured'; 5.28).

25. Examples of this kind of commentary include Marla J. Selvidge, 'Mark 5.25-34 and Leviticus 15: A Reaction to Restrictive Purity Regulations', *JBL* 103 (1984), pp. 619-23; Ben Witherington, *Women and the Ministry of Jesus* (Cambridge: Cambridge University Press, 1984); Ben Witherington, *Women and the Genesis of Christianity* (Cambridge: Cambridge University Press, 1990).

In contrast to all the doctors' failed healing, when she touches Jesus' clothes she is instantly cured (5.29), and in one moment the source of her suffering dries up, and even more importantly, she knows instantly in her body (τῷ σώματι) that the cause of her trouble has disappeared (5.29). The most remarkable aspect of this cure is that it is unintentional on the part of Jesus, and that the woman has orchestrated the whole episode on her own behalf. The narrative describes a woman afflicted with a horrendous medical problem, for which, as an independent person in search of a cure, she has sought help for many years. Disappointed with the failure of cures, though not willing to abandon herself to despair, she has boldly sought out a wonder-worker, whose reputation for curing the sick has spread throughout the countryside (5.27).

The narrative refocuses the action when Jesus realizes that 'power' has gone from him (ἐπιγνοὺς ἐν ἑαυτῷ τὴν ἐξ αὐτοῦ δύναμιν ἐξελθοῦσαν, 5.30), and he asks who has touched his clothes. Attention shifts from the woman to Jesus and his disciples, who seek to explain the obvious, that there are a lot of people around, and how could they control whether someone touched him. When the woman occupied the central action, the narrative was silent about Jesus' action. But, Jesus takes hold of the narrative when he senses he has been touched. In response to his irritated inquiry, the bold woman, who had for years endured her painful suffering, and who had fearlessly pushed herself forward through the crowds, was very afraid (5.33), but not so overwhelmed by her fear that she did not immediately fall at his feet and tell him the whole truth (5.33). Calling her θυγάτηρ ('daughter'), Jesus tells her that through her πίστις ('trust'), she has healed herself, ἡ πίστις σου σέσωκέν σε, (5.34) and she is forever rid of this affliction, ἴσθι ὑγιὴς ἀπὸ τῆς μάστιγός σου (5.34).

The intercalation of the Bleeding Woman story interrupts the crisis narrative to focus on the bleeding woman whose humanity has been suspended by her debilitating illness. As the narrator dwells on how the woman acts tenaciously and assertively on her own behalf to eliminate her affliction, the reader must see her condition from her point of view. Such 'focalization' forces attention on her as a dramatic figure, as a single-minded and forceful woman, and as a sufferer as she takes on the struggle against her own temporal suspension. On the one hand, she is a model of the self-motivated, autonomous person who has the capability to 'save' herself.[26] The woman wishes to escape her suffering, a source of enormous physical discomfort and obsessive focus on her health at the expense of all other interests. But the woman's persistent effort to overcome her affliction also shows that aggressive female action can eliminate isolation and marginalism caused by poor health or cultic traditions. Jesus' role in this story is passive, for he takes no action to heal the woman, for it is she who, unknowing to him, takes charge of her last desperate action to rid herself of this plague, which has made her an outcast.

Jesus ignores the purity issue altogether, attending rather to the woman's faithful and desperate action. As others have pointed out, the healing of the bleeding woman occurs solely at the woman's initiative (5.28-29), and Jesus' action is almost by default (5.30), as power goes from him and arrests her affliction. But Mark is not only presenting her story as a separate incident to build up Jesus' healing powers, for he also connects her story to the crisis storyline in two important ways. One, her suffering parallels Jesus', for he and the woman have something in common: they both endure 'suffering' ($\pi\alpha\theta o\hat{\upsilon}\sigma\alpha$, 5.26), a word only used about her and Jesus in the entire Gospel.[27] As with many of these intercalated narratives suspending time, the story points to the development of a new community of understanding in a time outside the narrated events. By ignoring the purity laws, the woman and Jesus take themselves outside the ethnic, gender and traditional boundaries the laws re-enforce. At the same time as these disintegrate, sufferers with faith form a new community. The woman's affiliation with Jesus as fellow-sufferer paves the way for the ultimate scapegoat sacrifice with the promise to eliminate all scapegoats for all time. Fellow sufferers, like Job, they share the accident of tragic, unaccountable events. Thus the woman has borne the suffering of the outsider, the impure and the exile, as determined by her physical condition, and as Jesus will be, has become a scapegoat for her people.

In this, she and Jesus are like the 'sufferer' of Psalm 21 (22), and there are important ways in which this parallel is drawn and contrasted through the woman's narrative, which like many of these

26. As Tolbert insists, 'faith is a prerequisite of healing for the Gospel of Mark, not its result' (*Sowing the Word*, p. 169).
27. Elizabeth Struthers Malbon, 'Fallible Followers: Women and Men in the Gospel of Mark', *Semeia* 28 (1983), pp. 29-48 (30); Marla J. Schierling, 'Women as Leaders in the Marcan Communities', *Listening* 15 (1980), pp. 250-56 (254).

suspended time narratives proves to be a synecdoche of, a commentary on, or an analogy to the crisis narrative. First, in the Psalm (21.18) and in the Passion narrative (15.24), reference is made to the humiliation of the sufferer as his clothes (ἱμάτια) are divided. These, of course, are the very same clothes (mentioned three times in the woman's narrative) that proved so powerful when the woman touched them (5.28). To be deprived of clothes is to be humiliated and to be made powerless, and Jesus, as such an object of humiliation, repeats the traditional suffering and humiliation of 'Israel', and its prophets, but the clothes, the source of humiliation, are the very source of salvation itself. As the woman says, ἐὰν ἅψωμαι κἂν τῶν ἱματίων αὐτοῦ σωθήσομαι ('If I touch even his clothes, I will be cured', 5.28). The New English Bible translates σωθήσομαι as 'cured', but its root is σῴζω, meaning 'save', used by Jesus as he tells her, ἡ πίστις σου σέσωκέν σε ('Your faith has saved you', 5.34). Later, when Jesus has been stripped of his clothes, like the sufferer of Psalm 21 who prays to be saved (21.21), he is taunted to save himself, σῶσον σεαυτὸν ('save yourself', 15.30), but instead he utters the first lines of Psalm 21 (22) first in Aramaic, ἐλωι ἐλωι λεμα σαβαχθανι, and then in Greek (15.34). The ultimate rejection, his death, is the complete humiliation of the self before the divinity in whom salvation resides. These locutions cannot be incidental, but they point to a careful parallelism between the accidental suffering of the woman, the sufferer of Psalm 21 (22), and the ultimate sacrifice of Jesus. All are scapegoats for their people, whether male or female, sharing a common trust and knowledge that the source of suffering and humiliation is likewise the source of salvation. Senseless suffering is the unfortunate lot of humankind, and only trust in the divinity's saving power can alleviate it. The story interrupts the crisis narrative, just as the woman arrests Jesus' action and directs attention to herself. As a suspended narrative, it parallels the woman's life which was suspended because of her illness. Her seizure of the narrative interrupts the main narrative and puts her story in the forefront, pointing outside the crisis narrative to another community that can exist beyond the actors and actions of the central narrative, though interacting with it.

Herod's court, the ostensible stronghold of insider political power, in contrast, is a parable of faithlessness, a site where moral insiders (John the Baptist) are political outsiders. The struggle between John the Baptist and Herod pits Israel's laws against those who possess the political power in Israel. Moving from the streets to the court, from outside to inside, from the politically and socially powerless to the powerful, in 6.14-29, through what Mieke Bal and Gérard Genette call an internal retroversion or analepsis,[28] Mark intercalates the novella of the final days of John the Baptist.[29] This anachrony grafts one story, whose connection may or may not be evident, onto the primary narrative. According to Bal such an internal retroversion may momentarily overtake the main narrative, which is precisely what happens with the John novella.[30] The retroversion functions first to fill in gaps in the audience's knowledge of important events or characters in the primary narrative. Almost parenthetically the reader was informed of John's arrest at the beginning of Jesus's public ministry: μετὰ δὲ τὸ παραδοθῆναι τὸν Ἰωάννην ('after John had been arrested', 1.14). But the narrator had withheld the circumstances of his arrest and his eventual fate. The 'flashback' to John's final days overtakes the Jesus narrative, causing a number of ironic contrasts and jostling the reader/listener into questions, the answers to which might remain inconclusive.

Interrupting the temporal sequence, the 'encasement' of the John story, directs the reader to contrast it with those it follows or precedes in the narrative and to construct its symbolic relationship to the sequence, thus creating a new meaning that is not apparent in the narrative fragment. As a 'part' encased in a larger narrative, its implications reach out to other events in the Gospel. The story exists in its own right as a historical interpolation, but its location in the Gospel contrasts with the central crisis story of Jesus as well as with other narratives which precede or follow it. Furthermore, through a flashback, its precise temporal relationship to the crisis narrative is made unimportant as it suddenly disrupts the series of events it follows and precedes. Although it prophecies the fate of Jesus and remembers the fates of other moral voices in the Hebraic tradition, it achieves this end by taking on an achronic relationship to the series of events recounted in the central Gospel narrative.

28. Bal, *Narratology*, p. 59; Genette, *Narrative Discourse*, pp. 48-67.
29. Some of this discussion of the John the Baptist novella appeared in Schildgen, 'A Blind Promise', pp. 115-31.
30. *Narratology*, p. 60.

The Herod story with its 'blind promise' echo from Esther and Judges, as discussed in the last chapter, functions as an ironic foreboding of Jesus' future. Jesus, like Esther and John, would find himself in conflict with the entrenched political authority of the foreign empire, with no reprieve possible for himself or his people. In the narrative, Herodias attempts to control the future, having plotted and waited for a propitious day, γενομένης ἡμέρας εὐκαίρου (Mk 6.21). The word εὐκαίρου is especially significant here because it, or a form of it, is used only three times in the Gospel. The second is at 6.31 (καὶ οὐδὲ φαγεῖν εὐκαίρουν), prior to the feeding of the five thousand, and refers to the 'appropriate' time to eat in the first food multiplication story. The third use at 14.11 parallels its appearance in the Herod story; when Judas seeks the right time to turn Jesus over to the authorities, εὔκαιρος works to show Judas and Herodias as comparable types whose momentary possession of time betrays the prophets. The word opposes καιρός, or the propitious moment, the right time, when Jesus begins his public ministry (1.15, ὅτι πεπλήρωται ὁ καιρὸς). εὔκαιρος, an adjective, characterizes the manipulation of time practiced by Judas and Herodias to satisfy their individual desires; καιρός, on the other hand, synthesizes a concept of time, intended to convey apocalyptic and salvific meanings. Herodias takes possession of time, because Herod abandons control over the future with his blind promise, making it possible for opportunists to seize the present and the future. Herodias captures the moment for her own nefarious designs. In Mark, in contrast to Esther, because the king values the folk tradition of the 'blind promise' over Israel's written laws, the 'blind promise' works against Israel as the future is abandoned to the miscreant plots of the enemies of its laws.

The man who fasted, lived abstemiously in the wilderness, eating locusts and honey, has his head served on a platter in a gross parodic foreshadowing of the last supper, to a degenerate king who lives in corrupt luxury with his venal wife. If the previous two stories about daughters, the Bleeding Woman and Jairus's Daughter, were examples of faithful women, the story of Herodias's daughter (6.22-28) is an example of perverted family loyalty. The three daughters connect the stories thematically, and Mark emphasizes their relationship by having Jesus address Jairus's daughter as κοράσιον, 'little girl', the same word he uses for Herodias's daughter.

Although this section is called the John the Baptist story, he never speaks in it, and actually never appears except as a severed head. In fact, beyond establishing John's motive for his indictment of Herod, the narrator makes John passive and silent once he is incarcerated and focuses instead on the internal motives of Herod, Herodias, and the daughter. Once again assuming an omniscient voice, the narrator tells us why Herod had John thrown in jail, which shows the action of this story was triggered by John's moral outrage. The story might better be called the Herod/Herodias incident since the narrator's omniscience directs the audience to recognize the corruption that has overtaken the political leadership in Israel. The Gospel narrator, without explicit moral judgment, discloses Herodias's manipulative plans and her role in killing John the Baptist. The narrator emphasizes Herodias's obsessive desire and her role in perverting both Herod's and her daughter's desires. In fact, the narrator tells us that Herod had incarcerated John precisely because of his brother Philip's wife (6.17); he tells us, again as omniscient narrator, that she held a grudge against John and that she took the initiative to kill him (6.19).

Herodias differs radically from the bleeding woman, for although they do share many features, as, for example, ostensible violation of Levitical laws, aggressive action, and desire to control their own lives, in the case of Herodias, the desires are corrupt and self-seeking at the expense of others, and more particularly, at the expense of Israel's laws and moral status. In the one case, assertive female action leads to a kind of salvation, whereas in the other, self-immersed depravity violates Israel's sacred laws. In one case, the woman seeks to overcome her scapegoat status, and in the latter, Herodias makes John a scapegoat. The 'bleeding woman' wants to bring her suspension to an end. Likewise, Herodias wants to conclude her own vulnerable situation but to do so, she must suspend Israel's laws and murder the prophet who remembers them.

The narrator, like the narrator of the Bleeding Woman story, conveys his omniscience as he tells us that John the Baptist indicted Herod for ignoring Levitical prohibitions against incest (6.18). The violation is emblematic, setting the heinous murder plot in motion, and revealing the desires for power and gratuitous self-satisfaction of both the queen and her daughter, while also showing that 'Israel' and all its divinely awarded traditions are under siege.

It is Herodias and not Herod who takes severe action against John for his rebuke, although Herod, like Samson, seems to cooperate willingly in his own manipulation. Herodias plans to commit murder when she fears what consequences might follow from John's public criticism. Her actions redraw boundaries, in which the Roman territorial borders and political machinations replace ethnic and cultural lines of division and absolute moral laws. In addition, Herodias goes further than abolishing the Levitical laws against incest, for she also violates a number of the ten commandments (first, fifth, and sixth), replacing Israel's laws with her own selfish interests.

Like the bleeding woman, Herodias is suffering. She has been assaulted and her security is in jeopardy, and she also decides to take action on her own behalf. In fact, though the action to arrest John is taken by Herod, the narrator specifically lets us know that Herod was afraid of John. The narrator informs us that Herod knew John was a holy man, although he lacked the capacity to understand what he had to say (6.20).

Fearlessly plotting to secure her status and arrogantly attempting to control the future, Herodias plans John the Baptist's demise. Waiting for a propitious day (6.21), she finds her opportunity at a banquet for her husband's birthday when she uses food and her daughter's sexuality to lure her husband into a foolish promise that he will be obliged to honor (6.21-23). Herodias appears to have been watching while her daughter seduced the king with her dancing, for after the promise, the girl goes out to her mother to ask what she should ask for (6.24). The daughter is too young to realize her own sexual power, yet mature enough to mesmerize the king with it. She turns to her self-seeking mother for a response to the king's generous but foolish offer (6.22-25). Although she sponsored the entire action, the only time Herodias actually speaks is after the king's blind promise when she answers her daughter's desperate question, 'What shall I ask for?' Revealing her single obsession, Herodias demands, τὴν κεφαλὴν Ἰωάννου τοῦ βαπτίζοντος ('The head of John the Baptist', 6.24). In addition to the cruelty and obduracy of the mother's request, however, the girl quickly learns how to express depraved yearnings, and repeating her mother's request, she asks εὐθὺς ('immediately') (6.25) in addition that the head be served ἐπὶ πίνακι ('on a platter')·

The young girl in the Herod story learns that female sexuality possesses power that can reap personal advantage. Such a manipulation of gender power contradicts the Gospel's revelation of the power of suffering and of powerlessness, found in the utopian family household of mutual cooperation, service and respect unfolded by the Markan narrative.[31] Herodias's ungracious request abruptly concludes the banquet, as the platter serves John the Baptist's head (Mk 6.28) and with it the hopes of victims and underdogs and those with moral courage, for 'Israel' has fallen to self-seeking manipulators. Symbolically rendering the limited power of charismatic leaders, the scene evokes images of a decapitated head served on a silver platter, as the *pièce de résistance* at a banquet that perverts table fellowship. The brief speaking engagements of these women reveal that premeditated malicious action, not their gender, ethnicity, or status is the source of their pollution and the reason for their specific moral status.

The John the Baptist intercalation raises serious questions about women's status. As an aggressive manipulator of men for her own benefit, Herodias practices a kind of inverse servility, in which her vulnerable status, anxiety about her insecure position and lack of power become the underlying motives for her 'gendered' choice of action as she seeks to undermine social, religious and political powers. The king, like Samson, seduced by women's sexual power, willingly conspires in his own manipulation. In the story, women's sexuality is perverted, prurient and murderous. The daughter's dancing is a foil for duplicity and cunning as she learns to deploy her emerging womanhood and sexual gifts for nefarious purposes. Juxtaposed against the paired stories of two faithful daughters, Jairus's and the Syrophoenician woman's (5.22-23; 7.24-30), the story of Herodias's daughter's seduction of Herod is an example of perverted family loyalty in which selfish, frightened women allow their personal desires[32] to take priority over all other claims, whether of the law or the rightful fear of the consequences of thwarting the power and prerogative of prophets. Herodias, in contrast to the two loving parents (one a Jewish father and the other a Gentile mother), who petition Jesus on behalf of their daughters, uses her daughter in her plot to kill John. The intercalation and juxtaposition

31. John R. Donahue, *The Theology and Setting of Discipleship in the Gospel of Mark* (Milwaukee, WI: Marquette University Press, 1983); Best, *Following Jesus*; Stephen C. Barton, *Discipleship and Family Ties in Mark and Matthew* (Cambridge: Cambridge University Press, 1994).

32. René Girard, 'Scandal and the Dance: Salome in the Gospel of Mark', *New Literary History* 15 (Winter, 1984), pp. 311-24.

of these stories draws out the ironic contrasts between loving parents, whether male or female, Jew or Gentile, and Herodias's corrupt manipulation of her daughter for her own selfish ends.

Herodias's choices, like Judith's, Esther's, or even Delilah's, are premeditated and violent. Like Delilah,[33] Herodias and her daughter have used their sexual powers not merely for their own benefit and to subvert the patriarchal prerogatives, but also to weaken or destroy Israel. Because ultimately it is not kings who rule 'Israel' but Israel's divinely originated laws, the destruction of kings or leaders is only important if 'Israel's' moral safety is endangered. Herod, while arranging Israel's political survival, has endangered 'Israel's' true identity by violating its laws.

The John the Baptist intercalation interrupts the crisis time narrative primarily to provide information about what had happened to John because Herod had heard of Jesus' fame and that people were saying Jesus was John raised from the dead (6.14-16). It is the narrator's opportunity to situate the Jesus story politically. The narrative disrupts linear time because it is a flashback to an earlier time. We really do not know how much earlier it happened, however, because the narrator doesn't provide such time clues in this story. Like other suspended time narratives, because of the contrasts it suggests, the John the Baptist novella is a commentary on the crisis narrative, an interpretation of contiguous stories (Jairus's Daughter and the Bleeding Woman), and a commentary on Hebrew salvation history. It is also a symbolic flashforward to the occasion when Jesus will fall into the hands of rapacious political and religious authorities who will allow their own vicious desires to dictate their actions. Although the narrative interrupts the crisis narrative, in fact, it works to tie its events together typologically and temporally. First, it explains what had happened to John earlier, but in addition, like the Parable of the Vineyard, it points to what will happen to the central character in the crisis narrative later and to how this future sacrifice belongs to an established pattern that even predates John.

In the intercalated story of 'Peter's denial', the loyalty of Jesus' closest disciple is pitted against the tenaciousness of an anonymous servant girl whose insistent allegations forced her entrance into historical time. She challenges and exposes Peter both as a member of Jesus'

33. Mieke Bal, *Lethal Love: Feminist Literary Readings of the Biblical Love Stories* (Bloomington, IN: Indiana University Press, 1987).

inner group and as a coward; the suspended narrative allows this persistent but humble appendage of the high priest's household to take center stage in a major drama in the crisis narrative.[34] She appears to act on her own initiative as she pursues and unveils Peter because her 'service' is not to her master, nor for herself, since we do not see that she gains anything from harassing Peter. Her challenge to Peter is particularly ironic since she is the high-priest's servant, that is, an insignificant member of society, though she is affiliated with one of the most powerful households represented in the Gospel, the owner of which has orchestrated Jesus' arrest. Her anonymity is poised against the designated leader of Jesus' fledgling discipleship in a critical struggle that will determine Peter's loyalty and commitment. While her persistent action forces Peter to confront himself, she performs an unplanned and incidental service, for her action compels Peter to realize his own cowardice, which results in his self-recognition:

καὶ εὐθὺς ἐκ δευτέρου ἀλέκτωρ ἐφώνησεν. καὶ ἀνεμνήσθη ὁ Πέτρος τὸ ῥῆμα ὡς εἶπεν αὐτῷ ὁ Ἰησοῦς ὅτι πρὶν ἀλέκτορα φωνῆσαι δὶς τρίς με ἀπαρνήσῃ· καὶ ἐπιβαλὼν ἔκλαιεν

Then the cock crowed a second time; and Peter remembered how Jesus said to him, 'Before the cock crows twice you will disown me three times.' And he burst into tears (Mk 14.72).

Though the servant girl's role is marginal, she functions mythologically like the guardian of the gate (or waterway), as the one who warns the main characters that there are sides, and a choice must be made. She makes Peter realize that he cannot choose to remain separated or suspended from the historical process underway, that situations beyond his control force him to accept the responsibility that friendship with Jesus has opened to him, and that he must either abandon himself to fear and ignominy or accept the challenge that Jesus' arrest offers him. It is this marginal character, essentially outside the crisis herself, who confronts Peter with this choice. Like the intercalation, which is not essential to the central narrative, the servant girl interrupts the scene of Jesus before the Sanhedrin that the reader imagines taking place, to

---

34. Erich Auerbach, one of the first to consider the literary features of the Bible used the scene as the basis for his discussion of the literary style of the New Testament; see *Mimesis*, pp. 35-43. René Girard, writes of Mark's servant girl, 'She shows initiative and stirs up the group' ('Peter's Denial', in Bloom [ed.], *Modern Critical Interpretation: The Gospels*, pp. 149-64 [153]).

face Peter and all other onlookers with the choice—to remain marginal or to accept the possible consequences of affiliation with Jesus. To remain marginal is to be suspended in time and to remain peripheral to the central action, as the narrative of his denial shows, but to take forceful action is to accept the historic mission Jesus has provided him, no matter what the consequences. This is not a comforting possibility, for it is personally endangering and therefore frightening, but this choice is thrust before Peter and before the audience by this unpretentious but persistent young woman in the intercalated story. Because of the known later history that followed the Gospel version of these events, we know that the event narrated turned out to be peripheral and a critical turning point in Peter's life.

By contrast, the John the Baptist novella, ostensibly a flashback to explain what happened to John, as a suspended time narrative intercalated with its adjacent stories, is about scapegoats, ancient laws and moral and political corruption. Herod, as the surrogate of a ravenous and venal empire is impotent against his own lusts, and Herodias as the heinous plotter of murder, are the main actors in a parable that typologically parallels the eventual death of Jesus at the hands of jealous and fearful powers. The parables also interrupt the main narrative time to synthesize the central themes and allegorically convey the Gospel's meaning. They are synecdoches of the crisis narrative, which briefly convey in their own cryptic style what the crisis narrative means and how the community of listeners to these stories can choose to respond. While they halt the main story line they simultaneously develop many of the main themes of the Gospel. Narrative outsiders themselves, they show how the Gospel brings its message to the vulnerable and the exiled, whether madmen, the sick, or the polluted (and this includes female Jew and Gentile children, a Gentile madman, and a woman whose condition makes her polluted). The narratives show how this exiled status can be overcome and point to the role of the exiled in their own salvation. In their appeal to those suspended in time and their deliberate drawing up of opposing sides, these narrative interruptions redefine insiders and outsiders, showing that insiders are not the powerful and privileged but the vulnerable and weak. They point to how a community of these exiles can develop beyond and outside the time and experience of the crisis narrative.

Chapter 4

THE END OF FEAR:
MYTHIC TIME IN THE GOSPEL OF MARK[*]

Myth

Myth deals in 'wonders', but not to avoid reality. On the contrary, the 'wondrous' hints at the possible. Myth describes a temporary environment where the conditions of biological and existential living outside of ordinary time and outside of conventional spaces can be fully explored. Yet, it is the fundamental condition of living in conventional space and ordinary time that forms the central concern of myth. As such, myth is a literary environment, the world of the imagination, whether bound by conventions or consciously transgressing the conventions (social, political, religious, or cultural) that regulate and rule human behavior. Myth is the extraordinary space-time where the extraordinary human possibility can be worked out. The conventions of ordinary space-time and ordinary life are abrogated during the extraordinary circumstances.

My working definition of myth is that it is an uncontingent announcement of a truth or truths, confronting humans with the 'absolutism of reality'.[1] Proclaimed as narrative, its primary vehicles being metaphor and symbol, this absolute reality presents itself as humans' innermost fears, whether fear of cosmic disorder, public, personal or moral chaos; personal, familial, 'tribal', or environmental annihilation; or fear of political, social and familial disjunctions; as a consequence of the intensity of these anxieties, humankind is led to doubt its own place in a predictable, knowable universe. This fear of potential chaos threatens

* A version of this chapter was published as 'The Gospel of Mark as Myth', in John C. Hawley, S.J. (ed.), *Through a Glass Darkly: Essays in the Religious Imagination* (New York: Fordham University Press, 1996).
   1. Blumenberg, *Work on Myth*, pp. 3-33.

to disrupt an individual's hope for tranquility at any point, whether, as
Clifford Geertz has written, at the boundary of his 'analytic capacities',
at the boundary of his 'powers of endurance', or at the 'limits of his
moral insight'.[2] As such, myths are maps of human consciousness, a
means for grasping the human condition, a timeless, though time-orig-
inated metaphoric vehicle to expose reality and a taxonomy of human
psychology as preserved in our most fundamental symbolic traditions.[3]

This symbolism adheres, as Paul Ricoeur has suggested, 'to the most
immutable human manner of being in the world, whether it be a
question of above and below, the cardinal directions, the spectacle of
the heavens, terrestrial localization, houses, paths, fire, wind, stones,
or water'.[4] Through looking at the Gospel outside of ordinary time
and history, and examining how it employs mythic themes and symbols,
we can approach some understanding of how the Gospel attempts to
say something about how to live in the world *sub specie eternitatis*.
However, conventionally myths are projected back into a time before
time, (Ramayana, Mahabharata, Oedipus, Odyssey, Gilgamesh, or
Genesis, for example), what Paul Ricoeur calls 'mythic time', but in
the case of Mark the narrative is set in the present time. Creation
narratives, in particular, set in this 'mythic time' represent an imagined period before 'fragmentation' overtook the human condition,
when all the differences, whether between the sky and the earth, male
and female, God and humankind, and so on were in harmony. Consciousness of differences did not exist, because human transgression
had not created them. Heroic myths often describe a critical time of
awareness of such fragmentation, when the forces of good must battle
the dangers of evil; or myths may also unfold the quest of the exemplary hero for a transcendence that is culturally defined. Obviously
the Gospel of Mark does not describe the loss of a golden age, or the
quest of the hero for personal triumph, but it does present a critical

2. I am applying Clifford Geertz's idea that religion is 'a system of symbols
which acts to establish powerful, pervasive, and long-lasting moods and motivations
in humans by formulating conceptions of a general order of existence and clothing
these conceptions with such an aura of factuality that the moods and motivations seem
uniquely realistic' ('Religion as a Cultural System', in *idem, The Interpretation of
Cultures* [New York: Basic Books, 1973], p. 90).

3. Mircea Eliade, *Myth and Reality* (trans. Willard R. Trask; New York: Harper
& Row, 1963).

4. *Interpretation Theory: Discourse and the Surplus of Meaning* (Fort Worth,
TX: Texas Christian University Press, 1976), p. 65.

moment in time when overcoming the fragmented human condition is presented as a possibility. By modeling a 'way of being in the world', Jesus lives out how this fragmentation can be harmonized. Thus 'mythic time' in the Gospel of Mark is an 'allegory of possible time' when human *communitas* can be restored.[5] The mythological dimensions of the Gospel show a way and point to a future opportunity to overcome the human alienated condition, thus bringing the imagined tranquility and loss of the mythic past into play as a dynamic utopian future.

We have generally slighted the mythological dimension of the Gospels whether by allegorizing as during the Patristic era, rationalizing as in the Enlightenment, historicizing in the nineteenth century, sociologizing and politicizing in the twentieth, spiritualizing, as in the mystical traditions of Christianity, moralizing and dogmatizing throughout the history of dogmatic and moral theology, or dismissing whatever failed to meet current religio-cultural-doctrinal-ideological standards and interests. Although the Enlightenment's rejection of this symbolic world as 'superstition' was reversed in the Romantic Period, when the continued opposition between myth and reason raised the 'mythical consciousness' as an ideal, nevertheless it merely replaced one absolute for human consciousness with another. Hans-Georg Gadamer has correctly argued, I believe, that Romanticism's 'presupposition of a mysterious darkness in which there was a mythical collective consciousness that preceded all thought is just as dogmatic and abstract as the Enlightenment's ideal of absolute knowledge'.[6] Because the Western intellectual traditions combine the Judeo-Christian tendency to historicize myth with the Greek tendency to philosophize and rationalize it and the Roman tendency to politicize it, we have overlooked how the central Christian myth or sacred story makes use of synchronic mythic patterns. These often symbolic narrative patterns may involve foundational subject matters critical to a particular culture, such as the human quest for knowledge, understanding, adventure, or personal transformation, the relationships between the sexes, family organization and related issues, the role of kings and priests, as well as narrative patterns using devices such as trebling, the journey, descents, ascents and crossings over.[7]

5. As described by Victor Turner in *The Ritual Process* (Chicago: Aldine, 1969), pp. 96-97.

6. *Truth and Method* (New York: Crossroad, 1986).

7. Ricoeur, *Time and Narrative*, I, p. 57. What I mean by culture here are those

Introduction: Myth in Mark

In the Gospel of Mark, the extraordinary events, their prime actor, and the 'way of being' he adopts, create a new community that temporarily replaces conventional structures and expectations. These changes direct the Gospel's readers or listeners to the possibility of a new community formed out of this utopian human opportunity. When spotlighted against 'mythic' or 'cosmic time', the powers ruling 'ordinary time' are exposed for their limitations. The mythological hero operates in ordinary or historical time but his activities and attitudes oppose the limitations and obsessions of ordinary time. However, he is not world-denying, for he focuses on world reforming, but he must bring the eternal horizon to the contemporary world in order to highlight the betrayals and corruptions of the present.[8] As a consequence, during his career, normal expectations, structures and understanding are momentarily overturned, questioned or brought into the foreground. Though his reforming activities turn out to be marginal as also the time when the activities take place, they simultaneously put this historical time action in a hierarchical and confrontational relationship with 'cosmic' or mythic time. Because of the mythic nature of his historical career, the time of its actions become a momentary interruption of ordinary time that shows how 'ordinary time' can be transformed into 'cosmic' or eternal time or at the very least, seen from the perspective of 'cosmic' time. Viewing the Gospel in this way opens us to psychological and ontological dimensions that may be less apparent in time-specific historical or sociological studies. An exploration of the mythic characteristics of the Gospel of Mark will suggest how Mark's Jesus is a mythological figure and conversely how Mark's Gospel redefines mythology.[9] I will be discussing some mythic themes

aspects of communal living enforced tacitly and preserved by narratives, beliefs, taboos and customs.

    8.   Though I do not agree with Cullman's radical division between Hellenic and Hebraic concepts of time, I believe he argues correctly that 'Primitive Christianity' never dissolves into metaphysics because it links redemptive history to a progressing time line (*Christ and Time*, p. 54).

    9.   For studies of myth, see Blumenberg, *Work on Myth*; Ernst Cassirer, *The Philosophy of Symbolic Forms* (trans. Ralph Manheim; New Haven: Yale University Press, 1957); Eliade, *Myth and Reality*. The first modern scholar to identify the New Testament specifically with mythology was David Friedrich Strauss. By the third

in the Gospel, and how the Gospel is both mythic and non-mythic.

Rudolf Bultmann's demythologization program proposed interpreting myth rather than dismissing it. However, his emphasis on finding a single meaning or 'kerygma' underlying the myth automatically denied the many symbolic layers in the mythic communication. Because of myth's parsimony of dialectic and plethora of symbol, it forbids a single meaning and continually re-opens itself to both new and potential meanings. This capacity for endless interpretation generally characterizes myths, whether of the ancient worlds, the major religions, or of traditional peoples, and also helps us to understand why these stories are so persistent. Despite an age of science that denigrated their importance, or an age of romanticism that sentimentalized them, many of them have the power to relocate themselves in different historical, social, cultural and intellectual climates. In fact, as Gadamer, among others, has reflected,

> To leave an enormous amount open seems to belong to the essence of a fruitful fable and to myth. Precisely thanks to its open indeterminacy, myth is able to produce constant new invention from within itself, with the thematic horizon continuously shifting in different directions.[10]

In his chapter 'The Exorcism Narratives' in *The Problem of History in Mark and Other Marcan Studies*, James Robinson writes, 'Jesus'

---

edition of his *The Life of Jesus Critically Examined*, which appeared in four editions between 1835 and 1840, he had developed a New Testament theology that showed the Jesus narrative with its mythic 'futuristic eschatology, apocalyptic fanaticism, and messianic delusions' as incompatible with the 'modern' sensibility (David Friedrich Strauss, *The Life of Jesus Critically Examined* [ed. with intro. Peter C. Hodgson and trans. George Eliot; Philadelphia: Fortress Press, 1972],), p. xl. Strauss's efforts were taken up again by Rudolf Bultmann in 'New Testament and Mythology', in Hans Werner Busch (ed.), *Kerygma and Myth: A Theological Debate* (trans. Reginald H. Fuller; London: SPCK, 1957), pp. 1-44, and in the later *Jesus Christ and Mythology* (New York: Charles Scribner's Sons, 1958). Adapted to the existential German philosophy of the twentieth century, Bultmann's essay, 'The New Testament and Mythology' defines myth as 'an expression of man's conviction that the origin and purpose of the world in which he lives are to be sought not within it but beyond it' (pp. 10-11). The essay was first published in 1941. Bultmann's collected commentaries on the New Testament and myth have been recently reprinted as *The New Testament and Mythology and Other Basic Writings* (trans. Schubert M. Ogden; Philadelphia: Fortress Press, 1984). The range of reactions in support and in conflict with Bultmann are reflected in both volumes of *Kerygma and Myth*.

10. *Truth and Method*, p. 454; Blumenberg, *Work on Myth*.

context is the cosmic language of the opened heavens, the voice of God, the Son of God, the Spirit, Satan, angels, and beasts', but he argues that 'cosmic language is rare in Mark' and the exorcisms are the points in the historical narrative where 'the transcendent meaning of that history is most clearly evident'.[11] I would add that Mark's attention to the miraculous and the extraordinary in which demonic powers oppose salvific ones specifically locates his historical narrative against the backdrop of cosmic time, thus emphasizing the eternal significance of the activities[12] and the human potential for reconciliation and conquest of the demonic, whether spiritual or physical, or in the form of devils, disease, physical handicap, hunger, moral depravity or death. Bultmann, also, despite the weaknesses in his 'demythologization' agenda, identifies the mythical characteristic of the *New Testament*:

> The world is viewed as a three-storied structure, with the earth in the centre, the heaven above, and the underworld beneath. Heaven is the abode of God and of celestial beings—the angels. The underworld is hell, the place of torment. Even the earth is more than the scene of natural, everyday events, of the trivial round and the common task. It is the scene of the supernatural activity of God and his angels on the one hand, and of Satan and his daemons on the other. These supernatural forces intervene in the course of nature and in all that men think and will do. Miracles are by no means rare. Man is not in control of his own life. Evil spirits may take possession of him. Satan may inspire him with evil thoughts. Alternatively, God may inspire his thought and guide his purposes. He may grant him heavenly visions. He may allow him to hear his word of succour or demand. He may give him the supernatural power of his Spirit. History does not follow a smooth unbroken course; it is set in motion and controlled by these supernatural powers. This aeon is held in bondage by Satan, sin, and death (for 'powers' is precisely what they are), and hastens towards its end. That end will come very soon, and will take the form of a cosmic catastrophe.[13]

This is all implied or stated in the Gospel of Mark. The mythic themes include among others, the journey on a road (1.3) which takes Jesus to the wilderness to confront Satan (1.12-13), and in which he travels from

---

11. P. 81.

12. Paul Ricoeur argues in discussing historical intentionality, I believe correctly, that the historian's long time-span is one of 'the paths by which historical time is led back to cosmic time', historical time building its 'constructions against the background of cosmic time' (*Time and Narrative*, I, p. 266 n. 51).

13. 'New Testament and Mythology', pp. 1-2.

one side to the other side, and across water, which he subdues to his own will (4.35-41; 6.48).[14] There is a God up above, a devil, and humans between these two opposites. Other themes are the wilderness-city contrast (1.6-8, 1.35-39), the threshold he crosses over when he begins his public ministry (2.2), and that is also the 'boundary' condition with which Jesus identifies the present time: 'the end is near, at the very door' (ὅταν ἴδητε ταῦτα γινόμενα, γινώσκετε ὅτι ἐγγύς ἐστιν ἐπὶ θύραις, 13.29). There is a promise of the eternal return (8.31; 9.9; 9.31; 10.33-34) and there will be a fiery end of time (13).

Mark, of all the Gospels, has an extraordinarily 'magical' setting: the large number of curing wonders (1.23-27, 1.29-33, 1.40-44; 2.3-5; 3.10-12; 5.21-43, passim); the commissioning of the disciples as 'proclaimers of the gospel' and 'drivers out of devils' (3.13-16); the identification of perverse human behavior with the devil and diabolic spirits (5.1-17; 8.33; 9.14-27, 9.38-40); the two multiplication of food stories (6.30-44; 8.1-13); the transfiguration (9.2-13); the taming of the sea (4.35-41; 6.45-52);[15] the three predictions of forthcoming suffering, death and resurrection; and the empty tomb and announcement that he had risen just as predicted (16.1-8). Many of these are standard folk-lore motifs as 'culture hero banishes demon',[16] 'dying culture hero teaches people how to die',[17] 'culture hero establishes customs',[18] and 'culture hero tames winds and regulates rivers'.[19]

Mark's exaggeration of perverted, disordered, dangerous, or suffering physical and mental conditions, whether hundreds of devils in a single person, excessive femaleness in a twelve-year menstrual flow, or the double provision of 'bread' to the starving thousands or death itself, serve to emphasize the power of Jesus' 'way of being' to transform the human experience of the natural world. In Mark, Jesus, as a mythic presence, a way of 'being in the world', shows how all the biological, environmental and existential dangers that oppress humans, even death

---

14. Malbon, *Narrative Space and Mythic Meaning* is an elaborate structural analysis of the topographical, architectural, and geopolitical spaces in the gospel.

15. Motif #D 2151.1, 'Magic Control of the Seas', in Stith Thompson (ed.), *Motif-Index of Folk Literature* 2 (Bloomington, IN: Indiana University Press, 1966), p. 386.

16. A531.1.1, *Motif-Index*, I, p. 122.

17. A565, *Motif-Index*, I, p. 124.

18. A545, *Motif-Index*, I, p. 124.

19. A532, A531 and A533.1, *Motif-Index*, I, p. 123.

itself, can be overcome. As he confronts the distress of 'living as humans' with all the fears, anxieties and dangers, Jesus consistently identifies fear (φόβος) as the source of the human environmental, biological or ontological crisis. He challenges the boundaries created and preserved by fear. If myth promotes a fearful view of the universe and re-enforces terror by showing what happens to transgressive humans who step outside the boundaries of human place in the cosmos and society, the Gospel of Mark's myth works against this hereditary fear. Just the contrary, it shows fear as perverse and destructive, and identifies the conquest of fear with the erasure of the 'different' or 'other' status of humans. Such fearful structures and taboos enforce the desires and taboos of the entrenched powers of the historical moment, but confronting or overcoming them shows their insignificance in cosmic time. I am using the term 'otherness' following Jacques Lacan's definition, which seems appropriate to this discussion. For Lacan, 'the Other' is the location of meaning that may be 'made present of the subject—it is the field of that living being in which the subject has to appear'. Working from Freudian pre-suppositions, he argues that the ways of being of male or female are abandoned to the 'field of the Other'. Language, parents, the unconscious and symbols, for Lacan, all constitute 'the Other', and they are the locus of individual and unconscious desire. Human alienation, the separation of the self from the Other, is located in the lack that occurs when the child separates from the mother at the same time that the father appears.[20] The application of this idea to a discussion of myth is not far-fetched, since the child's loss of the mother's company physically parallels the mythological human loss of the edenic status, when alienation between humans and God enters the human drama. Alienation is the human condition, and desire to retrieve a time before this differentiation overtook the human status inspires human activity, however elusive both the goal and the possibility of achieving it are. In the Gospel of Mark, Jesus' activities direct themselves towards dispelling fear and its sources in human institutions, taboos and conventions, pointing to the possibility, through his own experience, for humans to overcome estrangement and the 'ego-bound' status as they are recreated according to a divine cosmic order. Jesus' mission is a brief interlude in human historical time when this potential

20. *The Four Fundamental Concepts of Psycho-Analysis* (ed. Jacques-Alain Miller and trans. Alan Sheridan; New York: Norton, 1978), p. 203. The chapter, 'The Subject and the Other: Alienation', pp. 203-15, explores this concept.

is made present. Jesus' interruption of history is a confrontation between 'mythic time' and 'ordinary time'.

Fear

Although confusion over meaning, suffering and ethical paradox remain unresolved at the end of the narrative, the Gospel points to fear as one source of these human dilemmas, and as the cause of mankind's anxieties and desire to appropriate and own the world. As the emotion that seems to characterize the motives behind every major event in the Gospel, fear drives the actions in the Gospel.[21] This 'fear', as φόβος or a form of φοβέομαι, has been variously interpreted as both awe and cowardice, depending on who in the Gospel experiences it. Jesus, however, enjoins his closest associates not to fear, but to trust. Instead of explaining away fear, or providing a palliative or catharsis for it, as is more common in myth, the Gospel identifies fear as the emotion that threatens to return chaos, and therefore prompts humans to seize control of the world. Fear-laden taboos rule human relationships, whether between social and ethnic groups, families, political power structures, or ritual practices. Fear creates and controls the distance between human and human and human and the divinity; under such circumstances, mankind is disoriented and isolated. As a projection of mankind's deepest anxieties, 'fear' reminds humans of their fugitive status and makes them conscious of their own 'otherness' in relationship to the cosmos, to the society in which they sojourn, to their family, and most of all to their own consciousness. However, in revealing and preserving the human alienated status, 'fear' also makes possible the potential for reconciliation. If humans create and preserve their own alienation, they must also have the potential for reconciliation. Jesus' mission is a brief interlude in human affairs when this potential becomes present.

Fear undergirds taboos, and taboos control the world Jesus enters as heroic cult leader. He presents the antidote for these fears and their attendant desires, which is simply not to yield to fear, but to trust. Such

21. Robinson discusses 'fear' in the Gospel, identifying it with the presence of the numinous (4.40-41; 6.49-52; 5.15; 16.8), but also as cowardice (5.33, 36; 11.18, 32; 12.12). In both cases, however, 'fear' is due to lack of faith, suggesting their intimate association, whether experienced by perverse people or Jesus' intimates (*The Problem of History in Mark*, pp. 117-21).

an act of trust makes the numinous[22] present in human experience and closes the gap between the 'self' and the 'other'. When Jesus crosses over from the ontological territory of the habitual 'self', structured by rigid custom and taboo, and sustained by fear of the natural world or fear of social, political, biological, religious or other personal differences to the utopian world where such rigid structures collapse, his act restores the divine to the human experience. Jesus' radical actions subvert fear and the taboos enforcing it as he accepts the human's powerless and fragile place in the world. This vulnerability unsettles the boundary between the divine and humans, making possible the return of the divine to the human experience. The exposure of human weakness and fragility hints that to abandon the ego, with all its desires and fears, is simultaneously to abandon all the social and human structures that support it. It is, as it were, to retrieve the prelapsarian state before fallen mankind realized its own separation from the divine and constructed social mores and familial alliances in an effort to control the world in which its vulnerable 'self' might subsist.

The Gospel, therefore, presents Jesus as a mythic figure confronting his own ontological crisis, his 'aloneness', 'otherness', and 'isolation', as cosmic powers, social and political structures, family alliances and friends all flee from him, persecute him or fail him. His mission and death show that fear drives people to delude themselves into thinking they can control the world. Jesus' experience proclaims that fear promotes the desire for power over other people, both politically and social-culturally (as in the case of the High Priests, Pontius Pilate, and Herod); over tradition (as with the Scribes and Pharisees); over life and death (as the disciples and Jairus); over God (as shown by all the miscreant acts in the Gospel); and even over one's own will (as with Judas, Peter, and the women at the tomb). Fearlessness, on the other hand, as a declaration of the human's powerless place on earth, shatters the boundaries between humans (whether social, ethnic, familial or individual), between society and nature, and between the divine and the

22. See Rudolf Otto, *The Idea of the Holy: An Inquiry into the Non-rational Factor in the Idea of the Divine and its Relation to the Rational* (trans. John W. Harvey; London: Oxford University Press, 1923) for an extended discussion of the nature of the 'numinous', a word he invented from Latin 'numen'. Generally, it means something akin to the awe in the face of the *mysterium tremendum* (pp. 5-30); see also Otto, 'The Numinous in the New Testament', in *The Idea of the Holy*, pp. 82-93.

human, and reconciles them. Finally, fear thrives in ordinary-histor-ical time, but fearlessness is restored in mythic time.

Fear characterizes the emotions and propels the actions of the un-knowing as well as the evil characters in the Gospel. Fear defines the insiders and outsiders, aligning followers with betrayers and opponents with intimates. Almost every major character and many minor ones express fear, whether it be Herod, the disciples, the woman bleeding for twelve years, the disciples, the chief priests, Pontius Pilate, the elders and scribes or the women who attend Jesus at the tomb.

Mark identifies the motive for some of the most perverse actions in the Gospel as fear. Fear prompts the murders of the two holy men, John the Baptist and Jesus. In the John the Baptist story, 'Herod feared John' (6.20), which actually kept him alive though incarcerated (6.20), but Herodias nursed a grudge against him (ἡ δὲ Ἡρῳδιὰς ἐνεῖχεν, 6.19), prompted by her fear for her place as rightful wife of Herod, despite John's reminder that according to custom, Herod could not marry his sister-in-law (6.17). The ultimate consequence of this fear was the death of John.

Fear inspires the political and religious powers to conspire against Jesus. When Jesus assaults the established cultic practice and its prac-titioners (11.17), the chief priests and the doctors of law respond with a plan to kill him because 'they were afraid of him' (11.18) (ἐφοβοῦντο γὰρ αὐτόν). In addition to fearing him, their cowardice has spread to their fear of his power over people, their own religious constituency (11.32; 12.12). Although Mark does not use the word fear to describe Pontius Pilate's mood as he decides to capitulate to the crowd's demand to 'crucify him', he does make clear that Pilate's action is motivated by a desire to βουλόμενος τῷ ὄχλῳ ('satisfy the crowd', 15.15), sug-gesting that Pilate feared the power this mob might wield if not satisfied.

The other group of fearful is the 'unknowing' and it includes Jesus' closest followers and those for whom he performs miracles, in other words, those in the closest of relationships to him and therefore in a position to have understood the new way of being he reveals to them. I call them 'unknowing' because they do not seem to understand the meaning of Jesus' activities. The fact that these intimates do not under-stand does not, however, undermine the uncontingent truths of this new life. But it does show that new certainties will not easily displace or erode the old. It emphasizes that this new life is contingent on human behavior; it is a struggle and a journey, a ὁδός to be trod rather than assumed.

'Trust' opposes fear as the ontological condition that can conquer the power of fear over human's lives, but this message seems to elude all the characters in the Gospel. The first occasion when the disciples express their fear, during the first crossing of the water (4.41) introduces this opposition. The unknowing, when observers cannot understand how the Gerasene demoniac could be freed from a legion of devils (5.16), also opposes trust to fear. The hemorrhaging woman is afraid when she realizes that Jesus' magic has cured her, as also is Jairus when he finds out his daughter is already dead (5.35-36). But in both these cases, Jesus informs these distressed people that 'trust' can overcome the most oppressive dangers if one only abandons fear, μὴ φοβοῦ, μόνον πίστευε (5.37).

Again when Jesus predicts his forthcoming suffering, death and resurrection, his disciples do not understand this riddle, and are afraid:

οἱ δὲ ἠγνόουν τὸ ῥῆμα, καὶ ἐφοβοῦντο αὐτὸν ἐπερωτῆσαι.

they did not understand what he said and were afraid to ask (9.32).

On the way to Jerusalem, his disciples are astounded, while those who follow are afraid (10.32). These are examples of a confounding fear prompted by intellectual bafflement and emotional distress about the predicted but unknown future. Peter's failure to admit that he knew Jesus when challenged by one of the High-Priest's serving maids (14.68; 70), even though his motive is not provided by Mark, is another case where cowardice overcomes trust. The Gospel also paradoxically concludes with the word 'fear': καὶ οὐδενὶ οὐδὲν εἶπαν, ἐφοβοῦντο γάρ ('They said nothing to anybody, for they were afraid', 16.8). Even the women, who did not flee the crucifixion but watched from a distance (15.40), capitulate to fear when the empty tomb disrupts their normal human expectations.

'Limen' *and* 'Communitas'

This highlighting of fear points to the normal condition of humans, and at the same time shows Jesus opposing its power. However, his action is presented as a liminal experience. This 'limen', or margin is a brief interval or interruption of the normal, a boundary experience when the past is momentarily negated, suspended or abrogated, and the future has not yet begun; it is a time of possibility when every-thing known and assumed is suddenly tentative and contingent.[23] The 'limen' is the space between oppositions, the threshold where a new community unfolds. Victor Turner called this *communitas*, that is, liberation

> of human capacities of cognition, affect, volition, creativity, etc. from the normative constraints incumbent upon occupying a sequence of social statuses, enacting a multiplicity of social roles, and being acutely con-scious of membership in some corporate group such as a family, lineage, clan, tribe, nation, etc. or of affiliation with some pervasive social cate-gory such as class, caste, sex, or age-division.[24]

In this liminal space-time, the history of the final time of Jesus' life, his public ministry dominates. In contrast to most myths where the hero crosses the boundary into exile whether the forest, desert, or jungle, Jesus' crossing is into the public arena, the streets of local and distant villages and eventually Jerusalem itself. Rather than a with-drawal from the security of home into the unknown natural terrain, Jesus' exile from the security of home takes him into the hostile and unknown territory of contemporary Palestine and environs, that is, into contemporary history.

Liminality characterizes a number of narratives in the Gospel. For example, the narrative focus on the last, or only events in Jesus' life that the Gospel records, can itself be considered a 'limen'. It is a narrative of his public life, the boundary between his life as it was in Galilee, about which we learn very little, and his death. In this period of his life, a challenge to the conventional structures that regulate social, political, and religious life occurs, and we see how the fear and anxiety that sustain these structures can be subverted. After divine sanc-tion has been conferred on Jesus by the heavenly voice, Σὺ εἶ ὁ υἱός μου ὁ ἀγαπητός, ἐν σοὶ εὐδόκησα ('Thou art my beloved; on thee my favour rests', 1.11), communicating to Jesus his special status, he announces the beginning of the marginal but apocalyptic time when his public ministry begins (1.15). His proclamation, a cue to a turning point in the narrative, dismisses ordinary time, ordinary kingdoms, and ordinary messages in favor of μετάνοια and trust. This proclamation

---

23. Victor Turner, 'Liminal to Liminoid in Play, Flow, and Ritual', in *idem, From Ritual to Theatre* (New York: Performing Arts Journal Publications, 1982), pp. 20-60 (44).

24. 'Liminal to Liminoid', p. 44.

reverses worldly conventions whether of time, space, or being, suspending many contemporary worldly conventions (like family alle-
giances and cultic practices) while the marginal or liminal in the form
of charismatic wandering, wonder-working and teaching take their
place. The 'liminal' experience becomes a self-imposed exile from
human business as usual, when a totally new community or 'way of
being' can emerge. The liminal *communitas* emerging as a consequence condemns the normal condition of human alienation. This
alienation or separation is of two kinds: one is for humans to act only
in terms of social or political structures; the second is to accede to fundamental selfish urges no matter how much one harms fellow human
beings.[25]

While Jesus, his disciples and followers participate in the temporary
abrogation of social, cultic and familial convention and avoid self-
centered actions, the Gospel draws up sides that divide the world into
those who conform to codes and expectations and conspire in selfish
acts versus those who follow Jesus. In the liminal interlude, Jesus
creates a community where he abandons these structures and base urges
and where altruistic action replaces them. Here the liminal and exilic
conditions converge, as Jesus' self-chosen exile from the predictable
world he regularly inhabited momentarily becomes the prelapsarian
utopia that starkly contrasts with the normal 'exilic' or alienated human
status. This suspension recreates the prelapsarian conditions for human
existence, in the sense that reconciliation between the divine and human
and humans and other humans is possible, though not necessarily realized. The exilic and prelapsarian conditions merge during the liminal
space-time, creating a temporary harmony with the divine and con-
structing a utopian community. The narrative tension builds as the possibility of the restored utopia conflicts with humankind's obduracy. This
potential return to the idyllic and utopian ontological status does not
erase consciousness but rather focuses it on the basic choice between
fear and trust. 'Faith', 'trust', and 'openness', make possible this reconciliation, but the Gospel also shows that fear destroys it, and cements
the power that disruptive forces have over humans.

A number of incidents also can be characterized as liminal in that
they occur at the juncture between one social or physical environment
and another. These major turning points in the narrative include Jesus
crossing over his own doorway into the public arena of conflict, two

25. Turner, *The Ritual Process*, p. 105.

crossings over water from the known to the unknown, and three entrances into Jerusalem, through which he experiences the final encounter between life and death. He is the intermediary between living in the world as it is and the world as it might become or once was;[26] between the society he knows and sojourns in and the society or *communitas* he constructs.

In the liminal space-time all the conventional dichotomies in human experience, whether between male and female, life and death, old and young, culture and nature, or village and city, priests and kings, polluted and clean, for example (what Levi-Strauss called binary oppositions)[27] are present. The narrative of Jesus' life shows how to set aside these dichotomies, but whether anybody in the Gospel rises to the invitation and demonstrated possibility, the Gospel leaves open to interpretation. Jesus' command of μετάνοια, in fact, is not a demand for action but for ontological change, which may show itself in action. It is a reversal, an apocalyptic invitation to turn away from the normal and towards the marginal.[28] In contrast to the structured dichotomies, the mythic narrative reveals only one dichotomy: God's way and the human way, and this too can be reconciled. As the surface peripeteia of the Jesus narrative unfolds, two parallel reversals take place.[29] The conventional social and political structures are first exposed and undermined by Jesus' street actions, then restored, and during this time a contingent model for recovering the divine in the human emerges. The narrative exposes the difference between the eternal space and time of the divine world and the ephemeral human world and presents the model for overcoming the separation between these worlds by bringing the eternal into the ephemeral.[30]

26. Louis Marin in *The Semiotics of the Passion Narrative: Topics and Figures* (trans. Alfred M. Johnson, Jr; Pittsburgh, PA: Pickwick Press, 1980) constructs a structural analysis of the passion 'narrative', showing Jesus as a mediating figure.

27. Claude Levi-Strauss, *Anthropologie Structurale* (Paris: Plon, 1958); translated by C. Jacobson and B.G. Schoepf, *Structural Anthropology* (Harmondsworth: Penguin Books, 1968); *The Raw and the Cooked: Introduction to the Science of Mythology* (trans. John and Doreen Weightman; New York: Harper & Row, 1969).

28. Karl Jaspers, 'Jesus' in *idem, Socrates, Buddha, Confucius, Jesus* (trans. Ralph Manheim; New York: Harcourt Brace Jovanovich, 1957), pp. 64-86.

29. Bilezikian, *The Liberated Gospel*, was the first to apply this Aristotelian term to the Gospel.

30. See Paul Ricoeur, 'Interpretative Narrative', in Regina Schwartz (ed.), *The*

The Gospel of Mark seems uniquely prepared to overturn the conventional dichotomies, in fact, to present a story that probes and even opposes social adherence to custom.[31] For example, Jesus' attention to women (5.25-43) confronts the taboos separating the sexes; also he shows how to dismiss the opposition between Jew and Gentile (5.1-20; 7.24-30, passim). His choice of followers reflects his distrust of social conventions of status and political affiliation separating people into categories, for he includes rich, poor, political zealots, Roman collaborators, fishermen and bureaucrats (1.16-20; 2.13-14; 3.13-19). He also dispels the opposition between city and country because his mission takes him to both places. The structural conventions or dichotomies thus undergird the space where the liminal action of Jesus' public career takes place; they rule the world he enters, and we might assume that they hold sway at his death, but whether or not they triumph after his death is left paradoxically open for those who read the Gospel as adherents or deniers of 'the way'.

In his conflict with the doctors of the law (2.15–3.6; 7.1-3), Jesus addresses the oppositions between culture and nature; the Herod versus John the Baptist intercalation (6.14-29) exposes the struggle for power between kings and priests; Jesus identifies himself with a mission in the towns in contrast to John's mission in the wilderness (1.35-38); he is the purifier who cleanses those with πνεύματι ἀκαθάρτῳ (1.23, 32, 34, 39; 5.1-20, passim); Jesus promises a future life that will conquer the powers of death (Mk 8.34-8; 9.9, 31; 10.29-31); God versus Satan (8.33) is yet another opposition, as is land versus water (4.36-41; 6.45-52).[32]

Mark's narrative presents situations where Jesus modifies the conventions traditionally determining insiders and outsiders, that is, those who follow the authoritative teachings on the family, patriarchalism, sex and gender roles, eating and cleanliness rituals, and clan solidarity condoned in the Hebrew Bible, as discussed in Chapter 2. Although he re-affirms the law repeatedly, Mark's Jesus, nevertheless, redefines

Book and the Text: The Bible and Literary Theory (Oxford: Basil Blackwell, 1990), pp. 244-47, which suggests this interpretation.

31. In this respect, in contrast to Bronislaw Malinowski's theory about myth's functional role, the Gospel does not re-enforce social and moral responses or sustain the norms of social structure. See 'Myth in Primitive Psychology', in *Magic, Science and Religion and Other Essays* (New York: Doubleday, 1954), pp. 93-148.

32. Malbon, *Narrative Space*.

familial and clan alliances, choosing a group of followers who represent different social statuses and political affiliations (1.16-20; 3.13-19), specifically seeking those outside his own ethnic clan (7.24-30; 5.1-20), and rejecting his family on the grounds that 'Whoever does the will of God is my brother, my sister, my mother' (3.35).[33] Nor are Mark's negations of social and cultural conventions restricted to issues of status and familial alliances. His version of the Jesus story shows his hero confronting and undermining cultic practice, redefining insiders and outsiders by confronting the 'doctors of the law' and the priesthood, those who hold the religious, intellectual and cultural power in the setting of the story (2.13–3.6; 12.13-27; 14.1-2, passim).

Many myths, particularly those found in the Indo-European group represent power as equally divided between king and priest. This dichotomy may appear as thinker and warrior, warrior and magician; soldier and contemplative; pope and emperor; Brahman and Ksatriya, for example. The myths point to the necessary balance of power, as, for example, in Arjuna and Yudhishthira in the *Mahabharata*, Arthur and Merlin in the Celtic tradition, Romulus and Numa and Jupiter and Fides.[34] In the Gospel of Mark, Jesus' actions take place within these mythic political structures. Indeed, it could be argued that history has ruptured myth and challenged Hebraic-social-political practice. It has restructured the balance between king and priest because the Roman presence has made Israel a client state under the management of the Roman procurator Pontius Pilate, with the puppet king Herod in Galilee and the temple priesthood continuing cultic practice as usual in Jerusalem. Instead of the king and priest acting as mediating forces, the Gospel presents a perverse figure, Pontius Pilate, as the ironic or subversive mediator between these historically and mythologically balancing powers. Likewise, it could be argued that the mythic structures have adapted themselves to 'real' historical circumstances. In the balance of power between king and priest, Mark's Jesus is hardly a mediator. Rather his mission and activity seem to be directed against the structural mythic political conventions that maintain these powers in

---

33. See Stephan C. Barton, 'Jesus and His Own Family', 'Jesus' True Family', *Discipleship and Family Ties in Mark and Matthew* (Cambridge: Cambridge University Press, 1994), pp. 67-96, 179-91.

34. See Georges Dumézil, *Mitra-Varuna: An Essay on Two Indo-European Representations of Sovereignty* (trans. Derek Coltman; New York: Zone Books, 1988; repr. *Mitra-Varuna* [Paris: Editions Gallimard, 1948]).

their hereditary positions, even though he does not take a political position against the Romans, insisting perhaps ironically that Caesar, like God should receive his due (12.17). The Gospel, nevertheless, shows that king and priest have abandoned their traditional mythic roles as protectors of the certainties ruling the clan's life, sustaining its identity, and ensuring its survival. On the contrary, it is they who are violating 'Israel's' laws, traditions and customs by murdering its prophets and charismatic religious leaders (6.14-29; 14.1-2, 10-11; 14.55-64). Neither Jesus nor Mark spend much attention on the tyranny of the Roman presence, supported by self-evident military power, but Mark shows Jesus in direct confrontation with those holding cultural and social power as he attempts to expose the grounds for their righteousness presumed by tradition, taboo, habit and prejudice.

Elizabeth Struthers Malbon's study, *Narrative Space and Mythic Meaning*, reviews in great detail these structural oppositions as they appear in spatial configurations, so I will not repeat them here. Louis Marin's structural study, *Semiotics of the Passion Narrative*, also has shown that underlying narrative structures do not merely represent themselves figurally, but as Paul Ricoeur points out, this narrative surface is where 'initiatives get taken', introducing contingencies into the narrative and governing the transformations taking place on the deeper levels.[35] I want to emphasize that the narrative shows Jesus is not a mediator between these opposites, because he actively opposes them; he deliberately exposes them and shows a way of being that would eliminate their dichotomous power over humans. His public ministry, the only part of his life that Mark has chosen as his subject, though essentially a brief period in ordinary time when conventions are momentarily challenged, calls into action a new human being by questioning conventional structures and foregrounding their limitations. His actions call for a 're-ordering of power'.[36] As Turner points out, liminality invites critical thinking and even opposition to 'social structural man', but liminality also presents, whether directly or by

35. Ricoeur, 'Interpretative Narrative', p. 244.

36. Waetjen (*A Reordering of Power*) argues persuasively that Mark's Gospel exposes the 'guardians of the society' and proposes a 'new human being'. Similarly Fernando Belo (*Lecture matérialiste de l'évangile de Marc: récit, pratique, idéologie* [Paris: Editions du Cerf, 1975]; ET, *A Materialist Reading of the Gospel of Mark* [trans. Matthew J. O'Connell; Maryknoll, NY: Orbis Books, 1981]), examines the social revolution implicit in the Markan Gospel.

implication, a possibility for human society that is an unstructured but 'homogeneous' *communitas* composed of the human species.[37] Such a situation cannot be sustained for long, for it is an interval, a period in which all structural conventions are momentarily denied or abrogated.[38] Jesus' public ministry, therefore, is such a momentary period when the possibility of a new community outside these structural conventions takes hold of the people's imaginations and behavior.[39] Jesus' charismatic activities and fearless presence direct this momentary hiatus. Although this interruption of 'normal' time is told through the narrative resources provided by contemporary experience and an actual history, the courageous break with this conventional notion of time and business as usual temporarily stops time. While the actions of Jesus' public life unfold in an apparently temporal setting, they set up a paradigmatic mythological model that the social world normally can only allow to exist outside time. In this mythological environment, Mark's narrative moves outside conventional temporality into a bracketed temporal space where the normal and the ordinary no longer possess power over human behavior.

In addition to the Gospel narrating the 'liminal' final period in Jesus' life, a number of threshhold events also characterize Jesus' mission. The first of these liminal experiences occurs in ch. 2. Jesus is 'at home', that is, in Galilee, within the world of his tradition and his social and religious training. He proclaims his message from the security of this home environment, while the crowd listens in the 'space in front of the door' (πρὸς τὴν θύραν) (2.2). At this point in the Gospel, despite the fact that the 'time (ὁ καιρὸς) has come' (1.15), and Jesus' public ministry has begun, he has not crossed the threshold into the public arena, but remains within the domain of his home in Galilee, with all the security that offers. But there are so many people occupying the threshold that the crowd 'opens the roof', thus annulling the normal conventions of 'inside' and 'outside' and 'up' and 'down'. It is through this action, and Jesus' response to it, 'Your sins are forgiven', (2.5), that Jesus crosses the 'limen' that initiates the conflict with his opponents (2.6-8) and establishes the oppositions between 'good' and 'evil', between the fearful and the fearless. This 'limen' is between

37. 'Liminal to Liminoid', p. 47.
38. See 'Liminality and Communitas', in *The Ritual Process*, pp. 94-130.
39. For the socio-political implications of this structural change, see Waetjen, *A Reordering of Power*.

'things as they are' held together by fear and taboo—the security of home, family, clan, society, ritual, custom and culture—and a new, unknown territory where social, cultural and political predictability, with the exception of prophetic foreknowledge, disappears. Thus Mark deploys the mythic theme in which a culture hero crosses the threshold, but in contrast to myth, the journey the hero undertakes will redefine how to live in the world rather than confirm the cultural norms and conditions preserved in the οἶκος. This is why, for example, it is such an important detail that Jesus teaches his first recorded parable from the 'sea' (4.1) while the crowds listen from the land. The 'sea' also denotes a 'limen' as a metaphor for the mythic 'natural' environment, outside of civilization, culture and tradition as we know it, where he can preach a totally new social and moral message, a new way of being, a new *communitas*, told in The Parable of the Sower (4.3-34).

Immediately following this first parable, Jesus tells his disciples, διέλθωμεν εἰς τὸ πέραν ('Let us cross over to the other side of the lake', 4.35), traversing the mythical 'boundary' between the known and the unknown, the world as it is and the world he will show his disciples can exist. This is not an easy crossing for the disciples,[40] although for Jesus it is very tranquil, 'he was in the stern asleep on a cushion' (καὶ αὐτὸς ἦν ἐν τῇ πρύμνῃ ἐπὶ τὸ προσκεφάλαιον καθεύδων, 4.38). The cushion is a detail unique to the Markan version, a word that specifically denotes leisure and comfort, showing his sleep was peaceful and tranquil. It is in the crossing itself that this new ontology of being human is specifically presented because the disciples in their usual frayed state are terribly frightened, διδάσκαλε, οὐ μέλει σοι ὅτι ἀπολλύμεθα ('Master we are sinking! Do you not care?', Mk 4.38), and Jesus, having calmed the waters,[41] confronts them with their cowardice, τί δειλοί ἐστε? οὔπω ἔχετε πίστιν? ('Why are you such cowards? Have you no faith even now?', 4.40). Again, Jesus takes his disciples on to the dangerous and unknown mythic environment of the water, a physical threat to humans. It is a symbolic menacing environment precisely because it is nature uncontrolled by humans; it is outside social rules and habits, that is, the taboo-ridden world created out of human fears. At any moment it threatens to destroy the human need for predictability, in the normal fear-bound condition, the static world humans count on to continue their existence. But Jesus' actions

---

40. Jean Starobinski, 'Essai exégétique: Marc 5.1-20', pp. 95-121.
41. Motif #D.2151, 'Magic Control of Waters', in *Motif Index*, II, p. 385.

show the disciples that unknown, threatening natural forces and the unknown territories of human ontology or sociology they symbolically represent, are not menacing if we do not allow 'fear' to rule us. He is taking them across the boundary between the known and unknown, but he is showing them the ontological condition that must characterize this crossing. As the disciples recognize Jesus' power over the water, a moment of spontaneous *communitas* occurs; although the disciples are awestruck and confused by the event, it is, nonetheless, a moment of mutual understanding when all the anxieties that separate humans from one another, from God, and from nature, are suddenly exposed.

In the second sea journey, again a mythic crossing over the unknown, Jesus walks on the water,[42] while the wind exercises its will ἦν γὰρ ὁ ἄνεμος ἐναντίος αὐτοῖς (the disciples were 'laboring at the oars against a head wind', 6.48), showing the disciples it is possible to cooperate with the unknown, despite its dangers. The disciples are once more terrified (ἐταράχθησαν, 6.50) and Jesus tells them, θαρσεῖτε ('Don't be afraid'), giving the revelation formula for divine presence (ἐγώ εἰμι)—and advising them once more to avoid fear, μὴ φοβεῖσθε (6.50). The primal fear of water that threatens to conquer and destroy humankind's tranquility in the known and stabilized environment, can be diverted by abandoning fear, a transformation that makes the divine present in human experience. The danger of unknown and untamed nature, that threatens to break in on humankind and its known conventions at any moment, creates fear, but the human conquest of fear makes the numinous present to them.

The final threshhold Jesus crosses is the three-time entrance into Jerusalem (11.1, 15, 27). The confrontation with Jerusalem is between 'his way' and the practices of the times. In his first entrance, he is greeted as a leader, the traditional 'liberating' king (11.9-10), the savior who enters the temple in a traditional 'king' versus 'priest' pattern. He traverses the boundary between his established ministry in the towns and villages of the countryside into the ultimate confrontation with the 'city', the historical site of Israel's regal and religious past and its present form. Mark merely notes that καὶ εἰσῆλθεν εἰς Ἰεροσόλυμα εἰς τὸ ἱερόν καὶ περιβλεψάμενος πάντα ('He entered Jerusalem and went into the temple, where he looked at the whole scene', 11.11). He makes no comments on what Jesus might have

42. Motif #D. 2125.1, *Motif Index*, II, p. 376.

observed there, and Jesus himself is silent. Mark constructs a dramatic scene pitting the 'cult hero' against the locale of traditional sacred rite and priestly purview, leaving narrative gaps to be filled in by the second and third entrances into Jerusalem. Whether Jesus' reaction was fear, revulsion, anger or acceptance, we do not know, although all of these emotions will characterize his actions once the Jerusalem drama actually begins.

Prior to the second entrance, Jesus curses the 'fig tree', symbolic representation of Israel; as a precursor to his angry cleansing of the temple (11.15-18), and a link to the first entrance into Jerusalem, this frames the coming of the 'miracle worker'.[43] His cursing acts as a narrative clue to his emotional response to what he had seen in Jerusalem on his first visit. Righteous anger prompts both actions as he transgresses the boundaries of cult and prejudice overseen by the official powers who will determine his inevitable death (11.18-19). The fig tree's 'unripeness' parallels the unreadiness of the temple practitioners for the reforms Jesus demands. His violation of the fig tree confronts the complacency of Israel and its rigid refusal to change. In the final entrance, the authority for his actions are challenged (11.28), to which he responds by dismissing the conventions of temporal authority, telling the Parable of the Vineyard with its veiled allegory of Israel's historic rejection of its prophets or divine missionaries (12.1-9). Asked by what right he violates the sanctified boundary separating the priestly cultus from others, his fearless response in the form of The Parable of the Vineyard, answers that the right comes from the divinity, the right of prophets who are outside the priestly-aristocratic domain. He is not a mediator, but a divine presence interrupting ordinary time to put it in the context of eternity.

The temple practice, or religious business as usual, Jesus deems a profligate violation of *communitas*. His confrontation with the temple is his final act of opposing the established power and exposing its corruption. His actions frame the apocalyptic choice between contemporary social and religious custom in the temple and God's house. Excoriating the temple practitioners (11.17), he quotes Jeremiah, ὁ οἶκός μου οἶκος προσευχῆς κληθήσεται πᾶσιν τοῖς ἔθνεσιν ('My house shall be called a house of prayer for all the nations'), and dismisses all human structures, whether of cult, clan, or nation, and

---

43. See Broadhead, *Teaching with Authority*, pp. 168-70.

reminds his listeners of the utopian *communitas* where all humans are joined in common prayer in God's house.

The Gospel ending, nevertheless, makes paradoxical the possibility for a continued or renewed *communitas*, for only if its listeners accept the 'road' Jesus' mission reveals can *communitas* continue. When Jesus' followers (Judas, Peter and even the women) succumb to fear and desert him, they figuratively join his opponents as betrayers of the kerygmatic mission and its potential to restore the prelapsarian human condition. Their acquiescence to fear on the narrative surface also reworks the underlying structures defining insiders and outsiders, God's world and the human world, and convention and unconvention. If the arrest is the final turning-point in the narrative when the liminal period concludes and the restructuring that had overtaken Jesus' inner society and the narrative comes to an end, it is also at this point that the old structure returns, but it is God and Jesus on one side and all those who have forfeited their wills to fear on the other. From this point on, Jesus' magical power disappears,[44] just as it had when he visited his own home town earlier in the Gospel (Mk 6.4-6), which Mark had explained on the grounds of lack of faith. It is also from the arrest forward that Jesus withdraws as actor and subject, to whom everyone reacts, becoming instead the acted upon and object in the drama, although still the prime agent, as he assumes the role of scapegoat and passively inspires action in his opponents. Though superficially the narrative appears to restore the conventional structures as the priests and leaders re-establish their authority with all the people falling into their respective places, in fact a totally new structure has taken over, and it is no longer liminal. Jesus as a fearless, intensely suffering sacrificial offering offsets all the fear-driven agents who participated in or looked at the spectacle of the liminal events.

Just as power and prophecy desert him, so does speech, for he remains mostly silent, although his three utterances during this span of the narrative (from the arrest to his death) are central to the mythic communication. The first is to answer the question, σὺ εἶ ὁ Χριστὸς ὁ υἱὸς τοῦ εὐλογητοῦ (14.61) to which he responds by recalling the divine revelation formula, ἐγώ εἰμι (14.62) and quoting Daniel's prophecy of the coming of the son of Man (14.62). In the second, a response to Pilate's question, σὺ εἶ ὁ βασιλεὺς τῶν Ἰουδαίων ('Are

44. See Broadhead, *Teaching with Authority*, pp. 180-87, discusses the 'absence of miracle stories in Mark 14.1–16.8'.

you the king of the Jews?', 15.2), he passively returns the remark to the speaker, σὺ λέγεις ('The words are yours'). Recalling Psalm 22, ἐλωι ἐλωι λεμα σαβαχθανι? ('My God, my God, why hast thou forsaken me?'), the Aramaic words from the cross are his third and final statement. Including a statement of divine presence, a refusal to acknowledge human structures, and a lament about divine absence, all three emphasize Jesus' outsider status from worldly structures and his denial of their ultimate power, and at the same time show him accepting his vulnerable status in the cosmic drama. Unlike all the other characters in the Gospel, who, desiring to control the world, yield to fear, his death demonstrates he has embraced his vulnerability because he cannot control the world. The Roman centurion's statement, ἀληθῶς οὗτος ὁ ἄνθρωπος υἱὸς θεοῦ ἦν ('Truly this man was a Son of God', 15.39), conferring divinity on Jesus, points to his death as an act of reconciliation. Such a reconciliation closes the gap between God and humankind and the separation that accompanies it. Now the opposition is between the deserted person on the cross whose only appeal is his own forsaken condition and all the other compromised ways of being, whether of betrayal, power-seeking, cowardice or other malicious behavior that characterize ordinary time activities.

Though Jesus' mission points to the possibility of an uncontingent abrogation of the structural oppositions, whether the Gospel shows how this will happen is questionable. The Gospel can not absolutely erase these oppositions. The Gospel does not overcome the conflict between the chaos and order of life, or the tension between despair and integration in human experience, but it does reveal a way to encounter such crises without fear. While the liminal time may have temporarily overturned the ordinary human manner and expectation, the crucifixion and empty tomb, and all the human action of betrayal, abandonment, desire for power, and cowardice that made these events possible emphasize the contingency of human behavior and 'being in the world', in contrast to God's absoluteness as embedded in the kerygmatic communication of the narrative. The oppositions undergird Jesus' mythic journey; the narrative breaks through these underlying patterns because Jesus' action subverts their power. Restoring the oppositions at the end of the Gospel emphasizes the contingency of the impact of his journey. But the failure of his most intimate followers to live up to the challenge does not undermine them or the message; just the contrary, the narrative presents the model for the liminal experience, and leaves open the possibility for any listener to follow it, difficult as it may be.

Though Jesus' way is uncontingent, the capacity for humans to travel it is contingent. Here the structural approach to myth collapses because it fails to take into account human living in the world, an implication of the narrative that emerges as a consequence of interpretation rather than description or explanation of its structures. Jesus is not a 'divine figure', despite the fact that he is called 'the son of God' on three important occasions (Mk 1.11; 9.7; 15.39), but a human being who is the primary actor in the mythic and cultural drama. Mythic oppositions establish the terms of the sacred events. However, the radical action of the main character and his uncontingent acceptance of the mission set out before him, combined with the human reactions to his journey, determine their resolution. In other words, the mythic context is the occasion for working out the potential of a new uncontingent way of being.

Thus Mark's Gospel unveils a new ontology, ready to replace the old, which is in a state of collapse. This confrontation with fear, the 'ultimate' mythic kerygma, insists that we cannot own the world, we can only trust in it. Examining Mark in its mythic context reveals this new way of being or narrative truth. The essence of this revelation is timeless, for its message transcends the particular historical moment of the Gospel. In fact, the power of this opportunity for living without fear lies precisely in its confrontation with historic time. It opposes 'being' according to the rules, corruptions, and needs of historical time with 'being' according to 'eternal' terms.

In this brief hiatus, Jesus' career represents a liminal interruption of 'normal' time in which the central character accepts both the promise and the vulnerability of his mission and his own role in it. His trust in the 'world' shows how to retrieve the imagined 'mythic time' before divisions and fragmentation overtook the human condition. Mark presents this as a human possibility and a utopian hope for the present and the future.

CONCLUSION

THE END OF VIOLENCE:
RITUAL TIME IN THE GOSPEL OF MARK

Ritual is traditionally defined as the acting out of myth, the means by which particular cultic communities reaffirm and recreate their collective beliefs.[1] Other theories distinguish ritual's synchronic features because it is traditional and continuous in contrast to the diachronic, fluid and contingent nature of historic action.[2] Paul Ricoeur, in discussing time and ritual suggests

> If we oppose myth and ritual, we may say that myth enlarges ordinary time (and space), whereas ritual brings together mythic time and the profane sphere of life and action. By punctuating action in this way, it sets time and each brief human life within a broader time.[3]

These theories about ritual describe the practice of ritual. In this chapter, I examine the initial creation of ritual in the Gospel of Mark to distinguish Markan ritual time from the historic practice of Christian ritual. In Mark, the ritual time is a 'subversive flicker',[4] a gap between ordinary time and a return to ordinary time.

In the first food multiplication story in the Gospel of Mark, Jesus and the disciples have withdrawn to the ἔρημος, usually translated 'lonely place' (6.31-35), where some five thousand people (6.44) who have run from the cities (6.33), have joined him. Realizing it is late and that these followers are hungry, the disciples want to send them away to the surrounding villages where they will be able to buy something to eat. But Jesus intercedes and tells the crowd to sit on the

---

1. Emile Durkheim, *The Elementary Forms of Religious Life* (trans. J.W. Swain; London: George Allen & Unwin Ltd., 1976 [1915]), pp. 101-40.

2. Stanley J. Tambiah, *Buddhism and the Spirit Cults of North-East Thailand* (Cambridge: Cambridge University Press, 1970).

3. Paul Ricoeur, *Time and Narrative*, III, p. 105.

4. This is a term used by Turner, 'Liminal to Liminoid', p. 44.

χλωρῷ χόρτῳ ('green grass', 6.39), an expression not found in Matthew, who leaves out 'green', or Luke who does not give any information about where the people sat down. When the people are seated, Jesus 'taking the five loaves and the two fishes' he and his disciples had brought with them, 'looked up to heaven, said the blessing, broke the loaves, and gave them to the disciples to distribute' (6.41-42).

Both the food multiplication stories in Mark (6.30-44; 8.1-10) are eucharistic rituals, in which Jesus and his disciples have removed themselves to a remote area and halted their usual activities in the towns and villages. But the townspeople and villagers have followed them into this 'green world' where a spontaneous community outside the conventions of civilized space and time has formed. Markan oppositions are a steady topic of commentaries on Mark,[5] but this particular one is unique in that it opposes the villages, towns and seats of power to the remote ecology of the 'green world'. In addition, because of its ritual atmosphere, the setting stands apart from the central site of ritual observation in ancient Palestine, that is, the temple in Jerusalem, which had already been destroyed as a center of cultic life by the time Mark wrote his Gospel. Because the first food multiplication story in the Gospel, set on the χλωρῷ χόρτῳ, immediately follows the narrative of the perverted table fellowship that brought an end to John the Baptist's life (6.14-29), it contrasts with the banquet in the seat of temporal and religious power. Here two kinds of ritual enactments are juxtaposed and opposed: Herod is a king and Jesus is a charismatic wonder-working carpenter; Herod is afraid of John but swayed by his lust and by Herodias, but Jesus has fearlessly left his home and family to embark on a dangerous public mission; Herod is politically powerful, lacks moral courage and fears social criticism, while Jesus is powerless, ignores danger and is morally courageous. Herod can exercise conventional power even though he is a puppet of the Roman Empire. Jesus is impotent in conventional terms. Significantly, Herod's banquet takes place indoors and Jesus' eucharistic gathering occurs outdoors. Both the birthday party and the food multiplication stories are community celebrations, yet the first is a murderous and devious plot to override Israel's laws and their guardians, leading to the death

---

5. F. Neirynck, *Duality in Mark: Contributions to the Study of Markan Redaction* (Repr. Leuven: Leuven University Press, 1972); Malbon, *Narrative Space and Mythic Meaning*; Marin, *The Semiotics of the Passion Narrative*.

of an outspoken critic of the king. The second, on the other hand, is a spontaneous ritual that celebrates the coming together of all kinds of people, who leave behind the trappings of social and political power, and gender, ethnic, or other social distinctions, as they join together in eating and thanksgiving in a pastoral setting.

In my discussion of ritual time in the Gospel, I want to argue that the ritual initiated at the first food multiplication is a Markan version of the 'green world', where the world of history, politics, social, gender and ethnic hierarchies and taboos temporarily ceases and a new utopian end of the violence of human history takes its place. This retreat to the 'green world' is not an imaginary mirror of the ordinary time world but a visionary projection of the utopian experience made possible when humans retreat from the rules, structures and power conspiracies of the world of contemporary history and politics. It is a play interlude poised amidst all the serious endeavors of the conventionally powerful and fearful. Furthermore, it establishes a place for ritual experience that is 'space' rather than historic site. A place possesses some kind of stability; it can be identified and frequented; a 'space', on the other hand, is made up of 'intersections of mobile elements'; it is produced or made actual by situations that are not necessarily stable or repeatable. For De Certeau, it is like the 'word when it is spoken'.[6] Rather than the temple, which is a 'place' where ritual was observed and followed, here in the pastoral setting, the suspension of time and historic locale provides the space for the formation of a spontaneous community. This ritual interruption does not end time— just the contrary, it temporarily stops ordinary time, but then sends the participants and leaders back into real time and history. My discussion of ritual time will focus on four incidents in the Gospel: the narrative of the death of John the Baptist (6.14-29); the first and second food multiplication stories (6.30-44; 8.1-10); and the last supper (14.12-25).

---

6.   For this distinction between 'place' and 'space', see Michel de Certeau, *The Practice of Everyday Life* (trans. Steven Rendall; Berkeley: University of California Press, 1984), pp. 117-18; for other theories of space recognizing this distinction, see David Harvey, 'The Experience of Space and Time', in *The Condition of Postmodernity: An Inquiry into the Origins of Cultural Change* (Cambridge, MA: Blackwell, 1989), pp. 199-259; Jonathan Z. Smith, *To Take Place: Toward Theory in Ritual* (Chicago: University of Chicago Press, 1987).

'The green world', a second or alternate world to the 'normal world', is a term used by Northrop Frye in his essay 'The Argument of Comedy' in a discussion of Renaissance drama. Frye connects the green world to 'paganism' and folk ritual that was organized calendrically.[7] Meyer Abrams also discussed such spaces as the 'second world' or a 'heterocosm', 'created by the poet in an act analogous to God's creation of the world'.[8] Abrams' heterocosm may be an image of the real world or of its opposite—in either case, for him both are products of the poet's imagination. Writing about Renaissance drama, Harry Berger carries these ideas further, arguing that

> The green world seems to possess two essential qualities: first, since it is only metaphorically a place or space, it embodies a condition whose value should not remain fixed but should rather change according to the temporal process of which it is a part. It appears first as exemplary or appealing and lures us away from the evil or confusion of everyday life. But when it has fulfilled its moral, esthetic, social, cognitive, or experimental functions, it becomes inadequate and its creator turns us out. Those who wish to remain, who cannot or will not be discharged, are presented as in some way deficient. Thus the second quality of the green world is that it is ambiguous: its usefulness and dangers arise from the same source. In its positive aspects it provides a temporary haven for recreation or clarification, experiment or relief; in its negative aspects it projects the urge of the paralyzed will to give up, escape, work magic, abolish time and flux and the intrusive reality of other minds.[9]

Berger disputes Frye and shows how these two worlds in the Renaissance imagination are not opposites but fictional mirrors of each other. I am interested in these arguments because of their application to myth and ritual. I agree with Berger that the 'green world' invariably mirrors the real world and that the utopian 'green world' cannot tolerate disruptions or conflicts to its own vision. Rigid and codified social and political structures that ensure their own permanence no matter what tyrannical measures are necessary to secure their coercive powers control and direct the ordinary time world. The 'green world', on the

7. Northrop Frye, 'The Argument of Comedy', in Leonard F. Dean (ed.), *Shakespeare: Modern Essays in Criticism* (New York: Oxford University Press, 1957), pp. 79-89.

8. *The Mirror and the Lamp: Romantic Theory and Critical Tradition* (New York: Oxford University Press, 1953), pp. 272, 327.

9. *Second World and Green World: Studies in Renaissance Fiction-Making* (Berkeley: University of California Press, 1988), p. 36.

other hand, constructs its own counter-structure, which likewise requires rigid compliance for membership in its community. Thus,
though the utopian alternative draws attention to the rigidity, coer-
civeness or cruelty of the social structure of ordinary time, at the same
time, it shows its own limitations. In myth, heroes frequently remove
themselves or are exiled into the 'green world', the forest where they
must work out their own relationships to the power and desires of kingdoms and governments. This is the pattern in Valmiki's and Kampan's
versions of *The Ramayana* and in *The Mahabharata*, for example. The
heroes find themselves politically liminal and their retreat to the forest
for thirteen years is their opportunity for self-scrutiny and personal
development. The time lapse also allows them to learn to question the
merits of the ordinary time power they had lost or abandoned when
they entered the forest. Dante the pilgrim likewise finds himself in parallel circumstances at the beginning of the *Divine Comedy* in the *selva
oscura* ('dark wood'). In the forest environment, these mythic seekers
invariably encounter both the extraordinary in the form of magic or
divine presences as well as usurpations and corruptions that conjure
the worlds left behind.

In the Gospel of Mark, the retreat to the *locus amoenus* where the
spontaneous ritual occurs, however, is a communal act that recreates
history in completely new terms. At the moment of the eucharist, when
everyone is fed to satisfaction, a new community emerges. But it cannot remain in the *locus amoenus*. For the ritual to have meaning, it
must make possible the return to ordinary time society, no matter
what the consequences. This ritual opposes the history dramatized in
the story of the murder of John the Baptist (6.14-29), when self-seekers
abandon themselves to their desires for temporal power. The cult leader who initiated the ritual action in the *locus amoenus* is willing to
take on a similar death in order to bring such violence to a grinding
halt. When the ritual ends, the community returns to the towns and
cities, but, one assumes, with a totally new understanding of the relationships between human beings, for the power structures that rule
ordinary time have no place in this community. They must return out
of harmony with the real world, for their spontaneous communal experience in the 'green world' makes them alienated in the world of historical action and deeds. Jesus has not taught them during this sojourn.
An interesting aspect of this first food multiplication story besides the
fact that it occurs on a green field, is that verbal communication ceases

except for the concern over eating and the thanksgiving prayer itself. The primary function of the ritual is communion, not teaching or consoling, though it may do both of these without differentiating form and function.

In Mark, we have a Palestinian-Hellenistic milieu version of pastoral, a retreat to a *locus amoenus* where history and the deeds of humans are temporarily stopped. The incident suspends ordinary time, ordinary places, and the extraordinary public ministry of the main character in an interlude that creates its own ritual time as an answer to all the confusions and distortions of ordinary time. The incident establishes the ritual as outside history and outside time—as a marginal space and time where initiatives get taken that have the power to create an alternative history and society grounded in social values contradicting those that rule ordinary time.

In arguing for this Christian ritual as signaling the end of violence and the end of time as formerly experienced and anticipated, I am distinguishing it from other well-received theories about the origins, functions and forms of ritual. Ritual as 'the symbolic intercom' possesses numerous forms, functions and frameworks.[10] I would agree with many theorists who argue against a universal theory to cover all rituals, even though many rituals from different areas of the world may share common features. Rituals, whatever their originating moment, take on the symbolic traditions and social functions of the cultures to which they belong. Their meaning and performance, though predictable and conservatively conforming to established custom, nonetheless reflect the changes in the cultures where they continue to be practiced. In the major religions, another feature of rituals that contributes to their changing meaning or practice is the commentary traditions on the texts (narrative or myths) the rituals re-enact, which elaborate diverse and innovative meanings often only symbolically implied in the ritual actions themselves. This kind of elaboration has

---

10. 'Symbolic intercom' is Nancy D. Munn's term in 'Symbolism in a Ritual Context: Aspects of Symbolic Action', in J.J. Honigmann (ed.), *Handbook of Social and Cultural Anthropology* (Chicago: Rand McNally, 1973), pp. 579-612 (579). William G. Doty (*Mythography: The Study of Myths and Rituals* [Alabama: University of Alabama Press, 1986]) explores many of these theories of myth and ritual.

also occured when Western-trained anthropologists have studied and theorized about traditional people's rituals.[11]

Ritual theorists like Eliade, Turner and Van Gennep have been pre-occupied with describing the phenomenological characteristics of ritual.[12] In these theories, attention is drawn to the process undertaken and experienced during the ritual. Thus Eliade can talk about the installation of a king in a Fijian enthronement ceremony as a re-creation of the universe, a renewal rite that reiterates the cosmogony.[13] Other theorists or theories, as found in Clifford Geertz, V. Turner, C. Levi-Strauss and E. Cassirer seek to understand the underlying structures of rituals, whether as deep structures (Levi-Strauss) or symbolic structures (Geertz, Turner or Cassirer).[14] For Geertz, 'rituals of religion are symbolic models of a particular sense of the divine, a certain sort of devotional mood, which their continual re-enactment tends to produce in their participants'.[15] Cassirer, in contrast, stressed the 'reality' of the symbolic action experienced by ritual participants. Turner argues that 'ritual is the affirmation of communal unity in contrast to the frictions, constraints, and competitiveness of social life and organization'. It affords 'a creative "anti-structure" that is distinguished from the rigid maintenance of social orders, hierarchies, and traditional forms'. Psychological approaches to ritual include neo-Jungians, who argue that rituals play out archetypal prototypes, or developmentalists who perceive a pattern of human stages reflected in various rituals (Erikson), as for example, adolescent rites of passage, marriage rituals, initiation rites, or funerals.[16] J. Huizinga pinpointed the role of play in

11. See Catherine Bell, *Ritual Theory, Ritual Practice* (Oxford: Oxford University Press, 1992) for a thorough discussion of theories of ritual.

12. Eliade, *Myth and Reality*; Mircea Eliade, *Shamanism: Archaic Techniques of Ecstasy* (trans. Willard R. Trask; Princeton, NJ: Princeton University Press, 1964); Turner, *The Ritual Process*; Arnold Van Gennep, *The Rites of Passage* (trans. M.B. Vizedom and G.L. Caffee; Chicago: University of Chicago Press, 1960).

13. *Myth and Reality*, pp. 39-41.

14. Clifford Geertz, *The Interpretation of Cultures: Selected Essays*; Ernst Cassirer, *Language and Myth* (trans. Susanne K. Langer; New York: Dover, 1946); Ernst Cassirer, *The Philosophy of Symbolic Forms*. II. *Mythical Thought* (trans. Ralph Manheim; New Haven: Yale University Press, 1955); Levi-Strauss, *The Raw and the Cooked*.

15. *The Interpretation of Cultures*, p. 216.

16. Doty, *Mythography*, p. 80; Erik Erikson, *Identity: Youth and Crisis* (New York: W.W. Norton, 1968).

ritual and developed a theory of culture based on *homo ludens*.[17] In Huizinga's, for its time, radical theory, 'archaic ritual' is play in the Platonic sense of being 'outside and above the necessities and seriousness of everyday life'. The ritual act, for Huizinga, possesses all the formal features of play he singles out, including 'play as fun', as outside rational modes of thought, and as voluntary unusual activity in an out-of-the ordinary time and place that is satisfying in itself while also satisfying communal needs.[18] Jonathan Z. Smith took discussion of ritual in a new direction with his probing of how the spatial imagination undergirds the experience of ritual, drawing parallels and describing differences among the ritual environments or 'maps' of the Australian aborigines, Ezekiel 40–48 and the Christian liturgical year. Tracing the tradition of 'holy land' pilgrimages to the political context of the council of Nicaea in the fourth century, Smith argues that Constantine created a Christian 'holy land', which resulted in the building of the 'site of the resurrection in Jerusalem'.[19] Thus, what had begun as a ritual occasion separated from a specifically 'holy' site was transformed for political reasons (to strengthen Constantine's imperial power) in the fourth century. The struggle between a metaphorical Jerusalem and a political Jerusalem remains a central tension in Christian experience.

Those who study the historical origins or cultural situations out of which ritual arose have argued that violence is at the center of the ritual action.[20] Walter Burkert, for example, whose argument rests on the premise that 'all orders and forms of authority in human society are founded in institutional violence',[21] recognizes in ritual 'a form of communication' and a 'kind of language', a language that enacts how 'community arises' out of collective violence because 'collective killing' is 'an expression of loyalty'.[22] For the purposes of this discussion of ritual time in the Gospel of Mark, I will focus on four of these

17. J. Huizinga, *Homo Ludens: A Study of the Play-Element in Culture* (Boston: Beacon Press, 1950).

18. *Homo Ludens*, pp. 3-10.

19. Smith, *To Take Place*.

20. Walter Burkert, *Homo Necans: The Anthropology of Ancient Greek Sacrificial Ritual and Myth* (trans. Peter Bing; Berkeley: University of California Press, 1983); René Girard, *Violence and the Sacred* (trans. Patrick Gregory; Baltimore: The Johns Hopkins University Press, 1972).

21. *Homo Necans*, p. 1.

22. *Homo Necans*, p. 29, 35 and 37.

theories: Turner's idea of ritual as liminal, Huizinga's idea of ritual as play, and Jonathan Z. Smith's theory of the 'placelessness' of early Christian ritual, which I will oppose to Burkert's and Girard's conviction that violence lies at the center of ritual.

The primary deficiency in both Burkert's and Girard's theories of ritual is their claim for universality in ritual action, a claim which diffuses differences in cultural practices among the diverse people of the world. Thus Burkert can write, 'Sacrificial killing is the basic experience of the "sacred". *Homo religiosus* acts and attains self-awareness as *homo necans*'.[23] In ignoring distinctions between ancient Greek religions and Christianity, he writes that those 'who turn to religion for salvation from this "so-called evil" of aggression are confronted with murder at the very core of Christianity—the death of God's innocent son'.[24] '. . . The death of God's son is the one-time and perfect sacrifice, although it is still repeated in the celebration of the Lord's Supper, in breaking bread and drinking the wine'.[25] Burkert argues that this act of collective violence underlies the creation of a community more receptive to 'seriousness' than to compassion or friendliness; the murder justifies and affirms life and restores order or installs a new order to a society fragmented by communal difference or pollution.[26]

René Girard, in discussing the 'unity of all rites', asserts that 'all religious rituals spring from the surrogate victim, and all the great institutions of mankind, both secular and religious, spring from ritual'.[27] Girard argues that sacrifice has a cathartic function, for the unanimous violence against what he calls 'the surrogate victim' can stop the decay of the cultural order. This 'surrogate victim' substitutes for all the members of the community, protecting its members from violence through the mediation of the surrogate victim. But for Girard, this is not a morbid human pathology, for the rite is a 'lesser violence', a 'bulwark against a far more virulent violence'. He argues that a profound peace 'follows the sacrificial crisis and results from the unanimous accord generated by the surrogate victim'.[28]

23. *Homo Necans*, p. 3.
24. *Homo Necans*, pp. 2-3.
25. *Homo Necans*, p. 8.
26. *Homo Necans*, p. 35, 40.
27. *Violence and the Sacred*, p. 306.
28. Girard, *Violence and the Sacred*, p. 93, 98, 99, 101-103.

I want to point out some fundamental problems with these theories as applied to the ritual time in the Gospel of Mark. Jesus' death contrasts with Oedipus's demise, which I take as a paradigmatic example of a violent ritual to expel the diseased king. Oedipus, as the polluted king must be sacrificed to return order to the disordered community, but the death of Jesus at the end of the Gospel merely restores a corrupt political and cultic order, while the community he had formed during his public career is scattered. Secondly, Jesus, unlike the king in *Oedipus Rex*, is only a carnival king, and his death cannot install a new political order; rather it makes way for the old order to re-establish its power and control.[29] In other words, the sacrifice of the surrogate victim in the Gospel of Mark parodies acts of ritual violence, for political 'order', or ordinary time history, proves to be the very source of the ritual sacrifice. Similarly in *The Bacchae*, the ritual sacrifice of the king to restore civic-cosmic order shows the entire ritual decapitation as insane and irrational violence; the confrontation between the rational order and the irrational disorder in *The Bacchae* cannot result in a restored community; rather both sides are exposed for their irrational tyrannies.

Girard speaks of the violent ritual ending with the restoration of cultural order—but in the case of the Gospel of Mark, such an expectation is ironically reversed, for the violent political and cultic structures are reinstated. Rather than installing a restored community, the ritual sacrifice initially disrupts and destroys the spontaneous community that had emerged and replaces it with the entrenched social and political powers. The death of Jesus ushers in the triumph of the tyrannical anti-utopian forces in ordinary time human life.

The two food multiplication miracles as rituals in Mark, on the other hand, are closer to what Victor Turner called *communitas*:

> What is interesting about liminal phenomena for our present purposes is the blend they offer of lowliness and sacredness, of homogeneity and comradeship. We are presented, in such rites, with a 'moment in and out of time', and in and out of secular social structure, which reveals, however fleetingly, some recognition (in symbol if not in language) of a generalized social bond that has ceased to be and has simultaneously yet to be fragmented into a multiplicity of structural ties. These are the ties organized

29. Bakhtin, *Rabelais and his World*, links 'ritual spectacle' to carnival which parodies the high culture. Similarly, in the Markan ritual 'sacrifice', Jesus emerges from the 'culture of the marketplace', pp. 5-7.

in terms either of caste, class, or rank hierarchies or of segmentary oppositions in the stateless societies beloved of political anthropologists. It is
as though there are here two major 'models' for human interrelatedness,
juxtaposed and alternating. The first is of society as a structured, differ-
entiated, and often hierarchical system of politico-legal-economic positions
with many types of evaluation, separating men in terms of 'more' or 'less'.
The second, which emerges recognizably in the liminal period, is of
society as an unstructured or rudimentarily structured and relatively
undifferentiated *comitatus*, community, or even communion of equal indi-
viduals who submit together to the general authority of the ritual elders.[30]

In both food multiplication stories, the crowds have moved to 'liminal' pastoral environments, away from the world of social structure
where political and cultic hierarchies dominate. In both stories, the
normal 'structural ties' are suspended and secular distinctions are
homogenized as comradeship and community replace the normal
social divisions.

The miraculous actions and eucharistic festival seal the radical egalitarianism of the group, who together eat equally under the auspices
of the universal heavens (6.41; 8.6). In acts of spontaneous generosity
for the physical needs of the crowds who have followed him to these
remote areas, Jesus provides ἄρτων ἐπ᾿ ἐρημίας ('bread in the desert',
8.4). In fact, Jesus' pity is especially emphasized in the second story as
he remarks that he feels sorry for the people because they have been
with him for three days without anything to eat (8.2). Though there is
no specific teaching here, there is an implied condemnation of the
power-crazed selfishness of the ordinary time world of political and
social action and a recognition of the liberating power of charity.
Also, two kinds of assaults on the bond of *communitas* are condemned
here: the first is to act only in terms of one's social office or position;
the second is to abandon charitable instincts in favor of one's own selfish needs.[31] In both food miracle stories, these normal and ordinary
time actions are exposed, as the few loaves and fishes that could have
served only the twelve are made to serve thousands. Because of its
contiguous relation to the story of John the Baptist, the first food multiplication story is a direct answer to the destruction of the Hebraic
communitas once based on adherence to ancient laws and taboos, in
Herod's court. Both food miracle 'communions' are moments when the

30. Turner, *The Ritual Process*, p. 96.
31. Turner, *The Ritual Process*, p. 105.

political-social structures are temporarily replaced with an egalitarian anti-structure of mutual cooperation and sharing through the power of the almighty. In contrast, Herod's banquet subverts Israel's laws and ethnic and tribal community to secure the political structure for his own advantage.

Turner, in the style of Levi-Strauss also provides a useful list of the oppositions put into play by the liminal interlude, many of which are specifically appropriate to these Gospel rituals. In the spontaneous community, we find homogeneity, equality, anonymity, absence of property, absence of status, sexual abstinence, minimal gender distinctions, if any, absence of rank, humility, no distinctions of wealth, unselfishness, sacredness, silence, suspension of kinship rights and obligations, reference to divine powers, foolishness, simplicity and acceptance of pain and suffering. On the other side, and in the case of the Gospel, this means that among those who force all the selfish and malicious acts of the Gospel or those who just cannot join with this radical community, we find heterogeneity, structure, inequality, pride of name and position, property, status, maximum gender differentiation, sexuality, distinctions in rank, selfishness, deference to social structures that cement rank, kinship rights and obligations, established cultural definitions of sagacity, complexity and avoidance of pain and suffering.[32] Once more, the contrast between the John the Baptist story and the first food miracle exemplifies these differences. In a historical-political setting, named characters seek to control territories and property. Female desires to secure political position and maintain social power while avoiding the suffering of John's criticisms, undergird the treacherous multi-faceted plot to seduce Herod sexually, so that he will order the murder of John the Baptist. According to the terms of social and political power, Herodias's plan is selfish but wise, for John is undermining Herod's and her own security.

The opposition between foolishness and sagacity pits the liminal ritual time retreat into pastoral against ordinary time history and politics, and shows this abandonment of power as the act of fools, who choose *communitas*, which is 'celebration' and 'play', rather than the seriousness and the hard work of history.[33] This simple game, however,

32. *The Ritual Process*, pp. 106-107.
33. This is what Bakhtin calls 'carnival', the ritual time of 'folk' culture when 'fools' celebrate a utopian egalitarianism. Bakhtin, *Rabelais and His World*, pp. 7-9, 218-19, 220.

inspires counter-plots that will require its participants to accept pain and suffering planned by those who exercise control over the social structure. Those who have followed Jesus to the marginal green environment have freely chosen this path, stepping out into 'a sphere of activity' whose temporal duration is limited, for a gathering where all communal needs are satisfied. Here there can be no distinction between 'playing' and 'being', for 'identity', 'image' and 'symbol' are fused and the normal dichotomies cannot hold. In this marginal green environment, the numinous is present and merges with the human.[34] The celebration of ritual in these cases sets the Markan ritual apart in a number of ways. First, it is separate from the conventions and controls of the temple cultus or Pharisaic house rituals. Secondly, the place is so isolated that it corresponds to the apolitical 'dream time' where a new social community in which the hierarchies of rank, privilege and power ruling the temple cultus in Jerusalem cannot prevail. It is, furthermore, an imaginary space constructed by human desire for separation and freedom from the usual constraints. Thirdly, it represents ritual time as a breaking away from normal temporal and spatial associations, making it possible to transport it wherever humans desire to commune with God, thus making the ritual temporally spontaneous and spatially free, as discussed by Smith.[35]

The fourth incident which cannot be ignored in a discussion of ritual is the last supper. It introduces a knot into this argument and points dramatically to the ἀπορια and open-ended perplexities of time in the Gospel.[36] Like the food miracle stories, the last supper is also a eucharistic rite, in this case, also commemorating the Jewish passover from Egypt into the promised land, another ritual event which remembers the escape from Egyptian violence into the divine utopian promise. In the last supper rite, the *communitas* earlier experienced on the meadows has been disrupted. This change is spatially represented by the fact that this rite takes place indoors in the city of Jerusalem, in an upstairs room and according to Mark, only the twelve are with Jesus.

34. I am working here with Huizinga's ideas about ritual and play (*Homo Ludens*, pp. 1-26).

35. *To Take Place*, pp. 74-95.

36. See Vernon K. Robbins, 'Last Meal: Preparation, Betrayal, and Absence' (Mk 14.12-25) in Werner H. Kelber (ed.), *The Passion in Mark* (Philadelphia: Fortress Press, 1976), pp. 21-40, for a discussion of the perplexities in the last supper in Mark.

This is an urban, indoor environment where an ancient ritual is repeated. Gone is the spontaneous egalitarian community where the miraculous bread had appeared. Instead, we know that one of the twelve has already plotted to turn Jesus over to the authorities (14.10-11). In ironic narrative juxtaposition, just as in the John the Baptist narrative, Judas's plot is revealed immediately prior to the last supper narrative. The contiguousness of these narratives, particularly compared with the first food miracle story and the death of John narrative, contrasts the two rituals. Both juxtapose the plots to kill the prophets with the eucharistic rituals. The earlier spontaneous ritual and communion has now been replaced by a planned ritual (14.12-15); the sacred time and space of the initial spontaneous ritual has turned into a new structure, and members of the initiated group are no longer a united community, for one has raised his own selfish desires over the interests of the others, and Jesus warns that they will all fall away (14.27). Judas's act of betrayal against the marginal movement restores the cultic, social and political powers with their distinctions of rank and social and ethnic inequities, while simultaneously bringing an end to the simple but ludic interruption of ordinary time. In this sense, this ritual time is ambiguous and made murky because in the center of its celebration lurks a conspiracy of which the ritual leader is aware and which he deliberately makes public (14.18-21), thus undermining any transcendent sense of *communitas* formerly experienced by the group. However, though he predicts that one of them will betray him and that they will all fall away, he also predicts that they will be reunited when he rises from the dead, thus promising a future time when the former *communitas* will return.

The last supper ritual does not suspend time and history as the 'green world' ritual, for it is the first stage in the triumph of ordinary time and history over Jesus and his disciples. This ritual brings together history, in the σκάνδαλον, and ordinary time corruptions and desires in the form of hypocrisy, deceit and betrayal. Because ordinary time has intruded into the suspended time charismatic movement and threatens to fragment it, the last supper is rendered as a paradoxical ritual in which all the temporal contentions are played out: history versus eternity; the present against the future; the historic against the 'mythic'. This ritual time cannot restore cosmic order or undermine it. In gathering together the central paradoxes of salvation and failure, of community and selfishness, and of eternity and the moment, it enacts the 'aporia of time'—the indeterminate end of ritual time.

Its setting in Jerusalem, in the center of political and cultic power, combined with the atmosphere of distrust and deceit, is symptomatic of its problematic status as a ritual to celebrate community or restore order. In this ritual, in contrast to the food miracle rituals, radical dichotomies have replaced the spontaneous communal celebrations. 'Images' and false 'playing' have replaced authentic 'being', and as Judas dips into the same bowl with Jesus, symbolic action becomes form without meaning; a serious plot has exiled the power of the numinous from the communal action, and a dramatic false image assumed by one of the members becomes a ploy to entrap the ritual leader. If anything, this ritual forcefully recalls human failures, for it enacts the ritual practice in an ironic environment and dramatizes the human inability to heed or understand what the utopian opportunity in the 'green world' ritual had initiated. Here the opposition is between Jesus' simplicity, honesty and humility before God and all the fear-driven social cravings the ritual time had temporarily overcome. On the other hand, as the ritual that initiated an organizing ritual for practicing Christians, it also emphasizes the ambiguous tensions underlying its history and practice. The ritual itself re-enacts this paradoxical reminder of human failure and divine generosity.

In the green world, a community emerged while history was suspended by an egalitarian experience of selfless play. This community differs from the serious world of personally driven history where selfish desires rule. In Mark's Gospel, the 'green world' does not mirror the 'real-time' world. This is not the place for 'drama' and 'acting' that separate the real from the imaginary. It is the locale for the real and the imaginary to fuse in communal joy. Though it defers the ordinary time world, it can do so only temporarily, and its paradoxical power lies precisely in its inability to endure for long. On the one hand, it points to a time when all the structures, sufferings, and obsessions characterizing ordinary time can be overcome. On the other, it is a time that sets the standards for ritual time, for the 'green world' is defined in opposition to it. In the Gospel of Mark, the last supper rite returns the necessities and seriousness of everyday life in all their conspiratorial power to subvert the spontaneous ludic community that had temporarily swept ordinary time away.

In this sense, though it shares the idea of retreat and temporary escape with the 'green world' *topos* of literature, the green world ritual in the Gospel of Mark points to the radical difference between myth and literature. Though the green world of late medieval and Renaissance literature constructs an image of itself as a community where play and selflessness hold court, invariably it actually mirrors the serious world of history driven by personal desires and entrenched hierarchical structures.[37] But in the Gospel green world, the story proclaims its 'truth', the ritual is 'true', and rather than mirroring human life, it resists it. The ritual confronts the ordinary time world with a controversial egalitarian community. Thus the antinomies are 'true'. Human hierarchical structures and all the serious desires supporting them in the world of civilization oppose the divinely assisted joyful interlude in the country. While the literary green world seeks to console and teach by representing the ordinary time world from another vista, here there is no distinction between teaching and pleasing, for understanding is joy. Of course, this ritual time cannot last for long. Just the contrary, it is the last supper, with all its ambiguities, that is more characteristic of ritual time. The green world ritual is a bracketed moment, which can be repeated as the second food miracle shows, only to become a memory of utopian times but predicted also as occuring in the future. In the meantime, repetition and memory replace the spontaneous communal eucharist to emphasize the continuity of God's presence in human life despite the horror, suffering and betrayals of human history recalled by the repetition of the last supper ritual.[38]

The 'ritual time' enacted in the Gospel puts the events narrated in a broader time than its own historical setting. On the one hand, while it lasts, the green world ritual overcomes the ordinary time distinctions between the past and the future, and dismisses historical time in favor of ritual time, making all time eternally present. These pastoral rituals become a memory of past time when a spontaneous ritual overtook normal time. But the last supper institutes a paradoxical ritual that

---

37. *The Tempest, Midsummer Night's Dream*, and *As You Like It* or 'What passed between Don Quixote and some Goatherds', Chapter XI, *Don Quixote*.I. *The Romance of the Rose*, and the romances of Chrétien de Troyes offer good examples of this ambiguous opposition.

38. Turner discusses how *communitas* itself eventually leads to structure, and finally to structural oscification, as a new hierarchy comes to rule the originally egalitarian movement (*Ritual Process*, pp. 128-32).

memorializes human failure and God's generosity as a living tradition relevant in the present and the future. The contrast between these eucharistic rituals in the Gospel reveals yet another dimension of Markan meditations on time.

BIBLIOGRAPHY

Abrams, Meyer, *The Mirror and the Lamp: Romantic Theory and Critical Tradition* (New York: Oxford University Press, 1953).

Achtemeier, Paul J., 'Mark as Interpreter of the Jesus Traditions', *Int* 32 (1978), pp. 339-52.

—*Mark* (Philadelphia: Fortress Press, 1980).

Alter, Robert, *The Art of Biblical Narrative* (New York: Basic Books, 1981).

—*Rogue's Progress: Studies in the Picaresque Novel* (Cambridge, MA: Harvard University Press, 1964).

Auerbach, Erich, *Literary Language and its Public in Late Latin Antiquity and in the Middle Ages* (trans. Ralph Manheim; New York: Pantheon Books, 1965).

—*Mimesis* (trans. Willard Trask; Garden City, NY: Doubleday, 1957).

Aune, David, *The New Testament in its Literary Environment* (Philadelphia: Westminster Press, 1987).

Bakhtin, Mikhail, *The Dialogic Imagination: Four Essays* (ed. Michael Holquist; trans. Caryl Emerson and Michael Holquist; Austin, TX: University of Texas Press, 1981).

—*Rabelais and his World* (trans. Helene Iswolsky; Cambridge, MA: MIT Press, 1968).

Bal, Mieke, *Lethal Love: Feminist Literary Readings of the Biblical Love Stories* (Bloomington, IN: Indiana University Press, 1987).

—*Narratology: Introduction to the Theory of Narrative* (trans. Christine van Boheemen; Toronto: University of Toronto Press, 1985).

Barr, James, *Biblical Words for Time* (London: SCM Press, 1962).

Barthes, R., *et al.* (eds.), *Structural Analysis and Biblical Exegesis: Interpretational Essays* (trans. A. Johnson; Pittsburgh: Pickwick Press, 1974).

Barton, Stephen C., *Discipleship and Family Ties in Mark and Matthew* (Cambridge: Cambridge University Press, 1994).

Bartsch, Hans-Werner (ed.) *Kerygma and Myth* (trans. Reginald H. Fuller; London: SPCK, 1962).

Belinzoni, Jr, Arthur J. (ed.) *The Two-Source Hypothesis: An Appraisal* (Macon, GA: Mercer University Press, 1985).

Bell, Catherine, *Ritual Theory, Ritual Practice* (New York: Oxford University Press, 1992).

Belo, Fernando, *A Materialist Reading of the Gospel of Mark* (trans. Matthew J. O'Connell; Maryknoll, NY: Orbis Books, 1981).

—*Lecture matérialiste de l'évangile de Marc: récit, pratique, ideologie* (Paris: Cerf, 1975).

Benjamin, Walter, 'The Storyteller: Reflections on the Works of Nicolai Lenski', in Hannah Arendt (ed.), *Illuminations: Essays and Reflections* (New York: Schocken Books, 1988), pp. 83-109.

Berger, Harry, *Second World and Green World: Studies in Renaissance Fiction-Making* (Berkeley: University of California Press, 1988).

Best, Ernest, *Following Jesus: Discipleship in the Gospel of Mark* (JSNTSup, 4; Sheffield: JSOT Press, 1981).

—*Mark: The Gospel as Story* (Edinburgh: T. & T. Clark, 1983).

Bilezikian, Gilbert, *The Liberated Gospel: The Gospel of Mark Compared with Greek Tragedy* (Grand Rapids: Baker Book House, 1977).

Bjornson, Richard, *The Picaresque Hero in European Fiction* (Madison: University of Wisconsin Press, 1977).

Bloom, Harold, *The Book of J* (trans. David Rosenberg and interpreted by Harold Bloom; New York: Grove Weidenfeld, 1990).

—*Anxiety of Influence* (New York: Oxford University Press, 1973).

Bloom, Harold, (ed.), *The Gospels* (New York: Chelsea House, 1988).

Blumenberg, Hans, *Work on Myth* (trans. Robert M. Wallace; Cambridge, MA: MIT Press, 1985).

Broadhead, Edwin K., *Teaching with Authority: Miracles and Christology in the Gospel of Mark* (JSNTSup, 74; Sheffield: Sheffield Academic Press, 1992).

Bryan, Christopher, *A Preface to Mark: Notes on the Gospel and its Literary and Cultural Settings* (Oxford: Oxford University Press, 1993).

—'Mark as Hellenistic Life', in *idem*, *A Preface to Mark*.

Bultmann, Rudolf, 'New Testament and Mythology', in Hans Werner Bartsch (ed.), *Kerygma and Myth: A Theological Debate* (2 vols.; trans. Reginald H. Fuller; London: SPCK, 1957), I, pp. 1-44.

—*Jesus Christ and Mythology* (New York: Charles Scribner's Sons, 1958).

—*The New Testament and Mythology and Other Basic Writings* (trans. Schubert M. Ogden; Philadelphia: Fortress Press, 1984).

Burkert, Walter, *Homo Necans: The Anthropology of Ancient Greek Sacrificial Ritual and Myth* (trans. Peter Bing; Berkeley: University of California Press, 1983).

Burkill, T.A., *Mysterious Revelation* (Ithaca, NY: Cornell University Press, 1963).

—*New Light on the Earliest Gospel* (Ithaca, NY: Cornell University Press, 1972).

Burridge, Richard A., *What Are the Gospels? A Comparison with Graeco–Roman Biography* (Cambridge: Cambridge University Press, 1992).

Camery-Hoggatt, Jerry, *Irony in Mark's Gospel* (Cambridge: Cambridge University Press, 1992).

Carson, D.A., and H.G.M. Williamson (eds.), *It is Written: Scripture Citing Scripture. Essays in Honour of Barnabus Lindars* (Cambridge: Cambridge University Press, 1988).

Cassirer, Ernst, *Language and Myth* (trans. Susanne K. Langer; New York: Dover, 1946).

—*The Philosophy of Symbolic Forms* (trans. Ralph Manheim; New Haven: Yale University Press, 1957).

—*The Philosophy of Symbolic Forms. II. Mythical Thought* (trans. Ralph Manheim; New Haven: Yale University Press, 1957).

Certeau, Michel de, *The Practice of Everyday Life* (trans. Steven Rendall; Berkeley: University of California Press, 1984).

Charity, A.C., 'The Way of Jesus', in Harold Bloom (ed.), *The Gospels* (New York: Chelsea House, 1988), pp. 17-23.

Childs, Brevard S., *Old Testament Theology in a Canonical Context* (Philadelphia: Fortress Press, 1986).

Countryman, L. William, *Dirt, Greed and Sex: Sexual Ethics in the New Testament and their Implications for Today* (Philadelphia: Fortress Press, 1988).

Cox, Patricia, *Biography in Late Antiquity* (Berkeley: University of California Press, 1983).

Crossan, John Dominic, *Cliffs of Fall: Paradox and Polyvalence in the Parables of Jesus* (New York: Seabury Press, 1980).

—*In Parables: The Challenge of the Historical Jesus* (New York: Harper & Row, 1973).

—'The Parable of the Wicked Husbandmen', *JBL* 90. 4 (1971), pp. 451-65.

Culler, Jonathan, *Structuralist Poetics: Structuralism, Linguistics, and the Study of Literature* (London: Routledge & Kegan Paul, 1975).

Cullman, Oscar, *Christ and Time: The Primitive Christian Conception of Time and History* (trans. Floyd V. Filson; Philadelphia: Westminster Press, 1964).

Daube, David, *Appeasement or Resistance and Other Essays on New Testament Judaism* (Berkeley: University of California Press, 1987).

Deissmann, Adolf, *Light from the Ancient East* (trans. Lionel R.M. Stracham; Grand Rapids: Baker Book House, 4th edn, 1965).

Derrett, J. Duncan M., 'Mark's Technique: The Haemorrhaging Woman and Jairus' Daughter', *Bib* 63 (1982), pp. 474-505.

Derrida, Jacques, *Of Grammatology* (trans. Gayatri Chakravorty Spivak; Baltimore: The Johns Hopkins University Press, 1974).

Descamps, A.-L., 'Pour une histoire du titre "Fils de Dieu"', in M. Sabbe (ed.), *L'Evangile selon Marc: Tradition et Rédaction* (Leuven: Leuven University Press, 1988), pp. 529-71.

Dewey, Joanna, *Markan Public Debate: Literary Technique, Concentric Structure, and Theology 2.1–3.6* (Chico, CA: Scholars Press, 1977).

Dibelius, Martin, *From Tradition to Gospel* (trans. and rev. edn Bertram Lee Woolf; Cambridge: James Clarke & Co. Ltd, 1971).

Dix, Gregory, *The Shape of the Liturgy* (London: Dacre Press, 1945).

Donahue, John R., *The Theology and Setting of Discipleship in the Gospel of Mark* (Milwaukee, WI: Marquette University Press, 1983).

—*Are You the Christ? The Trial Narrative in the Gospel of Mark* (SBLDS, 10; Missoula, MT: Society of Biblical Literature for the Seminar on Mark, 1973).

—*The Gospel in Parable: Metaphor, Narrative and Theology in the Synoptic Gospels* (Philadelphia: Fortress Press, 1988).

Doty, William G., *Mythography: The Study of Myths and Rituals* (University, Alabama: University of Alabama Press, 1986).

Douglas, Mary, *Purity and Danger: An Analysis of Concepts of Pollution and Taboo* (New York: Frederick A. Praeger, 1966).

Drury, John, 'The Sower, the Vineyard, and the Place of Allegory in the Interpretation of Mark's Parables', *JTS* 24 (1973), pp. 367-79.

—*The Parables in the Gospels: History and Allegory* (New York: Crossroad, 1985).

Dumézil, Georges, *Mitra-Varuna: An Essay on Two Indo-European Representations of Sovereignty* (trans. Derek Coltman; New York: Zone Books, 1988; repr. *Mitra-Varuna*; Paris: Editions Gallimard, 1948).

Dungan, David L., and David R. Cartlidge (eds.), *Documents for the Study of the Gospels* (Minneapolis: Fortress Press, 1994).

Durkheim, Emile, *The Elementary Forms of Religious Life* (trans. J.W. Swain; New York: Free Press, 1965 [1915]).

Edwards, James R., 'Markan Sandwiches: the Significance of Interpolations in Markan Narratives', *NovT* 31 (1989), pp. 193-216.

Eliade, Mircea, *Myth and Reality* (trans. Willard R. Trask; New York: Harper & Row, 1963).

—*Shamanism: Archaic Techniques of Ecstasy* (trans. Willard R. Trask; Princeton, NJ: Princeton University Press, 1964).

Elliott, J.K. (ed.) *The Language and Style of the Gospel of Mark: An edition of C.H. Turner's 'Notes on Marcan Usage'. Together with other Comparable Studies* (NovTSup, 81; Leiden: E.J. Brill, 1993).

Elliott, John H., *Home for the Homeless* (Philadelphia: Fortress Press, 1981).

Ellis, E.E., 'The Date and Provenance of Mark's Gospel', in F. Van Segbroeck, C.M. Tuckett, G. Van Belle, and J. Verheyden (eds.), *The Four Gospels 1992: Festschrift Frans Neirynck* (Leuven: Leuven University Press, 1992), II, pp. 801-15.

Erikson, Erik, *Identity: Youth and Crisis* (New York: W.W. Norton, 1968).

Ferguson, Everett, *Backgrounds of Early Christianity* (Grand Rapids: Eerdmans, 1987).

Fernán-Gómez, Fernando, *Historias de la picaresca* (Barcelona: Editorial Planeta, 1989).

Fewell, Danna Nolan, 'Introduction: Writing, Reading, and Relating', in *idem*, (ed.), *Reading Between Texts: Intertextuality and the Hebrew Bible* (Louisville, KY: Westminster/ John Knox, 1992).

Fewell, Danna Nolan (ed.), *Reading Between Texts: Intertextuality and the Hebrew Bible* (Louisville, KY: Westminster/John Knox, 1992).

Finkel, Asher, *The Pharisees and the Teacher of Nazareth: A Study of their Background, their Halachic, Midrashic Teachings, the Similarities and Differences* (Leiden: E.J. Brill, 1974).

Fishbane, Michael, *Biblical Interpretation in Ancient Israel* (Oxford: Oxford University Press, 1985).

—*The Garments of Torah: Essays in Biblical Hermeneutics* (Bloomington: Indiana University Press, 1989).

Foucault, Michel, 'The Prose of the World', in *The Order of Things: An Archaeology of the Human Sciences* (New York: Vintage Books, 1973), pp. 17-45.

Fowler, Alastair, *Kinds of Literature: An Introduction to the Theory of Genres and Modes* (Cambridge, MA: Harvard University Press, 1982).

Fowler, Robert M., *Let the Reader Understand: Reader Response Criticism and the Gospel of Mark* (Minneapolis: Fortress Press, 1991).

Frye, Northrop, 'The Argument of Comedy', in Leonard F. Dean (ed.), *Shakespeare: Modern Essays in Criticism* (New York: Oxford University Press, 1957), pp. 79-89.

Funk, Robert W., *The Poetics of Biblical Narrative* (Sonoma, CA: Polebridge Press, 1988).

Gadamer, Hans-Georg, *Truth and Method* (New York: Crossroad, 1986).

Geertz, Clifford, 'Religion as a Cultural System' in *idem*, *The Interpretation of Cultures: Selected Essays* (New York: Basic Books, 1973).

Genette, Gérard, *Narrative Discourse: An Essay in Method* (trans. Jane E. Lewin; Ithaca, NY: Cornell University Press, 1980).

—*Palimpsestes: La littérature au second degré* (Paris: Editions du Seuil, 1982).

Gerhardsson, Birger, 'The Parable of the Sower and its Interpretation', *NTS* 14 (1968), pp. 165-93.

Girard, René, 'Peter's Denial', in Harold Bloom (ed.), *The Gospels* (New York: Chelsea House, 1988), pp. 149-64.

—'Scandal and the Dance: Salome in the Gospel of Mark', *New Literary History* 15 (Winter, 1984), pp. 311-24.

—*The Scapegoat* (trans. Yvonne Freccero; Baltimore: The Johns Hopkins University Press, 1986).

—*Violence and the Sacred* (trans. Patrick Gregory; Baltimore: The Johns Hopkins University Press, 1972).

Goppelt, Leonhard, *Apostolic and Post-Apostolic Times* (trans. Robert A. Guelich; Grand Rapids: Baker Book House, 1977).

Gottwald, Norman K., *The Hebrew Bible: A Socio-Literary Introduction* (Philadelphia: Fortress Press, 1985).

Grassi, Ernesto, *Rhetoric as Philosophy* (University Park: Pennsylvania State Press, 1980).

Gunkel, Hermann, *The Psalms: A Form-Critical Introduction* (intro. James Muilenberg and trans. Thomas N. Horner; Philadelphia: Fortress Press, 1967).

—*The Legends of Genesis* (New York: Schocken Books, 1964).

Hadas, Moses, and Morton Smith, *Heroes and Gods: Spiritual Biographies in Antiquity* (New York: Harper & Row, 1965).

Harvey, David, *The Condition of Postmodernity: An Inquiry into the Origins of Cultural Change* (Oxford: Basil Blackwell, 1989).

Hayes, Richard B., *Echoes of Scripture in the Letters of Paul* (New Haven: Yale University Press, 1989).

Herzog II, William R., 'Peasant Revolt and the Spiral of Violence', in *idem*, *Parables as Subversive Speech* (Louisville, KY: Westminster/John Knox Press, 1994).

Hollander, John, *The Figure of Echo: A Mode of Allusion in Milton and After* (Berkeley: University of California Press, 1981).

Holquist, Michael, *Dostoevsky and the Novel* (Princeton, NJ: Princeton University Press, 1977).

Huizinga, J., *Homo Ludens: A Study of the Play-Element in Culture* (Boston: Beacon Press, 1950).

Hultgren, Arland J., *Jesus and his Adversaries* (Minneapolis: Augsburg, 1979).

Jaspers, Karl, 'Jesus', in *idem*, *Socrates, Buddha, Confucius, Jesus* (trans. Ralph Manheim; New York: Harcourt Brace Jovanovich, 1957).

Jeremias, Joachim, *Rediscovering the Parables* (New York: Charles Scribner's Sons, 1966).

—*The Parables of Jesus* (trans. S.H. Hooke; New York: Charles Scribner's Sons, repr. 1972 [1954]).

Judge, E.A., *The Social Pattern of Christian Groups in the First Century* (London: Tyndale Press, 1960).

Kee, Howard Clark, *Community of the New Age: Studies in Mark's Gospel* (Philadelphia: Westminster Press, 1977).

Kelber, Werner, *The Kingdom in Mark: A New Place and a New Time* (Philadelphia: Fortress Press, 1974).

—*The Oral and the Written Gospel* (Philadelphia: Fortress Press, 1983).

Kennedy, George, *A New History of Classical Rhetoric* (Princeton, NJ: Princeton University Press, 1994).

—*Classical Rhetoric and its Christian and Secular Tradition from Ancient to Modern Times* (Chapel Hill: University of North Carolina Press, 1980).

—*The Art of Rhetoric in the Roman World 300 BC–AD 300* (Princeton, NJ: Princeton University Press, 1972).

Kermode, Frank, *Forms of Attention* (Chicago: University of Chicago Press, 1985).

—*The Art of Telling: Essays on Fiction* (Cambridge, MA: Harvard University Press, 1983).

—*The Genesis of Secrecy* (Cambridge, MA: Harvard University Press, 1979).

Kümmel, Werner, Georg, *Introduction to the New Testament* (trans. Howard C. Kee; Nashville: Abingdon Press, 1973).

Lacan, Jacques, *The Four Fundamental Concepts of Psycho-Analysis* (ed. Jacques-Alain Miller and trans. Alan Sheridan; New York: W.W. Norton, 1978).

Leenhardt, F.-J., 'An Exegetical Essay: Mark 5:1-20: "The Madman Reveals the Final Truth" (M. Foucault)', in R. Barthes *et al.* (eds.), *Structural Analysis and Biblical Exegesis: Interpretational Essays* (trans. A. Johnson; Pittsburgh: Pickwick Press, 1974), pp. 85-109.

Levi-Strauss, Claude, *Anthropologie Structurale* (Paris: Plon, 1958).

—*Structural Anthropology* (trans. C. Jacobson and B.G. Schoepf; Harmondsworth: Penguin Books, 1968).

—*The Raw and the Cooked: Introduction to the Science of Mythology* (trans. John and Doreen Weightman; New York: Harper & Row, 1969).

Lieberman, Saul, *Hellenism in Jewish Palestine: Studies in the Literary Transmission, Beliefs and Manners in Palestine in the I Century BCE–IV Century CE* (New York: Jewish Theological Seminary of America, 1950).

Lord, Alfred, *The Singer of Tales* (Cambridge, MA: Harvard University Press, 1960).

Lüderitz, Gert, 'Rhetorik, Poetik, Kompositionstechnik', in Hubert Cancik (ed.), *Markus Philologie* (Tübingen: J.C.B Mohr, 1984), pp. 165-203 (186-88).

Lührmann, Dieter, 'The Gospel of Mark and the Sayings Collection Q', *JBL* 108 (Spring, 1989), pp. 51-71.

Lukács, Georg, *Theory of the Novel* (trans. Anna Bostock; Cambridge, MA: MIT Press, 1971.

Malbon, Elizabeth Struthers, 'Fallible Followers: Women and Men in the Gospel of Mark', *Semeia* 28 (1983), pp. 29-48.

—*Narrative Space and Mythic Meaning* (San Francisco: Harper & Row, 1986).

Malherbe, Abraham J., *Social Aspects of Early Christianity* (Philadelphia: Fortress Press, 2nd edn, 1983).

Malinowski, Bronislaw, *Magic, Science and Religion and Other Essays* (Garden City, NY: Doubleday, 1954).

Marin, Louis, *The Semiotics of the Passion Narrative: Topics and Figures* (trans. Alfred M. Johnson, Jr; Pittsburgh, PA: Pickwick Press, 1980).

Marrou, H.I., *A History of Education in Antiquity* (trans. George Lamb; New York: Sheed & Ward, 1964).

Marxsen, Willi, *Der Evangelist Markus: Studien zur Redaktiongeschichte des Evangeliums* (Göttingen, Germany: Vandenhoeck & Ruprecht, 1956).

—*Mark the Evangelist: Studies in the Redaction History of the Gospel* (trans. James Boyce, Donald Juel, William Poehlmann, with Roy A. Harrisville; Nashville: Abingdon Press, 1969).

Matera, F.J., 'The Incomprehension of the Disciples and Peter's Confession (Mark 6.14–8.30)', *Bib* 70 (1989), pp. 153-72.

Meeks, Wayne, *The First Urban Christians: The Social World of the Apostle Paul* (New Haven: Yale University Press, 1983).

Miller, Dale, and Patricia Miller, *The Gospel of Mark as Midrash on Earlier Jewish and New Testament Literature* (Lewiston, NY: Edwin Mellen Press, 1990).

Miller, Stuart, *The Picaresque Novel* (Cleveland: Case Western Reserve University Press, 1967).

Momigliano, Arnaldo, 'Tradition and the Classical Historian', in *idem, Essays in Ancient and Modern Historiography* (Middletown, CO: Wesleyan University Press, 1977), pp. 161-77.

—*On Pagans, Jews, and Christians* (Middletown, CO: Wesleyan University Press, 1987).

—'The Origins of Universal History', in *idem, Pagans, Jews, and Christians* (Middletown, CO: Wesleyan University Press, 1977), pp. 31-57.

—*The Development of Greek Biography* (Cambridge, MA: Harvard University Press, 1971).

Moo, Douglas, *The Old Testament in the Gospel Passion Narratives* (Sheffield: Almond Press, 1983).

Munn, Nancy D., 'Symbolism in a Ritual Context: Aspects of Symbolic Action', in J.J. Honigmann (ed.), *Handbook of Social and Cultural Anthropology* (Chicago: Rand McNally, 1973), pp. 579-612.

Neirynck, Frans, *Duality in Mark: Contributions to the Study of Markan Redaction* (Repr. Leuven: Leuven University Press, 1988).

Neusner, Jacob, *Canon and Connection: Intertextuality in Judaism* (Lanham, MD: University Press of America, 1987).

—*Early Rabbinic Judaism: Historical Studies in Religion, Literature, and Art* (Leiden: E.J. Brill, 1975).

Niditch, Susan, *Underdogs and Tricksters: A Prelude to Biblical Folklore* (San Francisco: Harper & Row, 1987).

Ong, S.J., Walter, *Orality and Literacy* (London: Methuen, 1982).

Orchard, Bernard, and Thomas R.W. Longstaff (eds.), *J.J. Griesbach: Synoptic and Text-critical Studies 1776–1976* (Cambridge: Cambridge University Press, 1978).

Otto, Rudolf, *The Idea of the Holy: An Inquiry into the Non-rational Factor in the Idea of the Divine and its Relation to the Rational* (trans. John W. Harvey; London: Oxford University Press, 1923).

Parker, Alexander A., *Literature and the Delinquent: The Picaresque Novel in Spain and Europe 1599–1753* (Edinburgh: Edinburgh University Press, 1967).

Peabody, David Barrett, *Mark as Composer* (Macon, GA: Mercer University Press, 1987).

Pellón Gustavo, and Rodríguez-Luis, Julio (eds.), *Upstarts, Wanderers or Swindlers: Anatomy of the Picaro, A Critical Anthology* (Amsterdam: Rodopi, 1986).

Pesch, Rudolph, *Das Markus-Evangelium*. I. *Mark 1.1-8.26* (Freiburg: Herder, 1976).

—*Das Markus-Evangelium*. II. *8.27–16.20* (Freiburg: Herder, 1977).

Pomeroy, Sarah B., *Goddesses, Whores, Wives, and Slaves* (New York: Schocken Books, 1975).

Propp, Vladimir, *Morphology of the Folktale* (Austin, TX: University of Texas Press, 1968 [1928]).

Renan, Ernest, *Vie de Jésus* (Paris: Michel Levy, 1863).

Rhoads, David, and Donald Michie, *Mark as Story: An Introduction to the Narrative of the Gospel* (Philadelphia: Fortress Press, 1982).

Ricoeur, Paul, 'Biblical Time', in Mark I. Wallace (ed.), *Figuring the Sacred: Religion, Narrative, and Imagination* (trans. David Pellauer; Minneapolis: Fortress Press, 1995), pp. 167-80.

—'Interpretative Narrative', in Regina Schwartz (ed.), *The Book and the Text*, pp. 244-47.

—*Interpretation Theory: Discourse and the Surplus of Meaning* (Fort Worth, TX: Texas Christian University Press, 1976).

—'Existence and Hermeneutics', in Don Ihde (ed.), *The Conflict of Interpretations* (Evanston, IL: Northwestern University Press, 1974).

—*Time and Narrative* (3 vols., trans. Kathleen McLaughlin and David Pellauer; Chicago: University of Chicago Press, 1984–88).

Robbins, Vernon K., 'Last Meal: Preparation, Betrayal, and Absence' (Mk 14.12-25) in Werner H. Kelber (ed.), *The Passion in Mark* (Philadelphia: Fortress Press, 1976), pp. 21-40.

—'The Reversed Contextualiation of Psalm 22 in the Markan Crucifixion: A Socio-Rhetorical Analysis', in F. Van Segbroeck (ed.), *The Four Gospels 1992: Festschrift Frans Neirynck* II, pp. 1161-83.

—*Jesus the Teacher: A Socio-Rhetorical Interpretation of Mark* (Philadelphia: Fortress Press, 1984).

Robinson, James M., *The Problem of History in Mark and Other Marcan Studies* (Philadelphia: Fortress Press, 1982).

Rose, André, 'L'influence des psaumes sur les annonces et les récits de la passion et de la résurrection dans les évangiles', in Robert de Langhe (ed.), *Le Psautier: Ses origines. Ses problèmes littéraires. Son influence* (Louvain: Publications Universitaires, 1962), pp. 297-356.

Rousselle, Aline, *Porneia: On Desire and the Body in Antiquity* (trans. Felicia Pheasant; Oxford: Basil Blackwell, 1983).

Sanders, E.P., *Jewish Law from Jesus to the Mishnah: Five Studies* (Philadelphia: Trinity Press International, 1990).

Schierling, Marla J., 'Women as Leaders in the Marcan Communities', *Listening* 15 (1980), pp. 250-56.

Schildgen, Brenda Deen, 'A Blind Promise: Mark's Retrieval of Esther', *Poetics Today* 15.1 (1994), pp. 115-31.

—'The Gospel of Mark as Myth', in John C. Hawley, S.J. (ed.), *Through a Glass Darkly: Essays in the Religious Imagination* (New York: Fordham University Press, 1996).

—'The Gospel of Mark as Picaresque Novella', *Genre* (1998).

Schneck, S.J, Richard, 'Isaiah in the Gospel of Mark I–VIII' (Dissertation; Vallejo, CA: BIBAL Press, 1994).

Schneidau, Herbert, *Sacred Discontent* (Berkeley: University of California Press, 1976).

Schwartz, Regina (ed.), *The Book and the Text: The Bible and Literary Theory* (Oxford: Basil Blackwell, 1990).

Selvidge, Marla J., 'Mark 5.25-34 and Leviticus 15: A Reaction to Restrictive Purity Regulations', *JBL* 103 (1984), pp. 619-23.

Seters, John van, *In Search of History: Historiography in the Ancient World and the Origins of Biblical History* (New Haven: Yale University Press, 1983).

Shepherd, Tom, *Markan Sandwich Stories: Narration, Definition, and Function* (Berrien Springs, MI: Andrews University Press, 1993).

Sherwin-White, N., *Roman Society and Roman Law in the New Testament: The Sarum Lectures, 1960–61* (Oxford: Clarendon Press, 1963).

Smith, Jonathan Z., 'Good News is No News: Aretalogy and Gospel', in Jacob Neusner (ed.), *Christianity, Judaism, and Other Greco-Roman Cults: Studies for Morton Smith at Sixty* (Leiden: E.J. Brill, 1975).

—*To Take Place: Toward Theory in Ritual* (Chicago: University of Chicago Press, 1987).

Stambaugh, John E., and David L. Balch, *The New Testament in its Social Environment* (Philadelphia: Westminster Press, 1986).

Starobinski, Jean, 'Essai exégétique: Marc 5.1-20', in *Analyse Structurale et Exégèse Biblique*, pp. 95-121.

—'Le démoniaque de Gérasa', in R. Barthes *et al.* (eds.), *Analyse Structurale et Exégèse Biblique* (Neuchatel: Delachaux et Niestle, 1972), pp. 69-70.

—'Struggle with Legion: A Literary Analysis of Mark 5:1-20', in Harold Bloom (ed.), *The Gospels* (New York: Chelsea House, 1988), pp. 35-61.

Sternberg, Meir, *The Poetics of Biblical Narrative: Ideological Literature and the Drama of Reading* (Bloomington, IN: Indiana University Press, 1985).

Stock, Brian, *Augustine the Reader: Meditation, Self-knowledge, and the Ethics of Interpretation* (Cambridge, MA: Harvard University Press, 1996).

—*The Implications of Literacy: Written Language and Models of Interpretation in the Eleventh and Twelfth Centuries* (Princeton, NJ: Princeton University Press, 1983).

Stowers, Stanley K., *Letter-Writing in Greco-Roman Antiquity* (Philadelphia: Westminster Press, 1986).

Strauss, David Friedrich, *The Life of Jesus Critically Examined* (ed. with intro. Peter C. Hodgson and trans. George Eliot; Philadelphia: Fortress Press, 1972).

Talbert, Charles H., *What is a Gospel? The Genre of the Canonical Gospels* (Philadelphia: Fortress Press, 1977).

Tambiah, Stanley J., *Buddhism and the Spirit Cults of North-East Thailand* (Cambridge: Cambridge University Press, 1970).

The JPS Torah Commentary: Leviticus (Commentary Baruch A. Levine; Philadelphia: The Jewish Publication Society of America, 1989).

Theissen, Gerd, *Social Reality and the Early Christians: Theology, Ethics, and the World of the New Testament* (trans. Margaret Kohl; Minneapolis: Fortress Press, 1992).

—*Miracle Stories of Early Christian Tradition* (ed. John Riches and trans. Francis McDonagh; Edinburgh: T. & T. Clark, 1983).

Thompson, Stith (ed.), *Motif-Index of Folk Literature*, I, II (Bloomington, IN: Indiana University Press, 1966).

Tolbert, Mary Ann, 'The Gospel in Greco-Roman Culture', in Regina Schwartz (ed.), *The Book and the Text: The Bible and Literary Theory* (Oxford: Basil Blackwell, 1990), pp. 258-75.

—*Perspectives on the Parables: An Approach to Multiple Interpretations* (Philadelphia: Fortress Press, 1979).

—*Sowing the Gospel: Mark's World in Literary Historical Perspective* (Minneapolis: Fortress Press, 1989).

Trocmé, E., 'Why Parables? A Study of Mark IV', *BJRL* 59 (1977), pp. 458-71.

Turner, Victor, 'Liminal to Liminoid in Play, Flow and Ritual', in *idem, From Ritual to Theatre* (New York: Performing Arts Journal Publications, 1982), pp. 20-60.

—*The Ritual Process: Structure and Anti-Structure* (Chicago: Aldine, 1969).

Van Gennep, Arnold, *The Rites of Passage* (trans. M.B. Vizedom and G.L. Caffee; Chicago: University of Chicago Press, 1960).

Van Oyen, G., 'Intercalation and Irony in the Gospel of Mark', in F. Van Segbroeck (ed.), *The Four Gospels 1992: Festschrift Frans Neirynck II* (Leuven: Leuven University Press, 1992), pp. 949-74.

Vance, Eugene, 'Pas de trois: Narrative, Hermeneutics, and Structure in Medieval Poetics', in Mario J. Valdes and Owen J. Miller (eds.), *Interpretation of Narrative* (Toronto: University of Toronto Press, 1978), pp. 118-34.

Vermes, Geza, *The Dead Sea Scrolls in English* (London: Penguin Books, 1962).

Via, Daniel O., *The Ethics of Mark's Gospel—in the Middle of Time* (Philadelphia: Fortress Press, 1985).

—*Kerygma and Comedy in the New Testament: A Structuralist Approach to Hermeneutic* (Philadelphia: Fortress Press, 1975).

Voelz, J.W., 'The Language of the New Testament', *ANRW* 25.2 (1984), pp. 893-977.

Vorster, W.S., 'Meaning and Reference: The parables of Jesus in Mark 4', in B.C. Lategan and W.S. Vorster (eds.), *Text and Reality: Aspects of Reference in Biblical Texts* (Atlanta: Scholars Press, 1985), pp. 27-65.

Votaw, Clyde Weber, 'The Gospels and Contemporary Biographies', *AJT* 19 (1915), pp. 45-73; pp. 217-49.

Waetjen, Herman C., *A Reordering of Power: A SocioPolitical Reading of Mark's Gospel* (Minneapolis: Fortress Press, 1989).

Walker, Jr, W.O., *The Relationships among the Gospels: An Interdisciplinary Dialogue* (San Antonio, TX: Trinity University Press, 1978).

Walsh, P.G., *The Roman Novel: The 'Satyricon' of Petronius and the 'Metamorphoses' of Apuleius* (Cambridge: Cambridge University Press, 1970).

—' "Nachleben": The Roman Novel and the Rebirth of Picaresque', in *idem*, *The Roman Novel: The 'Satyricon' of Atronicus and the 'Metamorphoses' of Apuleius* (Cambridge: Cambridge University Press, 1970), pp. 224-43.

—'The Literary Texture', in *idem*, *The Roman Novel*, pp. 32-66.

Weisse, Christian Hermann, *Die evangelienfrage in ihrem gegenwartigen Stadium* (Leipzig: Breitkopf und Hartel, 1856).

- *Die evangelische Geschichte kritisch und philosophisch bearbeitet* (2 vols.; Leipzig: Breitkopf und Hartel, 1838).

Wengst, Klaus, *Pax Romana and the Peace of Jesus Christ* (trans. John Bowden; Philadelphia: Fortress Press, 1987).

Whitbourn, Christine J. (ed.), *Knaves and Swindlers: Essays on the Picaresque Novel in Europe* (University of Hull Publications; London: Oxford University Press, 1974).

White, Hayden, 'Interpretation in History', in *idem*, *Tropics of Discourse* (Baltimore: The Johns Hopkins University Press, 1974), pp. 51-80.

—*Tropics of Discourse* (Baltimore: The Johns Hopkins University Press, 1978).

—*The Content of the Form: Narrative Discourse and Historical Representation* (Baltimore: The Johns Hopkins University Press, 1987).

Wicks, Ulrich, *Picaresque Narrative, Picaresque Fictions: A Theory and Research Guide* (New York: Greenwood Press, 1989).

Williams, James G., *Gospel Against Parable: Mark's Language of Mystery* (Sheffield: Almond Press, 1985).

Witherington, Ben, *Women and the Genesis of Christianity* (Cambridge: Cambridge University Press, 1990).

—*Women and the Ministry of Jesus* (Cambridge: Cambridge University Press, 1984).

Yarbro Collins, Adela, *Is Mark's Gospel a Life of Jesus? The Question of Genre* (Milwaukee, WI: Marquette University Press, 1990).

INDEXES

INDEX OF REFERENCES

OLD TESTAMENT

NEW TESTAMENT

10.17	21	12.32-33	79	14.72	115
10.19	78, 79, 81	12.33	79	15	91
10.21	79	12.34-37	37	15.2	140
10.29-31	132	12.36	62	15.4-5	87
10.32	21, 128	12.38-40	33	15.6-15	37
10.33-34	25, 123	13.10-11	37	15.9-14	25
10.33	24	13.11	38	15.13	89
10.35-38	25	13.29	123	15.15	89, 127
11.1	21, 91, 137	14–16	88, 89	15.25	25
11.9-10	137	14.1-2	100, 133,	15.29	90
11.9	89		134	15.30	108
11.11	25, 137	14.1	25	15.33	25
11.12-14	100	14.3-9	100	15.34	25, 26, 90,
11.15-19	100	14.10-11	100, 134,		108
11.15-18	138		155	15.39	24, 140, 141
11.15	21, 22, 25,	14.11	110	15.40-41	36, 37
	137	14.12-25	144, 154	15.40	128
11.17	62, 82, 127,	14.12-15	155	15.42	26
	138	14.12	25	15.43	36
11.18-19	138	14.18-21	155	16.1-8	25, 36, 123
11.18	125, 127	14.18	89	16.1	26
11.19	33	14.24	80	16.8	125, 128
11.20-25	100	14.25	50		
11.27-33	33, 37	14.26	22	*Luke*	
11.27	21, 25, 137	14.27	87, 155	1.5	23
11.28	138	14.30	25	1.26	23
11.32	125, 127	14.32	22	2.1-3	23
12.1-11	97	14.34	25	2.41-42	23
12.1-9	138	14.37	25	3.1	23
12.9	99	14.40-41	25		
12.10-11	89	14.43	37	*John*	
12.10	62	14.47	38	7.8	17
12.12	99, 125, 127	14.49-50	62		
12.13-27	37	14.49	62	*1 Corinthians*	
12.13-17	33, 133	14.53-64	37	7.10-11	74
12.17	134	14.55-64	134		
12.18-27	33	14.56-64	25	*1 Thessalonians*	
12.19	72, 76	14.61	139	5.1	17
12.27	76	14.62	139		
12.28-34	33	14.64	71	*Revelation*	
12.28	81	14.68	25, 128	1.3	17
12.29	79	14.70	25, 128	22.10	17
12.31	79	14.71	25		